SOCIAL ISSUES

SOCIAL ISSUES

The Ethics and Economics of Taxes and Public Programs

JOHN C. WINFREY

New York   Oxford

OXFORD UNIVERSITY PRESS

1998

Oxford University Press

Oxford   New York
Athens   Auckland   Bangkok   Bogota   Bombay   Buenos Aires
Calcutta   Cape Town   Dar es Salaam   Delhi   Florence   Hong Kong
Istanbul   Karachi   Kuala Lumpur   Madras   Madrid   Melbourne
Mexico City   Nairobi   Paris   Singapore   Taipei   Tokyo   Toronto   Warsaw

and associated companies in
Berlin   Ibadan

Library of Congress Cataloging-in-Publication Data
Winfrey, John C.
Social issues : the ethics and economics of taxes and public
programs / John C. Winfrey.
p.   cm.
Includes bibliographical references and index.
ISBN 0-19-511432-9. — ISBN 0-19-511433-7 (pbk.)
1. Policy sciences—Moral and ethical aspects.   2. Social ethics.
I. Title.
H97.W564   1998
336.2—dc21   96-50900
                                                      CIP

1 3 5 7 9 8 6 4 2

Printed in the United States of America
on acid-free paper

To my colleagues at Washington and Lee, a true community of scholars

Contents

Preface

The aim of this book is to provide a framework for discussing and resolving several of our most pressing social issues. The government programs directed at these issues are the subject of intense debate and reform efforts. These issues include government activities and reform proposals for taxes, welfare, education, health care, Social Security, and environmental protection.

Given the competition among policy makers to cut taxes and social programs, these issues are likely to persist and to continue to occupy public attention. As reforms are considered and adopted, many of the issues will spark even more controversy.

I begin by developing a pluralistic approach to moral reasoning termed *social ethics*. It owes much to W. D. Ross's theory of *prima facie* duties. The argument is that there is no one principle from which all others are derived, nor is there a unique order of principles. Moral reasoning requires that moral principles be evaluated in terms of their relevance to a particular situation, or for our purposes, their relevance to a particular social issue.

Many of the arguments presented in public discussion of these social issues appeal implicitly or explicitly to widely held moral principles. Unfortunately the rhetoric of political debate is often designed to obfuscate rather than to clarify.

Almost by definition, social issues involve juxtaposed moral arguments and principles. In order for these moral conflicts to be satisfactorily resolved, a much better understanding of the moral and economic dimensions of the issues and the proposed reforms is required.

In chapter two, a number of concepts from economic and political theory are presented. These are useful for understanding the particular characteristics of existing social programs and possible reforms. Many recent reform proposals seek to enhance the efficiency of social programs by deregulation and privatization. Here the role of economic analysis becomes crucial. It is important to ask why the market originally failed to address and resolve the issues. The success of reforms depends on an appreciation of the special characteristics of the related goods and activities.

As each issue is considered in subsequent chapters, an attempt is made to clarify the moral, political, and economic dimensions that must be weighed as current programs and reform proposals are evaluated. Fortuitously, the social ethics approach provides a forum for open discussion in which the moral values and the political and economic assumptions from different viewpoints are entertained, discussed, and evaluated. The goal is to come to agreement on the social policies, but when that does not occur, the process should at least narrow our differences.

Acknowledgments

This book owes much to a wide range of people and institutions. My wife Barbara gave technical expertise as well as moral support. Lynda Bassett-deMaria contributed at every stage of the production process. I greatly appreciate the editorial support of a Lexington friend, Matt Paxton. Over the years, I have received generous support from Washington and Lee and the National Endowment for the Humanities. More recently, I have enjoyed visiting Duke University; University College, Oxford; and the Department of Social Economics at the University of Utrecht. Inspiration has also come from David Schrader at Washington and Jefferson College, Eric Mount at Centre College, and Rob Hudson at Boston University. I have dedicated the book to the collegial atmosphere at Washington and Lee. My special thanks to Ken Ruscio, John Gunn, Eduardo Valesquez, Lad Sessions, and Charles Boggs. Finally, many thanks to the editors and readers of Oxford University Press.

SOCIAL ISSUES

1

A Social Ethics for Social Issues

Let us start this exploration by simply acknowledging that we, like most other members of society, have some commitment to moral principles. We each have moral commitments and duties to other individuals and groups within society, and we intend to honor those commitments and duties.[1]

Some philosophers attempt to explain how prudential reasoning can lead one to choose to be a moral person. Whether or not such arguments can ever be successful is problematical. Fortunately that is not our task here. We will proceed with the understanding that each of us has made a commitment, say as an act of will, to be a moral person. We act morally when we honor our commitments and duties even when that seems to go against our more narrow, or "selfish," interests. Religious belief is an important source of moral commitment for many persons. Although the particular language may differ, the laws, commandments, and teachings of many religious beliefs are imbedded in the moral principles we will consider here. Of course the part played by one's own religious belief can be decisive not only in the nature and level of commitment but in the weights given particular moral principles.

Our society is continually evolving as different cultures and sets of values are faced with new technologies and new social, economic, and political institutions. It follows that our specific moral duties as family members and as members of neighborhoods, cities, states, and nations must at times be reinterpreted.

From an individual and social point of view, what sort of moral behavior can we expect from our fellow citizens? There are special cases in which others perform heroic acts that go far beyond our expectations of duty. Most moral behavior is not overly demanding; more often we behave morally simply because we want to see ourselves as basically good and trustworthy. We see ourselves as persons of integrity, true to the moral principles we hold dear. We do not bother to calculate how some small advantage may be gained through an immoral act. From a social point of view then, we can expect that most people will usually behave morally; but we recognize there are limits to what we can and should expect. There are periods during wars when the duties of soldiers, sailors, and aviators are extremely demanding. Even in peacetime it is often the duty of police officers, fire fighters, and rescue workers to perform heroic acts. As we analyze and evaluate our social institutions and programs, it will be important to ask what moral responsibilities are being placed on our fellow citizens. When we ask whether or not we can expect moral behavior, it is not necessary to take our bearings from extreme cases.

In addition to the question Will a person choose to be moral? there is also the question How do we choose when two or more moral demands are made? The definition of a *moral dilemma* does not involve the question of whether or not to act morally. A moral dilemma arises when we must choose between two or more apparently conflicting moral duties. This choice is our primary focus here.

Social Ethics: A Pluralistic Approach to Applying Moral Principles to Social Issues

The approach we will now develop, *social ethics*, is a variation of pluralism. It owes much to W. D. Ross's theory of *prima facie duties*. Ross (1877–1940) argued that there is no unique principle from which moral duties can be derived. Similarly, there is no unique ordering of principles. Instead there are several kinds of moral duties. Some duties are general to all humans, some are associated with our roles as children, parents, citizens, and so on. Other duties are created, as when we make promises or when others make sacrifices on our behalf. When we wrong someone we create a duty of reparation. Other duties include realizing our potentials, being generous, and seeking justice. We become aware of the various ways these duties relate to each other as we are confronted with circumstances that involve several complementary or conflicting duties. A prima facie duty such as keeping promises is one that should always be fulfilled, unless it is counterbalanced by other duties that have greater weight. When keeping a promise means great harm to an innocent person, the prima facie duty of promise keeping may be overridden.

Ross argued that "in many situations there is more than one claim upon our actions, that these claims often conflict, and that while we can see with certainty that the

---

Social ethics is a methodology of applying moral principles to social issues. The purpose is to clarify the moral principles and social goals inherent in social issues and public initiatives. It asserts that the relative strength of various moral claims can only be compared within the context of a particular social issue.

W. D. Ross's theory of prima facie duties is an ethical theory based on pluralistic intuitionism. The words *prima facie* mean "at first glance"; thus a prima facie duty is one all humans must undertake unless it is overridden by stronger prima facie duties. The selection and weighting of prima facie duties relies on intuition.

claims exist, it becomes a matter of individual and fallible judgment to say which claim is in the circumstances the overriding one. In many such situations, equally good men would form different judgments as to what their duty is. They cannot all be right, but it is often impossible to say which is right; each person must judge according to his own individual sense of the comparative strength of various claims."[2]

It would be nice if all moral principles could be assigned permanent weights, but that is not the case. When we examine the diversity of opinion on moral questions, it does not rest completely on disagreement about fundamental moral principles. It rests in part on "differences in the circumstances of different societies," and in part on "different views which people hold, not on moral questions but on questions of fact."[3]

We will extend Ross's views concerning prima facie duties to the balancing of a wide range of moral principles inherent in the major ethical theories. This is entirely consistent with Ross's method and is especially appropriate to our purposes. We want to present various moral principles in both the language of the major ethical theories and the language we encounter in public debate. Our approach is *pluralistic* in that we will describe the moral principles in the contexts of the major ethical theories.

The role of intuition comes at the final phase of the process. The role of intuition here is not to "spontaneously" intuit moral principles without resort to a reasoning process. What is meant here is that, in the process of making social choices, we cannot avail ourselves of a theory in which universally agreed-upon weights can be assigned moral principles. They have different weights according to the context of the particular situation.

Although no set weights can be assigned moral principles, our judgements as to how they should be balanced in various situations become better informed with experience. Indeed, this is the whole point of our present endeavor. According to Ross, one's moral intuitions evolve with experience. Creative morality involves new and better appreciation of how moral principles can be applied. "It recognizes that new circumstances sometimes abrogate old claims and sometimes create new ones, and that we must be constantly alive to recognize such changes and to act on them." [4]

The dynamic of policy making does not require that every participant agree that the final policy is the perfect choice, their own preferred balance among social values and goals. Much of policy making is finding compromise even though the participants simply agree to disagree and move forward. We do not presume that being clear about what moral principles are involved will bring unanimity as to how they should be balanced. Nor do we expect complete agreement on the economic and political analyses of a given social issue. The purpose is to better clarify the issue and to identify, and perhaps narrow, the points of disagreement.

Our pluralistic approach mirrors the nature of social issues and public discussion. The issues being debated engender arguments that appeal to one or more of our moral values. By their very nature, social issues pose moral questions that need to be clarified. Moreover, they usually contain moral principles that are in conflict. Our task is to unravel and clarify the moral dimensions of the issues and to suggest how they may or may not be balanced.

In public discussion, appeal is made to our moral values and virtues in the contexts of specific social issues. For public discussion to be better informed requires a better understanding of moral principles as they relate to particular political, economic, and social situations.

Our approach will not invariably lead to finding *the answer*, however, a better understanding of the issues and the most promising government responses will often lead to their resolution. A more analytical approach may open opportunities for reorganizing social programs so that goals that seem in conflict may be simultaneously accomplished. Our major social programs such as health care, Social Security, education, and welfare have a number of social goals. It is crucial that we understand all of their moral dimensions.

When we consider the issue of welfare reform, we will find that it involves a number of conflicting social goals. For example, we are concerned that all families have access to the basic needs of life; at the same time, we worry about the counterproductive incentives created by current programs. As with most social issues, there are tradeoffs between fairness and efficiency. We will also consider several social goals inherent in the Social Security program. One purpose is to meet the basic needs of the elderly poor. The system also functions as a retirement plan. All individuals are required to contribute during their working years, with the expectation that, if they live to retirement, a retirement base will be provided. Most participants add other investments in order to build a more comfortable retirement. These goals are in some ways complementary and in other ways in conflict. What are our social responsibilities to meet the needs of the elderly poor? And how are these responsibilities to be balanced against the claims of other retirees who have contributed during their working years? The Social Security programs also present some interesting questions of intergenerational justice, particularly with respect to the demography of the baby-boomer generation as it relates to the Social Security trust fund.

The government's programs in health care, education, and the environment are replete with social issues. We will attempt to get past the political rhetoric and ask what are the moral principles at issue. As we will discover in chapter two, there are some analytical perspectives from economic and political theory that help to clarify the social issues' contexts and show how moral principles can be applied. Our next step is to consider the major ethical theories and how their inherent principles can be applied to social issues.

Modern ethical theories have developed following one of two basic approaches, the *teleological* and the *deontological* approaches. The Greek word *telos* refers to consequences of one's acts, while the term *deon*, meaning "duty," focuses on the motivation behind those acts. Both approaches appeal to our most basic ideas of justice. We may ask what

> **Teleological ethical theory** is a theory of ethics that gauges the worth of an action by its consequences. The term *teleological* is derived from the Greek word *telos*, which means "end."

are the consequences of our actions: Are the results good or bad? Or we may ask what *principles* guide our actions: Do we behave morally?

> **Deontological ethical theory** is a theory of ethics that gauges the worth of an action by whether or not it is done out of a sense of duty. The term is derived from the Greek word for "duty."

TELEOLOGICAL ETHICS

The common feature of the various theories under the teleological umbrella is a focus on consequences rather than on duty or moral obligation. Consequences can be evaluated in terms of a concept of the good or the humanly desirable. Acting out of duty has value if, and only if, it leads to the good.

For centuries most philosophers in the classical, medieval, and early modern traditions took for granted the proposition that a life led according to moral principles was synonymous with the good life, or rather, with producing the good. Many, like Socrates in *The Republic*, proposed that a life led by principles of justice was inevitably more satisfying; acting out of duty to principle naturally leads to the good. While deontological criticisms were raised, it was left to Immanuel Kant (1734–1804) to formulate a consistent deontological theory.

Aristotle's Concept of the Good

The good for Aristotle (384–322 B.C.) was simply whatever one was aiming for or seeking. The good for a human is whatever that person *by nature* seeks. It may not always be what one thinks one is seeking or what one seems to be wishing for. But ideally one is seeking *eudaimonia*, that which fulfills one's natural function. This may not be the same thing as happiness. There may be conflict between the aims of one's soul and one's desires and appetites. The *rational* control of *irrational* desires is a moral virtue. One has virtue when one develops the habit of doing what one is supposed to do, or rather, what one is ordained to do.

We will not attempt to trace all of the ways Aristotle's writings have been interpreted and elaborated. At times they have taken directions that Aristotle himself would not have taken. Our point here is that the idea of what end or good we seek or should seek is many-faceted. A consistent theme of the various Aristotelian traditions is that the good is realized when one achieves those goals that are his or hers by nature.

Utilitarian Theory

The most important theory using the teleological approach is the Utilitarian Theory. We ask whether or not our actions make everyone better off. A basic question we ask of social programs such as education, welfare, Social Security, and health care is how their costs relate to the benefits received. Are net benefits maximized? The theory has great appeal to our ideas of efficiency and social welfare. We are constantly choosing among alternatives so as to find the best course of action, the one that will produce the most satisfaction or "utility." Origins of modern utilitarian theory can be traced to classical Greek philosophy, through Renaissance scholars (particularly those in Italy), and to its flowering in Scotland and England in the eighteenth and nineteenth centuries. The major figures in Scotland and England were David Hume (1711–1776), Jeremy Bentham (1748–1832), James Mill (1773–1836), and John Stuart Mill (1806–1873).

Bentham and his followers, the Philosophical Radicals, were very influential in changing the way people looked at social issues. Many of the reforms in Scotland and England in the eighteenth and nineteenth centuries were promoted by utilitarian arguments. There are some similarities with the Aristotelian emphasis on man's natural goals; but Aristotle focused on the happy, or blessed, condition of the soul, whereas Bentham focused simply on happiness defined as pleasure. The fundamental distinction is between the desires a man expresses in his real, everyday life and the desires he expresses when he is fully rational enough to include his moral virtues. When John Stuart Mill presented his more sophisticated version of Bentham, he argued that value must be judged in terms of quality, not simply quantity. At times there may be conflicts between our immediate appetites and what we know to be best for society, but according to Mill it is possible for us to "become attached" to social virtues.

The role of utilitarianism in modern political and economic theory is paradoxical. The original version features the moral credo, "the greatest good for the greatest number." It is egalitarian to the extreme. No individual counts any more than another. All that counts is to maximize total welfare. Moreover if we acknowledge that an extra dollar has less utility to the wealthy person than to the poor person, the "greatest good" can only be achieved by radical redistribution of income and wealth. When I ask what the demands of the Utilitarian Credo are on me as an individual, the requirements are equally challenging. I should be willing to sacrifice my own utility if by so doing I can give a greater amount of happiness to others.

Actually, many modern theorists in economics and politics attempt to avoid questions of morality by restricting their analyses to "value-free problems." It is the methodology of welfare economics, with its emphasis on maximizing, that gives the impression that it has a utilitarian philosophical foundation.

The *theory of welfare economics* is the attempt to specify the conditions necessary for efficient resource allocation. This idea of efficiency is normative, in that resources are to be allocated to the production of those goods that maximize society's welfare. Modern methodology traces back to the 1870s, when a revolution occurred in welfare theory. Leon Walras (1834–1910), Karl Menger (1840–1921), and William Stanley Jevons (1835–1882) conceived the idea that individuals acting independently to maximize their own utility could simultaneously achieve maximum utility for all, in other words, "the greatest good." Each individual economic agent is seen as making marginal adjustments that lead to the maximization of utility, happiness, profits, or income. The theory demonstrates that, when this sort of maximizing behavior takes place in an economy made up of competitive markets, the resulting allocation of resources will be the most efficient possible. Competition requires that firms produce at the lowest cost possible, and it requires that they produce that combination of goods that gives consumers the most satisfaction. Theoretically, since resource allocation is efficient and since each individual is maximizing his or her own welfare, total welfare is also maximized.

> An **ideology** is a cohesive system of values and beliefs. It provides its believers answers to questions about human nature, politics, economics, society, and the natural order.

What is paradoxical and ironic about this vision of the economic system is that it involves no moral demands on individuals or society. Welfare is maximized when each person follows his or her own narrow self-interests. For many, this vision of an economy composed of perfectly competitive markets has become an *ideology*. It is an ideology that gets in the way of a realistic assessment of political and economic systems. The French term *laissez-faire* ("hands off") carries with it the idea that markets usually work better with a minimum of government interference. Economists generally agree with this idea; but as we will see, there are many exceptions to the rule. Indeed, most of the social issues we are about to consider arise because some particular market has failed in one way or another.

> **Utilitarianism** is the doctrine that states that the rightness or wrongness of an action is determined by the goodness or badness of its consequences for everyone involved.

The role of *utilitarianism* in economic theory and in the assessment of social issues remains unclear. As noted, most analysts try to avoid questions of morality by addressing value-free problems. But for some, the utopian vision of the laissez-faire economy provides a philosophical foundation for their advocacy of free markets. In any case, this vision has little relation to social issues in the real world. Even if all markets were perfectly competitive, there is no reason to believe that the incomes generated and the goods consumed would go to those who would benefit the most; and if that is not the case, then total welfare would not be maximized.

The original utilitarians addressed questions of philosophy, politics, and economics, questions in which the normative content was straightforward and explicit. The utilitarianism of modern welfare theory has been truncated and deformed; however, the basic idea of calculating and maximizing welfare remains important. As we focus on social issues and programs, we invariably will ask what are the benefits and costs of the alternatives. This brings us to a central difficulty with the utilitarian approach: how do we calculate benefits and costs? While political and economic theorists often proceed as if there were a standard measure of utility, none has been found. It is not quite legitimate to assume that market prices are a reliable measure. The "measurement problem" will remain challenging, first because the social issues and social programs involve goods and services that the market does not handle well (and thus does not "price" well); and second because we are not solely committed to the idea of welfare maximization even if it could be measured precisely.

Act and Rule Utilitarianism

Although utilitarians focus on the goodness of results rather than actions, they are aware that the world is so complex that we must rely heavily on rules to guide our behavior. Utilitarians divide themselves into *Act Utilitarians* and *Rule Utilitarians* when debating how such rules should be formulated and under what conditions they can be broken. The Act Utilitarian takes into account that, while breaking a rule in a particular situation may have a good consequence, it also has the consequence that others may follow the example. All of the immediate and long-term consequences of an act must be considered.

> **Act Utilitarianism** focuses on particular actions and judges rightness or wrongness according to their consequences.

A Rule Utilitarian starts with the idea that the universal following of certain rules will maximize utility. The rightness of the act is defined in terms of conformity to a rule. The two theories differ as to the origin of rightness. Does it come from the act that has accounted for all of the consequences? Or does it come from conforming to a rule that, if universally followed, will increase social welfare?

> **Rule Utilitarianism** does not consider the consequences of particular actions but the consequences of adopting general rules for actions, such as "keep promises." Different rules are compared on the basis of their consequences.

Both Act and Rule Utilitarians generally support rules such as "Tell the truth" and "Don't bribe public officials." Telling a lie to promote one's own self-interest at a greater expense to others is clearly immoral by both approaches. The particular act is immoral because the welfare lost by others is greater than that gained by the liar. But telling a lie to protect an innocent family, say, from a campaign of ethnic cleansing, would obviously be moral as a one-time act. But it would go against the rule of telling the truth, a rule that, if generally followed, leads to greater social welfare.

Suppose you are a public official reviewing the qualifications of welfare mothers for certain benefits. Should you condone their practice of falsifying applications in order to receive greater benefits?

Bribing of foreign public officials in order to gain a favorable contract is usually both illegal and immoral. But there may be situations in which bribery would increase total welfare in both the short and the long run. Say, for example, that an official must be bribed so the company can import a life-saving medicine that would otherwise be unavailable.

As we focus on certain public issues and programs the questions of rules versus results will appear regularly. One point we should keep in mind is that both Act and Rule Utilitarians base their evaluation of rules on their efficacy in promoting total welfare, that is, on the final result.

DEONTOLOGICAL THEORIES

Deontological theories focus on processes rather than results. How should I live my life? What are the principles I use when I evaluate my own actions? What are my rights, duties, liberties, and obligations?

When we reason from these perspectives, we may often encounter moral dilemmas in which several obligations conflict. We must somehow rank various duties. Most theorists agree that no definitive hierarchy has been devised. Instead each moral dilemma must be approached on its own terms.

Immanuel Kant

Deontological theories rely primarily on the arguments first advanced by Immanuel Kant (1734–1804). He argued that what is important is how we live our lives. We should live in willful submissiveness and duty to the essential moral principles. No action has moral worth unless it is done from a sense of duty. If I act out of narrow self-interest even though the act may give great benefit to others, it has no moral worth. Kant's *categorical imperative* provides a necessary condition for an act to be moral: one ought never to act except in such a way that one could will that his or her maxim for that act would become a universal law. This condition requires that we have equal consideration for others and for society as a whole.

A related moral principle concerns the inherent value of every person. Kant would enjoin us to treat others as "ends" not simply as "means." Of course the taxi driver is a means for us to get to our destination, but she or he is also a person and as such deserves our respect and consideration.

> The **Categorical imperative** In Kant's ethics, an unconditional moral law not dependent on any ulterior motive or end: "Act only according to that maxim by which you can at the same time will that it should become a universal law." A related Kantian formula states: "So act as to treat humanity, whether in your own person or in another, always as an end, and never as only a means."

Moral credit for an action depends therefore on two elements. First, the motive for the action must be one of duty to principle for its own sake. Second, it is understood that the principle itself must be worthy. We can judge the validity of the principle by its universality: Could we will that the rule become a universal law? The criterion is essentially moral because all persons are given consideration. As a student or businessperson I cannot justify lying, cheating, or stealing simply because it will increase my own immediate welfare. I have no right to make an exception on my own behalf. Suppose I decide to cheat on exams and claim that everyone else is also free to cheat. The relationship among students and teachers would become more adversarial, the validity of grades would be brought into question, and more resources would have to be spent on the prevention of cheating. Obviously I would be worse off, along with everyone else. My rule that everyone be free to cheat fails Kant's conditions.

Evaluating a principle or an action by asking if everyone would be worse off sounds suspiciously utilitarian. In fact, most Rule Utilitarians would argue that deontologists are actually utilitarians since the principles they espouse all seem to trace their validity to their effect on total welfare. It is true that most moral rules can be justified by either utilitarian or deontological argument. But Kantians would argue that there is a fundamental difference in the respect given persons *as individuals*. This respect extends to the individual's autonomously chosen life plan.

One familiar counterexample to the utilitarian rule involves the question of exploiting one person for the greater good of others. Suppose the disutility that one person would suffer by being a slave would be overbalanced by the benefits enjoyed by another person; total welfare would be increased. But the Kantian respect for each person and his or her own goals would disallow such a tradeoff. One justification for the prohibition against cheating is that it unfairly disadvantages any individual who does not cheat. Respect for individuals and their initiatives demands that the system of rewards be fair. The ideas of fair games and fair play are elaborations on this theme.

While Kant's theory provides a structure for moral thinking it does not resolve all of the issues we have presented. Our understanding of a dilemma, such as lying to protect the innocent, may be enhanced by describing it as a conflict between duties, but the dilemma remains unresolved.

It is important to remember that, in the Rossian framework, which we have adopted, there can be a conflict among prima facie duties; but after due consideration, only one thing will be one's actual duty. Similarly, in our social ethics approach, the best social choice will emerge as moral principles are weighed in the contexts of particular social issues.

The Libertarian Argument

Libertarianism is deontological in that results are justified by fair processes. No matter how unequal the distribution of wealth or income, it is justified if the processes used are fair, say, for example, the process of fair competition in free markets. The libertarian argument places a high value on the liberty of the individual. Essentially I, as an individual, start with a clean slate, that is, with no obligations to anyone else. If I have no obligations or duties to anyone else, that means, correlatively, that they have no claims on me. I recognize no obligation to others' rights—"human," "natural," or otherwise—until these rights and obligations are created by mutual agreement.

The libertarian argument is perhaps the

> **Libertarianism** is a movement in political philosophy based on the rights of individuals. These rights derive from the absolute right that each individual has to self-ownership. Each individual has the right to any previously unused resource, such as virgin land, by expending personal energy to claim it. It is argued that the entire structure of private property rights is built upon these basic rights.

strongest possible statement of individualism. Individuals are free to make contracts with each other, and they may even set up governmental bodies that undertake the production of social goods. But governmental activities are legitimate only if all of those affected have given unanimous consent. Generally, individuals have the right to do anything they wish that is not proscribed by a contract they have agreed upon previously.

The question of rights is problematical for libertarians. While most would argue that rights and duties can only be created by mutual agreement, others make use of the idea of natural rights. Although not a libertarian, John Locke (1632–1704) presented the case that the natural rights to liberty and property originate *prior* to the state. Locke's intention was to demonstrate that rights did *not* originate with the sovereign. They do not exist at the whim of a sovereign nor can they be abolished at the sovereign's discretion. Some ethical theorists state that we have fundamental rights just because we are human. This quality is possessed by all human beings equally; therefore, all have a right to equal, impartial consideration: equal justice, equal freedom, and equal opportunity.

Some libertarians claim that property rights are not dependent on mutual agreement and thus are not dependent on the existence of a government. Appeal is made to arguments similar to those of John Locke and Adam Smith in which man is seen in a "state of nature" creating value by "mixing" his labor with heretofore unclaimed property. The hunter has a claim to the deer he kills; the settler has a right to the produce of the land he clears and plants.

The rights created in the libertarian world need not have strong intuitive appeal in and of themselves. They win the day primarily because no prior claims are recognized. For example, suppose I am the first to arrive at a waterhole in the desert and I lay claim to it, say by erecting a sign to that effect. Then the next person to come along has no right to a drink of my water. I have no obligation to give him any simply to save his life—he has no "human rights." Again the erecting of the sign would seem to be a weak claim, but it is sufficient since no other claims are admitted.

Robert Nozick's entitlement theory[5] begins with the origin of property rights and then describes how the legitimacy of ownership can be preserved through fair trading within a market system. Procedural justice is preserved because the voluntary nature of trades make them fair to all concerned. The results are legitimate because the starting points are fair and the processes are fair. If, at the end of the day, I wind up with more wealth than you, you have no complaint.

> **Robert Nozick's entitlement theory** is a theory of property rights based on procedural justice. Transactions in free markets are fair because they are voluntary. Since no other claims are admitted, the final owners of property gained through this process are entitled to the results.

There are obvious difficulties in using Nozick's entitlement theory to justify the present distribution of wealth. There may have been a few cases in the settlement of the United States in which it could be argued that no Indians had a direct claim on a particular piece of land. In most parts of the world, the acquisition of land and other forms of wealth has had a history that fails the test of procedural justice. Oddly enough the purpose of Nozick's argument is to show that property owners can do what they want with their property since no one else has claim to it. Notice, however, that the results are justified only if the entire process has been fair. The argument fails, therefore, if at any point in history an unfair transfer of property took place. It is safe to say that no present claim to property has such a perfect history. We would be left with no claims to property at all.

The difficulties the libertarian approach encounters in establishing property rights as prior to society and government are not crucial to our social ethics approach. We are more interested in several of the moral principles often associated with libertarianism. Many of these are held to be important by most citizens. We ask what weight they should be given in moral decision making. For example, the "process," or "the way the game is played," is an important ethical consideration. The argument that a person has at least some claim to wealth earned by hard work in a fair game appeals to our basic values. As we shall see, however, it is only one of many valid claims. It must be compared to others in the hierarchy of claims and intuitions.

John Rawls and Justice as Fairness

In his *Theory of Justice* (1971) John Rawls develops a theory that draws heavily on moral intuitions, widely held religious beliefs, and values and culture of Western democracies. His arguments are primarily deontological and, more specifically, Kantian. At the same time his principles can be used to evaluate results, and thus they often take on the strengths and weaknesses of the teleological approach.

Rawls focuses on the level of economic opportunity available to each individual. Respect for the individual is expressed in a recognition of the fact that each has personal goals whose attainment will require some access to *primary goods*. Rawls would have us conclude that we should distribute all primary goods equally except in those situations in which unequal distribution would work to the advantage of the least-well-off groups. He defines primary goods as "things every rational man is presumed to want. Those goods normally have a use, whatever a person's rational plan of life."[6] They include rights, liberties, powers, opportunities, income, and wealth. They even include natural endowments such as health, vigor, intelligence, and imagination.

> **Rawlsian primary goods** are goods every person needs in pursuing her or his rational plan of life. They include rights, liberties, powers, opportunities, income, and wealth, as well as natural endowments such as health, vigor, intelligence, and imagination.

Rawls takes care not to limit his egalitarian criteria to the final results of society's economic political processes. That is, he is not interested solely in how the pie should be divided, a point inherent in so many egalitarian theories. Instead, he focuses on the availability of primary goods and on the fairness of society's background institutions that govern economic and political processes. At the same time, his principles require that just patterns of distribution somehow be achieved.

The mechanics of Rawls's just society would seem to require continual reassessment of the "background institutions" and "rules of the game." While Rawls would rely primarily on free markets to allocate resources and distribute income, the rules of the game (especially taxes and transfers) could be adjusted to insure a distribution of income that could also be considered fair.

Moral Principles from Behind a "Veil of Ignorance"

Rawls invites us to consider ourselves our society's founders creating a social contract complete with moral principles and political and economic institutions. Here again Rawls appeals to widely held cultural intuitions and myths, especially those surrounding the births of the Western democracies. We are asked to imagine the rules we would make if we were behind a veil of ignorance, that is if we were ignorant of our own individual fortuitous characteristics— our race, sex, intelligence quotient (IQ), family wealth and connections, religious belief, and even our own individual talents and handicaps. The veil of ignorance would guarantee equal consideration for others. According to Rawls, the society's founders would adopt two principles for organizing and evaluating our society.

> The **Rawlsian difference principle** states that, in a just society any social and economic inequalities are to be arranged so that they are to the greatest benefit of the least advantaged and attached to positions open to all.

First: Each person is to have an equal right to the most extensive basic liberty compatible with a similar liberty for others.

Second: Social and economic inequalities are to be arranged so that they are both (a) reasonably expected to be to everyone's advantage, and (b) attached to positions and offices open to all.[7]

The second principle may be elaborated as the *difference principle*: "All social values—liberty and opportunity, income and wealth, and the basis of self-respect—are to be distributed equally unless an unequal distribution of any, or all, of these values is to everyone's advantage."[8] A further interpretation of the second principle reads as follows:

Social and economic inequalities are to be arranged so that they are both to the greatest benefit of the least advantaged and attached to offices and positions open to all under conditions of fair equality of opportunity.[9]

As we apply Rawls's theory we will find that it allows for a wide range of interpretation. For some interpreters, the maxim of equal liberty it proposes is not simply a "freedom from"; it also implies a "freedom to." Therefore it does not carry with it the libertarian assumption that liberty is primarily a matter of reducing government intervention into what otherwise would be a free society with ample opportunity for all. Instead it assumes that society must at times intervene if fair opportunities are to be made available. On the other hand, Rawls would argue that the difference principle does not require that we continually redistribute income according to a strict pattern; that is, a pattern that keeps reducing the wealth of the better off until the least advantaged are brought up to the highest level possible. Instead we are to pay attention to the background institutions that guarantee fair play. Of course we must account for the effect of redistribution schemes on incentives. Certainly there are limits to redistribution schedules; at some point they will damage work and saving incentives so much that even the least-well-off groups will be hurt. Much depends on how incentives are affected by taxes and transfers. Under the assumption that high taxes do little damage to work incentives, the difference principle would seem to require radical redistribution of income. Under the assumption that higher taxes greatly reduce work effort, and thus gross domestic product, much less redistribution would be possible. All of this leaves us with a wide range of possible interpretations. Moreover, as we will see when we attempt to apply his theory to the question of intergenerational justice, Rawls himself is willing to depart from his principles when they seem inadequate to the task.

Communitarianism

In recent years, several movements have arisen in reaction to what is seen to be the excessive individualism in American philosophical and social thought. One of these, the communitarian movement, places high value on community, insisting that it is natural for all of us to have social, as well as individual, needs. The emphasis on individual rights in Western culture, and especially in America, must be balanced with social responsibility.

> **Communitarianism** is a social movement rather than an ethical theory. It argues for a pluralistic deontological approach to ethics (as opposed to the teleological approach of utilitarianism and neoclassical economics). The ideal society is cooperative and participatory.

Many communitarians, such as Robert Bellah and Amitai Etzioni,[10] see individualism, self-centeredness, and adversarial relationships as very damaging to the social fabric. They argue that important social institutions such as families, churches, schools, towns, cities, and the nation are being seriously weakened.

The communitarians would argue that most current ethical theories follow the lead of Enlightenment philosophers in attempting to use reason to develop a morality based on the sanctity of the individual. They would claim that Kant, Kierkegaard, J. S. Mill, and more recently, Robert Nozick and John Rawls have failed in this attempt. None of us are individuals as such. The myth of the rugged, self-reliant loner exploring the wilderness has some appeal to our imagination but is hardly a viable starting point for ethical theory. Moral principles have to do with how we relate to each other. We can express our individuality only in terms of various social relationships. These social relationships are rich and varied. The communitarians argue that we cannot expect to start with a vision of the rights of an autonomous individual and use reason to arrive at a complete moral theory.

According to the communitarian view, social responsibilities do not originate in the way autonomous individuals make marketlike contracts. We are simply born into some relationships, and, with varying degrees of acquiescence, we find ourselves committed to others. We acknowledge certain virtues as important within these contexts. For example, when a person trains to become a physician, he or she takes on certain responsibilities toward patients. A narrow view of physicians as profit maximizers assumes that they will take advantage of their superior knowledge and prescribe expensive, unnecessary treatments. But few physicians actually see themselves as profit maximizers. As we consider policies to curtail health care costs, the question of how health care professionals regard themselves and their professional duties will be important.

The communitarian perspective would caution us *not* to approach social issues such as education, health care, social security, welfare reform, and the environment simply as marketlike contracts between the individual and the state.

We should ask how new policies may change individual responsibilities within the affected social institutions. How would a change in Social Security taxes or benefits affect the responsibilities of working-age children toward their parents? How are family responsibilities affected by various welfare reforms? More generally, can economic and social institutions be organized so that the inherent interpersonal relationships better reflect our ideas of community?

As noted, an ideology links moral values with beliefs about politics, economics, and, more generally, how the world works. Thus, communitarianism, along with libertarianism, individualism, egalitarianism, and other belief systems, will be a useful point of departure as we develop political and economic perspectives and apply them to social issues.

Deontological Theories as Rights-Based Theories

We will frequently ponder the question of the relationships between rights and duties (as well as the related ideas of privileges, obligations, expectations, responsibilities, liberties, proscriptions, and so on). Who is owed what by whom? Usually we expect that, if someone has a right, then someone else must have a correlative duty; when I have a duty to pay you five dollars, you have a right to be paid five dollars by me. To say you have a right to be paid five dollars but that no one has a correlative duty would be nonsensical. On the other hand, we speak as if one's right to life imposes duties on every other person; but we are not always clear as to what is involved.

As we survey the nature and distribution of rights and duties within our society, we will observe that there are several ways rights and duties can be arranged and several ways they can be categorized. Our commercial and legal systems provide rules for a wide range of transactions in which parties can assume various sorts of obligations. Although the specifics differ among cultures, parents have duties to their children and children have rights. These systems of rights and duties often have complex arrangements of subsidiary and supplementary rights and duties. My contract with you may be insured by cosigners. If a child's parents cannot fulfill their duties, other family members may be held responsible, or final responsibility may be seen to rest on society as a whole, say in the form of a state welfare agency. Some rights may be matched with only generalized duties. Consider the case in which a nation has declared that it will insure job opportunities to all citizens. No particular citizen or firm has an obligation, but each citizen has a right vis-à-vis the government.

Within theories of rights various accounts are given as to the origin of rights. Obviously individuals may create rights and obligations in business and other transactions. But can we also speak of God-given rights, human rights, natural rights, universal rights? In recent years our nation and others have used such forums as the United Nations to demonstrate concern over human rights violations by several national governments. The social issues we will address in this study do, in fact, involve human rights. We will proceed under the assumption that all moral persons recognize that all human beings have some basic rights and that they and others have duties correlative to those rights. We are left with interesting questions as to what those rights and duties are in the contexts of the specific social issues of our concern.

We will focus on how rights are given definition within the institutions of society. Rights are observed in cultural conventions, religious and philosophical beliefs, and legal rules. The social issues of our concern cut across a wide range of economic and political institutions and activities.

Social Ethics: The Methodology of a Pluralistic Approach

We now ask how we can account for the various moral theories and principles within a pluralistic approach. We must reaffirm our position that those theories that attempt to derive all rules from a single, fundamental principle are unsuccessful. For example, utilitarianism does not adequately account for the obligations we make, such as promises. Similarly, the Kantian criteria of duty and universality fail to capture many of the principles we consider important in moral decision making.

The real test of the pluralistic approach comes when we examine the moral content of specific moral issues. We invariably find a number of conflicting moral principles. Each requires our consideration as we decide upon the best course of action. We have argued that the relative weight given each moral principle may change according to the situation. Thus our approach must be *pluralistic* in the sense that no one ordering of principles is available. Similarly it must be *intuitionist* in the sense that, when no strict ordering is available, one must use her or his own considered judgment.

To iterate, the definition of intuition as used here does not include the popular notion of "spontaneous knowing" without resort to the reasoning process. It is true that the reasoning process is limited, in that following strict rules and priorities will not guarantee "the answer." But reasoning is important at every stage. We must use reasoning to learn from our experience as we make moral choices. How good are we at predicting the ramifications of our actions? On previous moral choices, were the weights we gave the various moral principles consistent with our assessments of the possible outcomes? Were our moral judgements in tune with others whose judgements we have learned to respect?

There is considerable controversy as to the role intuition plays in the context of pluralistic ethics. In recent years intuitionism has come to mean that moral principles can *only* be grasped by the process of intuition. In our social ethics approach we do not make that claim. We affirm that moral truths can be found or revealed through various means. These means are not limited to intuition but may include the operation of reason and judgment.

In summary, the important role for intuition in our social ethics approach comes in situations in which we are required to make moral choices. It is assumed that there is an array of known moral principles that must be compared when the moral decision is made. We define the faculty we use in this weighting process as intuition. It is not simply the calculation of previously agreed-upon weights. It is not spontaneous but relies on our faculties to reason.

What can we say to the complaint that the methodology of social ethics gives no definitive answers? We can predict that persons will differ in the weight they give the various moral principles. Thus, although we may agree about the facts of a given policy issue, we may arrive at different policy prescriptions. This is to be expected in a pluralistic ethical approach. The aim of the methodology is simply to encourage consideration of all the relevant facts and moral principles. Even if unanimity were reached, there would be no guarantee that the right answer had been found. But social issues continue to arise and policy decisions must be made. The idea is that in this ongoing process we can have greater faith in our moral intuitions if we take greater care in gathering and analyzing the facts and in weighing the moral principles.

The process will be employed over and over again in this exploration of social issues. We will ask what moral principles appear to be important to the issue in question. Then we will attempt to give them relative weights according to the situation. Of course, our understanding of the situation should be well informed. For this purpose in chapter two we will outline a number of analytical perspectives, especially those from political and economic theory.

THE ANALOGY OF A FAIR GAME

One technique we will use to organize moral principles is to cast them in terms of the "fair-game" analogy. The idea is that this will give some insight into how several moral principles are related. It also will provide a bridge between the moral principles and the real-world situation. For example, we often use the analogy of a fair game to evaluate the opportunities open to individuals and groups within our society. Often the reference is to an individual as he or she is born, educated, and follows a profession. Certainly one of the more important social goals is that every individual be afforded a wide array of opportunities at every step of the way. We often use the terms fair starts, fair rules of the game, fair play, and fair results. We also talk about a level playing field. Moreover we appreciate games in which competition is fair. Since risks are involved in our economic system, as well as in the sports we play, it seems fair to provide "safety nets" such as unemployment insurance, bankruptcy provisions, and welfare programs for those who are unlucky.

Fair Starts: Some Conflicting Principles

The idea of equal starting points is appealing. Strictly speaking, starting points in one's economic life can never be exactly equal since differences in talents, IQ, health, and family situation cannot be compensated for. Surely we would not want to equalize opportunity by imposing burdens on those with advantages such as natural talents. One of my youthful ambitions was to be a professional basketball player. But to give me an equal starting point would have required that thousands of players with greater talents be hindered in some way—perhaps they should have been required to play while carrying weights ranging from 100 to 200 pounds.

The idea of equal starting points also conflicts with other principles. Within limits, we allow individuals some freedom to use their wealth to improve the opportunities of others. In particular, we allow parents to buy educational toys for their children and to read to their children. Of course it would be possible to restrict parents in the use of their money and even in the time and energy they spend improving the starting points of their children. That tradeoff would seem to be a poor one. Indeed, we want to encourage parents to be responsible and loving towards their children. We want to encourage the virtue of generosity in general.

Should we allow generosity by parents and others to curtail the opportunities open to some children? Here there is a real conflict that requires that principles somehow be balanced. If our social goal regarding opportunity is interpreted in terms of insuring not an "equal opportunity" but an "acceptable range of opportunities," then we may find that most of the advantages parents give to their children do not conflict with that goal. The important question is whether or not there is still a wide range of opportunity open to all.

A general rule promoting both fairness and efficiency stipulates that positions in government and industry should be filled by those most qualified. It is certainly unfair for political or monetary influence to be used in filling positions that should be open to all. On the other hand, parents should certainly be allowed to help their children become better qualified for various desirable positions.

The fairness of one's starting point can be enhanced by programs such as Head Start that are designed to mitigate disadvantages some children face.

Again the appropriate question is whether or not a young person can be given a fair start. Will she or he have an acceptable range of opportunities?

Fair Games and Fair Results

If we consider the intertemporal aspects of a game, we immediately see how principles focusing on results and processes may conflict, or rather, need to be balanced. Consider the terms fair starts, fair rules of the game, fair play, and fair results. They cover the whole range of teleological and deontological perspectives and address many of the most fundamental questions of just how we are to balance our moral principles. How could the results of a game be fair if the starting points were unfair or if some of the players cheated?

What strategies in politics and economics are to be considered fair? What penalties should be imposed when the rules are broken? Under what conditions do we provide for a second chance? A third chance?

In chapter two we will outline the various ways government sets the rules of the game for our economic system. We will ask how they may be evaluated in terms of efficiency and fairness. There always seems to be a tension between our ideas of fair results and fair rules of the game. Our egalitarian moral principles suggest that the economic results, that is, income distribution, should be more equal; but would it be unfair to redistribute income earned in a fair game? On the other hand, there is nothing sacrosanct about the current set of economic institutions. Fairness and efficiency could be preserved, or even enhanced, under other rules of the game, to include other taxes and transfers. As we develop perspectives for evaluating our tax and expenditure structures, questions of income and wealth distribution will be important. The point is that we cannot simply look at starting points, rules of the game, or results. We must consider each in terms of the other.

A LIST OF MORAL PRINCIPLES

Let us summarize by listing some of the moral principles we have discussed. These ideas could be expressed in a number of ways according to the language used in the various moral theories. Therefore our list is somewhat arbitrary. It includes no attempt to prioritize. Moreover, there are obvious conflicts among the principles. But, of course, that is just the point of our pluralistic approach.

1. Individual actions should be judged on their *results*. Do they create the greatest good for the greatest number? This is known as the Utilitarian Credo.

2. Society's goal should be to maximize total utility; such maximization involves fine tuning, that is, making marginal adjustments. The rule would require that one person's utility be sacrificed if, by so doing, the total utility for society would be greater.

3. Actions should be evaluated in terms of motivation rather than results. According to Kant the only proper motivation is one of duty.

4. One ought never to act except in a way that one could make one's maxim a universal law (Kant's categorical imperative).

5. One should treat each person always as an end and never simply as a means. Each person has moral worth, and his or her dignity should be respected.

6. Each person should be afforded a fair chance to achieve her or his own goals in life. According to Rawls, the "primary goods" necessary to achieve one's life goals should be divided fairly. The difference principle says that all social values should be distributed equally, unless unequal distribution is to everyone's advantage. Specifically, inequalities should be arranged so that they give the greatest benefit to the least advantaged.

7. Distribution should be based on principles of justice:

   a. to each an equal share
   b. to each according to need
   c. to each according to effort or sacrifice
   d. to each according to contribution to society (i.e., to the welfare of others)
   e. to each according to his or her rights
   f. to each according to some other recognized merit

One theme running through these principles is respect for the dignity of every person. That this is so pervasive suggests that it is more than a principle to be balanced against others. Indeed when I choose to be moral, I necessarily choose to respect others. It is the essence of being moral. Ethical theorists suggest various ways to gain this moral perspective. One way is simply to follow the golden rule: do unto others as you would have them do unto you. Kant enjoined us to treat others as ends not simply as means. His categorical imperative requires that we give others due consideration. We may also use the device of pretending we are founding a new nation. Rawls would add the condition that we attempt to place ourselves behind a veil of ignorance. In each case the process would lead us to respect others in the same way we respect ourselves.

How Are We to Apply These Moral Principles to Social Issues?

The social ethics approach we have outlined is well suited to social issues. It is pluralistic precisely because the various arguments used in public discussion employ different moral perspectives. If we are to gain critical appreciation of these arguments it is necessary that we explore each in its own right. They can then be compared and balanced with other moral arguments. Each social issue must also be analyzed and evaluated on its own political and economic terms. What are the moral questions embedded in the issue's institutional context? Understanding the *causes* of a misallocation of resources or an inequity in income distribution may suggest how it can best be resolved or mitigated.

Different arrays of rights and duties are defined within different institutional contexts: individuals and families, and business firms, as well as educational, religious, charitable, professional, and other organizations. Consider how society can provide for the well-being, education, and economic opportunity of children. What should be the responsibilities of the parents? What are the roles we expect of schools and teachers? How are schools to be financed? How do we evaluate the educational opportunities available to each child?

In the next chapter we will review some useful analytical concepts from economic and political theory and ask how these relate to our moral intuitions. We start with the basics, an economic system based on free market capitalism and a political system based on representative democracy. The understanding of most Americans as to what constitutes fair play and fair results has evolved within this institutional setting.

Basic moral principles, such as respect for each individual and her or his opportunity to follow individually chosen goals, are embedded deeply within our ideas of how our economic and political system should work. Correspondingly, we have ideas and intuitions as to what constitutes unfair competition, exploitation, coercion, and misuse of monopoly power. By contrast, in fair competition all are free to compete and none have unfair advantage. As noted, we often resort to sports analogies to describe fairness in economics and politics; we demand that a fair game with fair rules be played on a level playing field.

We believe that fairness and efficiency are enhanced by competitive markets. The "perfectly competitive market" of economic theory features such conditions as free entry and exit of inputs and firms. All competitors should be "perfectly" informed. Moreover the earnings of each productive factor, that is each worker, each executive, and each stockholder should be based on their marginal contributions to the productive process. Their earnings, therefore, would be based directly on how well they contribute to the welfare of others, in other words, consumers. This is one of our widely held ideas of fairness, that those who contribute talent and hard work are due greater rewards. This idea is deontological in that the results are justified by the fairness of the process. It does not follow, however, that we must accept Nozick's version of the argument that discounts all other possible claims. In the real world we observe that some players in the game may be unfairly disadvantaged or simply have bad luck. We recognize their needs and would balance them against other claims.

The free market often involves economic risk taking. The players in economic games can usually avoid some risks by taking out insurance, hedging, and diversifying. Some risks, say a general economywide recession, are uninsurable. What are our obligations to players who take great risks and experience bad luck? Taking a broad, founders-of-the-nation view, we would probably agree that some risk taking is a matter of individual choice and that the risk takers deserve the consequences, good or bad. Even here we would want safety nets in place. Broad social programs should be designed to insure against certain kinds of otherwise uninsurable risks. These risks, such as massive un-

employment during a severe recession, are known as social risks. They are beyond the capabilities of private insurance companies.

There are several necessary conditions if the attributes of perfect competition are to be realized in a given industry. There must be a large number of
buyers and sellers, free entry and exit, and knowledge of relevant prices. All
benefits and costs must be captured by market prices, that is, the processes
must not create "externalities" such as air or water pollution. Several of the
concepts we will consider in the next chapter are defined in terms of depar-
tures from the competitive norm. These imperfections, known as *market failures*, may justify various types of government intervention. Where the numbers
of buyers and sellers are insufficient, as in monopoly or oligopoly, output may
be restricted so that prices do not reflect costs. Such results are considered unfair as well as inefficient. A second category of market failure occurs when information is imperfect. Erroneous estimates of costs, sales, weather conditions,
and so on can lead to bad consequences. Situations in which one party has an
important informational advantage, called "asymmetric information," may also
lead to unfair, inefficient results.

A third category arises in cases where various benefits and costs are not
captured by market prices. We define *public goods* as goods whose benefits are
not exhausted in consumption. In addition, it is often difficult to exclude consumers from enjoying the goods' benefits. The classic example, national defense, exemplifies these characteristics. If one hundred thousand new citizens
were born tomorrow, the protection they would receive would not diminish
the protection received by everyone else. Moreover, it would be impossible to
exclude them from being protected.

Externalities involve benefits or costs to third parties when regular
market transactions take place. When a paper mill manufactures and sells paper products, many transactions are necessary, and prices for inputs and products are set. But suppose the process involves the firm's polluting a river. Suppose further that no price is set, and the users of the river have no market
organization. These costs then are external to the mechanics of the market.
The market has failed and, once again, questions of efficiency and fairness
arise.

Similarly many of our ideas of fairness in political matters are drawn from
our centuries of experience with democratic institutions. The ideal of democratic government, government by the people using majority rule, also includes
the principles of equality of rights and safeguards for minorities. These principles are inherent in the checks and balances and separation of powers built into
our political processes. It is within this political context that we will evaluate
our approaches to certain social issues.

As we proceed we will also use *social choice* perspectives. The central question is how the preferences of citizens can be efficiently and fairly reconciled
using political processes such as voting and representative government. Ideally,
democratic political processes can be used to allocate resources in ways that
complement the allocation processes of competitive markets. *Government failures* may be defined as cases in which there are imperfections in government's

political and economic activities, say where government officials have incentives that undermine the fairness and efficiency of a program.

Each of the social issues we will consider has its own particular economic and political problems. Obviously, if competitive markets could efficiently produce and fairly distribute education, social security, health care, and so on, then fewer social issues would arise. We would not be called upon to ask What is the nature of the market or government failure? and What economic and political remedies are possible?

SUGGESTIONS FOR FURTHER READING

Ross's Theory of Prima Facie Duties

W. David Ross, *The Right and the Good* (Oxford: Oxford University Press, 1930).
——, *Foundations of Ethics* (Oxford: Oxford University Press, 1939).

Aristotle on "The Good" and "The Virtues"

There are numerous translations of Aristotle's *Nicomachean Ethics,* such as W. David Ross, ed., *The Works of Aristotle Translated into English,* 12 vols. (Oxford: Oxford University Press, 1908–1952). For some modern interpretations, see Amélie O. Rorty, ed., *Essays on Aristotle's Ethics,* (Berkley, Ca.: University of California Press, 1980).

Utilitarian Thought

Jeremy Bentham, *The Principles of Morals and Legislation* (Oxford, 1789).
John Stuart Mill, *Utilitarianism,* 1861, in *Collected Works of John Stuart Mill,* ed. F. E. L. Priestley (Toronto: University of Toronto Press, 1969).

Two Modern Utilitarian Moralists

Richard B. Brandt, *A Theory of the Good and the Right* (New York: Oxford University Press, 1979).
Peter Singer, *Practical Ethics* (London: Cambridge University Press, 1979).

Kantian Ethics

Immanuel Kant, *Groundwork of the Metaphysics of Morals,* trans. H. J. Paton (New York: Harper and Row, 1964).
Onora O'Neill, *Constructions of Reason: Explorations of Kant's Practical Philosophy,* (Cambridge: Cambridge University Press, 1989).

Libertarianism

Robert Nozick, *Anarchy, State, and Utopia* (New York: Basic Books, 1974).

Rawls's Theory of Justice as Fairness

John Rawls, *A Theory of Justice* (Cambridge: Harvard University Press, 1971).

Communitarianism

Amitai Etzioni, *The Moral Dimension* (New York: The Free Press, 1988).

ENDNOTES

1. As this discourse proceeds I will often use the term *we*. My hope is that the points being made are not controversial, at least between author and reader. I will try not to be too presumptuous. Indeed the purpose is to present a rather wide range of moral, political, and economic principles and perspectives. When the term *we* is used in a broader sense such as "we as a community," or "we as a nation," I will try to make those differences clear.
2. W. David Ross, *Foundations of Ethics* (Oxford: Oxford University Press, 1939), p. 189.
3. Ibid., p. 18.
4. Ibid., p. 190.
5. Robert Nozick, *Anarchy, State, and Utopia* (New York: Basic Books, 1974).
6. John Rawls, *A Theory of Justice* (Cambridge, Mass. Harvard University Press, 1971), p. 60.
7. Ibid., p. 60.
8. Ibid., p. 62.
9. Ibid., p. 83.
10. See Amitai Etzioni, *The Moral Dimension* (New York: The Free Press, 1988).

2

Social Issues

Some Analytical Perspectives from Economic and Political Theory

We start by retreating to utopia. The laissez-faire[1] model makes an excellent starting point for presenting several concepts that will be useful as we analyze social issues. This model of a free market economy features perfect competition in every market and a minimal role for government. Within this utopia there are few social issues. This starting point permits us to introduce the imperfections of the real world one at a time, affording us a better understanding of the nature of the market failure and any attendant social issue. There are also norms and values inherent in the model as a utopian ideal, and these in turn can be evaluated in the larger context of social ethics.

The chapter is organized around this point of departure. We first consider the laissez-faire model as a utopia and then the various ways real world markets may differ from the model. This allows us to analyze the nature of each type of market failure and the social issues it creates. It turns out that this analytical process often suggests ways to efficiently and fairly resolve the issue.

We begin with the idea that a capitalistic economy is composed of many economic entities whose behavior is somehow coordinated by market forces. The incentives at work include consumers maximizing their own welfare, firms maximizing profits, and workers and other input owners maximizing their own incomes. It was the genius of Adam Smith that he saw how market forces could act as an "invisible hand" to coordinate these functions. Moreover, government interference could easily do more harm than good:

> Projectors disturb nature in the course of her operations on human affairs, and it requires no more than to leave her alone and give her fair play in the pursuit of her ends that she may establish her own designs. . . . Little else is required to carry a state to the highest degree of affluence from the lowest barbarism but peace, easy taxes, and a tolerable administration of justice; all the rest being brought about by the natural course of things. All governments which thwart this natural course, which force things into another channel, or

which endeavor to arrest the progress of society at a particular point are un-
natural, and, to support themselves, are obliged to be oppressive and tyranni-
cal.[2]

No altruism is required. Consumers choose those goods that provide them the
greatest satisfaction. Firms profit by anticipating consumer wants and organizing production at the lowest cost possible. Firms compete for the most productive inputs and must reward them accordingly. These workers and other input owners have incentives to employ their talents where they are most
productive.

SOME DEFINITIONS OF EFFICIENCY: ALLOCATIVE EFFICIENCY, PARETO EFFICIENCY, EQUALITY OF MARGINAL BENEFITS AND MARGINAL COSTS

A system populated by perfectly competitive industries exhibits *allocative efficiency*. This term combines two attributes: responsiveness to consumer preferences and production at the lowest costs possible. Firms can make abnormal
profits in the short run by responding to changes in consumer tastes, thus the makeup
of goods produced tends to maximize con-
sumer satisfaction. Although firms can make
abnormal profits in the short run, competition inexorably drives prices down to the lowest costs possible (i.e., each price reflects the
lowest long-run average cost per unit).

> **Allocative efficiency** is an effi-
> ciency concept that relates con-
> sumer preferences to efficiency in
> production. Competitive markets
> organize production in response to
> consumer tastes. Competitive
> forces within those markets insure
> that goods and services will be pro-
> vided at the lowest cost possible.

The idea of a "circular flow" of money
within the economic system illustrates how
output and input markets are tied together.
In output markets, prices are determined by
consumers' demand and producers' supply,
and money flows from consumers to firms. Similarly, prices in input markets
are established by the firms' demand and input owners' supply, and money
flows from firms to input owners. As input owners use that money to buy re-
tail goods, the circular flow continues. The price mechanism provides the communication network for all of this, prices rising and falling in response to changes
in demand and supply.

> **Pareto efficiency** refers to situa-
> tions where it is not possible to
> make one person better off with-
> out making another person worse
> off. The concept was developed by
> the Italian welfare economist, Vil-
> fredo Pareto (1848–1923).

A related idea of efficiency focuses on
the trading that takes place in competitive
markets. Individuals and firms have
incentive to trade as long as they can gain
from doing so. When they have exhausted
the possibilities of gains from trade they
reach an equilibrium we term *Pareto efficiency*. Since the gains from trade have

been exhausted, no one can be made better off unless another is made worse off.

The fine tuning of resource allocation can be described best in terms of marginal benefits and marginal costs. Allocative efficiency is achieved when the production of a good is carried to the point at which marginal benefits (that decline as more is produced) are equal to marginal costs (that increase as more is produced). On the demand side, consumers are making tradeoffs among goods according to the utility they get from additional units of each. On the supply side, firms face rising marginal costs for added production. Costs rise in accordance with the familiar law of diminishing returns as inputs are added to productive processes. In perfectly competitive markets the output of the good is carried to the point at which demand and supply are equal. Since market demand reflects the marginal benefits enjoyed by consumers and market supply reflects the marginal costs incurred by producers, we see that this equilibrium achieves the best allocation of resources possible.

We will use the idea of equating marginal benefits and costs in several contexts to include questions of how far we should carry governmental programs. The obvious answer is "to the point at which marginal benefits equal marginal costs." The less obvious question is how we measure benefits and costs.

Several conditions must be met for markets to operate efficiently. These necessary conditions for perfect competition are as follows:

1. Large numbers of buyers and sellers
2. Free entry and exit, with perfect mobility of inputs and firms
3. Perfect knowledge of all relevant prices
4. All goods must be "private goods," all associated benefits and costs included in market prices

Large numbers of buyers and sellers insure that prices will gravitate toward the lowest possible cost per unit. Of course buyers and sellers must have good information on the available alternatives and their prices. There must be no externalities; prices must reflect all of the benefits associated with production and consumption.

If any of these conditions are missing, various kinds of imperfections and market failures may appear. According to the nature of the particular imperfection or market failure, different types of social issues arise.

Moral Values in the Free Market Utopia

Before analyzing the different types of market failure let us briefly return to the question begun in the previous chapter: What moral values and principles are inherent in the mechanics of our economic system, especially the utopian model of the laissez-faire economy?

Implicit in the title of his book *The Wealth of Nations* is Adam Smith's candidate for a social goal: material wealth.[3] The allocative efficiency of competitive markets will bring a state to the "highest degree of affluence." The focus is *consequentialist*; there will be a larger pie to divide. But there are also attributes that score well from *deontological* perspectives. Competitive markets offer many opportunities for individuals to pursue their own life goals. Individuals and firms are free to compete on a level playing field with fair rules of the game. It is the market that determines what rewards firms, workers, and other economic units receive. There can be no misuses of monopoly power; no economic exploitation of one person by another.[4]

Interestingly enough, there is no crucial role for *duty* to play in economic affairs. As Smith pointed out, every individual is assumed to follow "his own advantage . . . not that of society." Fortuitously, by following his own advantage he is led to do what is "most advantageous for society." Although such behavior and its results score well on utilitarian criteria, Kant would give it no credit whatsoever.

The most controversial feature of the laissez-faire model is its distribution. Even here it scores well on one of the principles of distributive justice: to each according to his or her contribution to society (i.e., to the welfare of others). As we have seen, competitive markets reward firms and individuals solely on the basis of how well they anticipate the wants of consumers. Indeed, this is what makes the system utopian from the consumer's point of view. How better to have an economy organized than to have everyone rewarded according to how well they anticipate your own wants and desires?

Being rewarded according to contribution seems intuitively fair and just, but this principle may at times conflict with others such as "to each according to need." If both principles are to be satisfied, we must augment the free market system with a program of income redistribution. Suppose the needs of our concern are the basic needs of food, clothing, shelter, and health care; it may be possible to fulfill both principles. It may be possible to allow for distribution to be based primarily on productivity but with the added contingency that everyone's basic needs be met. Individuals who are disadvantaged, who have bad luck, or who, for some other reason, cannot afford to meet their basic needs would be provided for through some process of redistribution. Obviously, there is much more to be said about distributive justice. It will be a major concern in all of the social issues to be addressed.

Market Failures, Monopolies, and Oligopolies

As we turn from the utopian model to the reality of free markets, we observe that market failures arise due to "imperfections" in competitive conditions. We will examine the various ways the market can fail and the social issues that arise from these failures. As we shall see, a better understanding of the *nature* of the market failure will often suggest ways that the market failure can be addressed and perhaps resolved. In each case there are fairness as well as efficiency considerations. We first focus on the condition that competitive markets must have large numbers of buyers and sellers. When there are large numbers of buyers and sellers, competition sets the price at the lowest cost possible. When there is only one seller, a monopoly, we expect it to make greater profits by cutting back on output and raising price. Since prices are higher and output lower, allocative efficiency is not achieved. Production is not carried to the point at which marginal benefits are equal to marginal costs.

Monopoly profits do not fare well when evaluated in terms of *just distribution criteria*. Income distribution no longer reflects the contribution made to the welfare of the buyers. In order to maximize profits, the price set by the monopolist is kept above the cost per unit; thus, neither efficiency nor fairness criteria are met.

Of course monopoly represents the extreme case in which there is only one firm in the entire market, but a similar type of misallocation can occur in oligopoly markets. We use the term oligopoly to cover a wide range of competitive behavior in which there is only a small number of firms competing. In small-number situations, anything can happen. Possible outcomes range from cutthroat competition to complete collusion; but allocative efficiency will not be achieved in any case.

On the input side, similar problems occur when there are not enough firms demanding inputs or when there are not enough input owners (say, workers). The single-buyer case is termed a *monopsony*. We would expect the monopsony, say a large textile producer in a small mill town, to curtail employment in order to keep down the wage rate. The term *oligopsony* refers to situations in which a small number of buyers compete. Here again anything can happen, according to whether they collude or compete.

In addition to questions of misallocation and inefficiency there are questions of a lack of fairness. We have observed that, when the prices monopolies or oligopolies charge exceed market determined costs, we can no longer justify their income on the basis of "to each according to contribution." Similar efficiency and fairness questions arise when monopsonists and oligopsonists restrict employment to keep wages down. Wage earners are paid less than their contribution (i.e., less than the value of their marginal product).

Government uses several approaches to improve the results of these sorts of market failure. It may encourage more competition through removing barriers to entry and subsidizing the start-up costs of potential competitors. When that is not possible, it may regulate the monopoly or oligopoly so as to lower prices and increase output. If price regulation is used, the regulating authority sets price so that output will be closer to the point at which marginal benefits equal marginal costs.

Government actions to improve allocation and fairness in input markets are similar. In labor markets, various educational and employment information services may improve mobility. Over the years, the union movement has been regarded as a counterbalance to the power of monopsony employers. In theory, this countervailing arrangement of power can lead to greater efficiency and fairness. Another method of overcoming monopsony and oligopsony power is the minimum wage. A higher minimum wage can, in certain situations, actually increase both wages and employment, since the monopsonist's incentive to keep wages down by curtailing employment is overridden. Both unionization and the minimum wage are blunt instruments. In some situations, wages are unaffected, say when the union is weak or the minimum wage is below the market-determined wage. In other situations, the wages set by unions or set by the minimum wage may be above those set by market demand and supply. Here we get the expected result: higher wages lead to less employment. New questions arise in the latter cases: How do we trade off higher wages for some workers against loss of jobs for others?

A Digression on Oligopolies and Game Theory

We have stated that anything can happen in markets in which there are a small number of firms. The familiar language of game theory is useful in describing the range of possibilities. One game, the prisoners' dilemma, provides insight into the options open to most oligopolists. The basic problem is one of cooperation among interdependent individuals. Both will be better off if they cooperate. Unfortunately, each also has incentive to defect.

The story of the game opens with two robbery suspects being apprehended and kept in separate cells. The district attorney is certain that they committed the crime but needs a confession for conviction in court. He therefore attempts to get a confession by playing on their mutual distrust and their inability to communicate. The deal he offers gives each incentive to confess and substantial disincentive to remain silent.

If neither suspect confesses, the district attorney is reduced to prosecuting minor charges such as illegal possession of a weapon, resisting arrest, and possession of stolen goods. The penalty will be one year. If one suspect turns state's evidence, he will get off with a six-month sentence while the district attorney will throw the book at the other, say a sentence of five years. If both confess, neither will have to turn state's evidence, but each will receive three years. Obviously both would be better off if they could cooperate and agree not to confess; in that case they would both receive one year. But there is strong incentive to confess. Consider the options. If I confess I will either receive three years or six months depending on whether or not the other suspect confesses. If I do not confess I will get either five years or one year. My fellow thief is faced with the same options. He also has incentive to confess so as to avoid getting the five-year sentence.

The resolution to the dilemma is that both confess and receive three years. The best mutual result, neither confessing and receiving only one year, is reached only if the adverse incentives are somehow overcome. Suppose, for example, one were able to communicate with the other and threaten death if he confesses. This new set of incentives would then achieve the best mutual result.

Query: Can Competition Be Too Severe?

In oligopoly, as in game theory, the players can follow various strategies that lead to various results. Oligopolists can fail to cooperate and, instead, engage in ruinous price competition. In many oligopoly situations the firms involved experience economies of scale in that, as each expands, its average costs fall. It becomes necessary, therefore, to be the first to cut price and expand. The competition becomes cutthroat as each opponent reduces price below cost in the hope of surviving longer than the opposition.

In some markets a price leader emerges, and firms, having learned not to wage price warfare, honor the market price. In other markets, firms engage in tacit or overt collusion. The ultimate resolution to the prisoners' dilemma is for oligopolists to form a cartel and to behave as a monopoly, setting the monopoly price.

In summary, anything can happen in market situations that feature small numbers of competitors. It follows that there is no one way for society to best regulate and set parameters. Each industry must be analyzed and evaluated in its own context. It is clear that in monopoly and oligopoly situations, allocative efficiency is lost. Prices do not reflect the costs of goods and thus consumer choices lead to misallocation. Moreover, competition is usually insufficient to require production at the lowest cost possible. Similarly, a lack of competition in the factor markets, such as labor, capital, raw materials, and so on, can lead to inefficient and unfair allocation.

So what should be the role of government? What regulation, if any, is appropriate for the various competitive and noncompetitive market situations? Let us briefly consider the history and present status of regulation.

Some Complexities of Regulation and Deregulation

In recent years the regulation and deregulation of several important industries have been the subject of much attention and debate. In most Western democracies a number of industries, particularly in transportation, communication, public utilities, and natural resources, have been run by government or have been closely regulated. In Western Europe the tradition has been that these industries are nationalized, while in the United States, government agencies at the federal, state, and local levels have been used to administer various aspects of production, especially pricing. In the United States, many cities have public transport systems in addition to water and sewage systems. Public corporations of the federal government provide post office and passenger rail service. Most public utilities are privately owned but regulated by a state or local agency. Federal, state, and local governments have created agencies that regulate prices, set standards for safety and health, and attempt to promote efficiency in telecommunications, electric utilities, airlines, and trucking.

In 1887, the Interstate Commerce Commission (ICC) was established in response to abuses of monopoly power by the railroads. Later the powers of government to regulate were extended beyond the railroads to other industries. The establishment of the Federal Power Commission (FPC) in 1920 and the Federal Communications Commission (FCC) in 1934 were followed by a substantial increase in regulatory agencies under the New Deal of Roosevelt. The New Deal initiatives were made during the Great Depression, when it appeared that unregulated, free market capitalism had failed. These agencies have evolved over the years. Those with primary focus on controlling prices and output are the ICC (regulates railroads, trucking, pipelines, and barges), the FCC (regulates telecommunications), and various federal, state, and local agencies that regulate electrical power and natural gas.

The complex roles of regulatory agencies have always been subject to criticism, especially by economists. This criticism, along with the more general loss of faith in government in the last three decades, has led to a wave of deregulation. Under President Carter, the airlines were deregulated in 1978. Deregulation under Presidents Reagan, Bush, and Clinton has continued, to include trucking, railroads, banking, and telecommunications.

Before deregulation, the airlines were regulated in terms of prices and routes, as well as safety. Entry was closely regulated. Airlines were allowed substantial returns on the more well-traveled routes but were also required to serve the marginal airports. This amounted to a form of cross subsidization. Since deregulation, competition in the airline industry has realized the worst and best of what was expected. Prices have fallen and competition has been fierce, especially on the well-traveled routes. Cutthroat competition has led to the bankruptcy of most of the original airlines. The price competition has taken several forms; lower prices are charged for vacation than for business travel. Frequent-flyer benefits are designed to encourage customer loyalty. Like price competition, these programs show the cutthroat character of a prisoners' dilemma game. Leveraged buyouts and mergers have allowed for consolidation and some economies of scale. Service to smaller cities has declined and prices have been raised where lack of competition permits. The gains to most consumers have been substantial; however, there have been losers as well.

Other transportation industries have also been deregulated. Trucking and railroads were closely regulated with respect to rates and entry into geographical regions. Since deregulation, rates have been reduced and the industries have substantially reorganized. Rail passenger service would have virtually disappeared had not the government begun Amtrak.

Several dramatic and ongoing regulatory questions involve the market reorganization in the telecommunications industries. In the telephone industry American Telephone and Telegraph (AT&T) was a closely regulated, natural monopoly. It was assumed that a monopoly was required because the stringing of copper wires and other fixed costs called for substantial investment and involved economies of scale. But, as the technology of transmitting signals by microwave developed, the monopoly was ended and MCI and Sprint were allowed to compete. The monopoly held by local telephone companies will be further eroded by other technological changes such as the development of cellular telephones.

Cable television has gone through several iterations of regulation and deregulation as technology has concentrated and then weakened various types of market power. Further developments in linking television, personal computers, telephones, and electronic communication for business and entertainment purposes will create an ongoing challenge for government to provide some guidelines and regulation.

The makeup of our economic system is constantly changing, as consumer tastes and new technology create new economic possibilities. Some industries grow and others recede. The proper role for government differs with each industry. It would be impossible for government to insure that there would be no winners or losers in this process. The general role for government would seem to be to keep the process efficient and fair. The most appropriate analogy for the government's role would seem to be to keep the "game" fair: fair starts, fair rules, fair play, and fair results. We do not expect the government to make everything right for the inevitable losers. We accept the fact that with economic development there are risks. On the other hand, it does seem appropriate for government to keep safety nets in place for those individuals whose losses reduce them to poverty.

Antitrust Policy

In 1890 the Sherman Antitrust Act was passed after decades of abuse of monopoly power by an arrogant breed of entrepreneurs known as "the robber barons." The case of John D. Rockefeller, Sr., and the Standard Oil Company was but one example. Under its leadership, a cooperative of refiners was formed and dictated prices to the railroads. The railroads were to give discounts to the cooperative's members but were to raise prices to its rivals; moreover, the railroads had to pay the cooperative "drawbacks," a percentage of the fees collected from rivals. In 1882, the group formed a more closely knit trust that closed down inefficient refineries and further constricted output so as to maximize monopoly profits.

Trusts were soon established in other industries on national and regional bases in whiskey, sugar, meat processing, milk, banking, railroads, lead, cottonseed oil, and linseed oil. Figures such as Philip Armour, J. P. Morgan, and W. H. Vanderbilt regularly voiced their contempt for the public, as exemplified by Vanderbilt's statement, "the public be damned."

Eventually countervailing political power arose. The Sherman Act prohibits contracts, combinations, and conspiracies "in restraint of trade" and monopolies of interstate and foreign trade. The Clayton Act (1914) prohibits price discrimination and any acquisition of another firm's shares that reduces competition. The Cellar-Kefauver Act (1950) was a further attempt to prohibit corporations from reducing competition or creating a monopoly by acquiring the assets of other corporations.

In summary, the government's role in regulation and antitrust is similar to that of a referee. The object is to keep the game fair. Restraint of trade and other attempts to collude and gain unfair advantage are punished either by regulatory authorities or in the courts.

Query: Does OPEC Play Fair?

The basic social goal of antitrust laws in the United States is to limit monopoly power. Competition in free markets, we assume, will promote both efficiency and fairness. Firms that collude instead of competing are punished.

Oddly enough, most Americans do not condemn the oil cartel, the Organization of Petroleum Exporting Countries (OPEC), for behavior that by our standards is clearly unfair. The stage was set for OPEC by several international oil companies, to include U.S. companies, organized so as to control the price of oil. The OPEC countries have simply expropriated this cartel arrangement. The member countries collude and use their monopoly power to keep the price well above what it would be under competition. What is less clear is why those countries that are being exploited do not attempt some countermeasures. Why is it that other countries do not form cartels around those goods and services that only they produce and use that leverage to bargain with OPEC? The point we make here is that our laws and what we consider fair rules of the game may be different from those in other countries.

The Basic Model of the Natural Monopoly: Price Regulation

The phenomenon of a natural monopoly arises because of economies of scale. A *natural monopoly* is an industry in which economies of scale make it possible for a single producer to supply the entire market at lower cost per unit than a larger number of smaller firms. Within the relevant range, the firm experiences *economies of scale*.

> **Economies of scale**, or, increasing returns to scale, occur when increases in output make for a lower average cost (cost per unit). The relationship between average cost and marginal cost is as follows: As output increases the cost of each additional unit, i.e., marginal cost, keeps falling, and this continually brings down the average, or, the average cost. Throughout the range where average costs are decreasing, marginal costs (the cost of adding another unit) are below the average cost.

There are two different approaches to the price regulation of a natural monopoly: average cost pricing and marginal cost pricing. The mechanics are simple. The regulatory commission dictates the price, and it is in the interests of the monopoly to supply all that is demanded at that price. Most regulatory commissions use the average-cost (or full-cost) approach. Here the regulatory authority simply sets the price so that all costs are covered at the quantity demanded. Calculating the costs is not quite as simple as it sounds. For example, some return must be included for the capital that has been invested, and these calculations can become complicated.

The second approach, marginal-cost pricing, is more difficult. Recall that, in the relevant output range, economies of scale mean that average costs are decreasing and marginal costs are below average costs. Thus, when the monopoly supplies all that is demanded at the marginal cost price, the revenue received will be lower than the cost per unit. The firm will be losing money! In order to break even, the firm requires a subsidy.

While this result may not seem plausible, it is, in fact, the most efficient. To understand why, we need to return to the definition of allocative efficiency. If all prices reflect marginal costs, then production will be taken to the point at which marginal benefits are equal to marginal costs. Monopoly is inefficient because the monopolist maximizes profit by restricting output, to keep prices higher than costs. Both average-cost pricing and marginal-cost pricing improve welfare and efficiency by lowering price and increasing output. The greatest possible efficiency, the fine tuning of resource allocation, requires that we carry output to the point at which what we add in welfare (marginal benefits) is just equal to what additional units cost (marginal costs).

If the regulatory commission uses the marginal-cost price approach it must also subsidize the firm. This raises the question of how the subsidy is financed. Presumably, general revenue sources will be employed. The firm's customers are not a logical source of extra revenue. They cannot be charged an extra "user charge," since that would defeat the purpose of having price reflect marginal costs.

Query: Should City Buses Lose Money?

We observe that many public utilities are candidates for regulation. Several, such as water, electricity, and telephone, have high fixed costs. Once the water pipes are laid it is relatively inexpensive to hook up additional houses. Similarly, once electricity and telephone lines are installed additional houses are easily added.

Now let us put all this together. Industries that require a large initial investment also require substantial output and sales in order to average out the costs. This is just another way of describing the idea of economies of scale. Over the relevant range of output, average costs are decreasing and the extra cost per unit, the marginal cost, is less than average cost. In order for the most efficient level to be produced, the price must be set at marginal cost, below the cost per unit.

Consider the case of a city-run bus service. The initial organization costs, driver training, scheduling, and, of course the city streets, are relatively fixed costs. As service is expanded, the cost per ride is lower, and as explained, the cost of each additional ride (the marginal cost) is lower than the average cost. If the service were to be expanded to where price reflects marginal costs, the bus company would lose money. It should lose money. This is not to say that mismanagement is to be tolerated. On the contrary, it would be inefficient not to carry service to the point at which the price of an additional ride just covers the cost of that additional ride.

There are a number of other efficiency arguments for keeping the price of bus service below the average cost. A city bus service lowers the cost of shoppers' getting to stores and the cost of employees' getting to work. It also creates less air pollution, produces less traffic congestion than the use of individual cars, and reduces the need for parking places. These positives should be included in the calculation of benefits and costs.

We have argued that regulating market power promotes efficiency, and that often moral considerations go beyond questions of efficiency. In many urban settings the lower income groups depend on buses. Lower bus fares help the poor in many ways, including greater access to employment opportunities and to a wide range of public services such as health care. It follows that a number of the moral principles outlined in chapter one are applicable, especially those that deal with the dignity of each person and his or her ability to choose and pursue legitimate goals in life.

MARKET FAILURES WHEN INFORMATION IS LESS THAN PERFECT

Now let us turn to the condition that all parties in a perfectly competitive market must have perfect information. This condition seems plausible if interpreted using common sense. It does not require that all parties know everything about the past, present, and future. It simply requires that consumers, firms, and input owners have the information necessary to make rational, efficient choices. It also requires that the various parties have equal access to relevant information.

In many situations an individual or firm may not have relevant information but may be able to obtain it at a cost. The question then becomes how much one is willing to pay for better information; the general rule is that an individual or firm will be willing to invest in better information up to the point at which the additional benefits of using the information are equal to the extra costs of obtaining it. This is just another example of maximizing by equating marginal benefits and costs. At this point, there may still remain informational deficiencies for one or more of the parties who take part in a transaction.

Asymmetric Information

The market failure termed *asymmetric information* refers to situations in which one party has better information and thus a strategic advantage in its transactions with another party. This asymmetry may affect both the efficiency and the fairness of the market. A familiar example is the market for used cars. When a person buys a new car, there is some probability that it will be defective. Some cars are so defective as to earn the appellation of "lemon." When the original buyer of the car sells the car to a used-car dealer he or she has much better information about the car than the dealer. By the time the dealer sells the car to another buyer the dealer will probably have driven the car for a time and had it thoroughly checked. At this point the dealer has better information than the next buyer.

> **Asymmetric information** is defined as a situation in which the various parties engaged in an economic transaction possess various levels of strategic information.

The market is influenced in two ways. First, the original buyers are more likely to trade in a lemon after owning the car for a short time; newer cars on the used-car market have a high probability of being lemons. Second, the price of all used cars is substantially lower because potential buyers have difficulty differentiating good cars from lemons.

How can the problem be overcome? Often used-car dealers will encourage potential customers to check with the car's former owner. They may also offer guarantees of free service. One basic solution here and in other cases of asymmetric information is to deal with trustworthy people. If you are fortunate enough to know a used-car dealer you can trust, the "lemon problem" will work to your advantage.

The employer searching for conscientious and efficient employees is also at a disadvantage. One hiring strategy is to hire several workers and then let some go. This is expensive, especially if it involves training programs, severance pay, and so on. In some cases a *signal* such as education can be used to differentiate among candidates. While a given diploma may not pertain directly to the job, it demonstrates a certain level of intelligence and perseverance.

When we consider health care as a social issue several questions of asymmetric information will be asked. Economists often claim that in the doctor–patient relationship, the doctor has incentive to prescribe expensive treatment whether or not it is needed. This tendency leads to greater health costs, especially when a third party, say Medicare, Medicaid, or an insurance company, will pay the full costs. Alternatively, when the doctor works for a health maintenance organization (HMO), in which the incentive is to keep costs down, it is assumed that she or he will prescribe less expensive and less effective treatment. Health care reform must account for these and other incentives faced by health care providers. As the health care industry undergoes change, it will still be necessary to rely on the professional ethics of the health care providers and on relationships of trust among doctors and their patients.

The moral questions raised by asymmetric information differ according to the situation. In many situations known as principal–agent relationships one person, the principal, must rely on another, the agent, to provide a service. The client must rely on his or her lawyer, stockbroker, or car mechanic. In each case, some part of the information gap must be overcome by trust, professional ethics, and integrity.

There are other situations in which it is considered fair for parties with superior knowledge to exploit their advantage. A chess player is not required to point out that his opponent is about to make the wrong move. In business, corporations are not expected to share plans for new products with their competitors. On the other hand many types of industrial espionage are both illegal and immoral.

In summary, there are many activities in which asymmetric information will influence the results. But the applicability of efficiency and fairness criteria must be considered in the particular context.

Other types of market failure may be attributed to information imperfections termed

> **Adverse selection** is defined as a situation that arises in insurance markets when the persons who choose to purchase a particular policy will be those persons who are at greater risk than the population for whom the policy was designed.

adverse selection. When an insurance company designs a policy, say for fire insurance, it makes actuarial calculations of probability and costs of fires that occur within a given population. The rates it assigns reflect the average incidence of fire and some additional costs for administration and marketing. We assume that some potential customers are "good risks" and some are "bad risks." It may be that the good risks consider the rates to be high relative to their own situation. The bad risks see the policy as a good buy, and consequently the final makeup of policyholders is adversely selected. The experience of the insurance company will be worse than expected, rates will be raised, and the process will continue. One possible result is that certain forms of insurance simply may not be offered. If the insurance company had better information and if it were able to better differentiate among individuals on the basis of risks, this type of market failure would be resolved.

The phenomenon of adverse selection is one of several factors that may cause an *incomplete market.* Historically, the government has entered several markets in which there was a clear social need but an inadequate response by the market. In the 1930s government used the Tennessee Valley Authority to demonstrate the viability of producing and selling low-cost electricity where private electric utility companies had shown inertia. It was also during the 1930s that a need for retirement plans for the elderly became a public concern. At that time, the market for retirement plans was incomplete, in part because of the adverse selection problem and in part because of the depression. Private insurance companies cannot be expected to insure against *social risks.* The depression affected the entire population. A large percentage of the elderly suddenly found themselves permanently unemployed and their savings destroyed. Even if retirement insurance plans had been available, it is unlikely that they would have been honored. Other social risks include inflation, war, and epidemics. In extreme cases, weather-related disasters such as floods, drought, and hurricanes qualify as social risks.

> An **incomplete market** occurs when firms have insufficient incentive to offer goods or services desired by the public. The market may fail for several reasons. These include the inexperience of firms in an emerging market, the lack of observations on which to base estimates of revenues and costs, and adverse selection.

> A **social risk** refers to a disaster that creates losses to a large number of people at one time. Private insurance companies can insure only against losses that occur with a relatively predictable frequency to a small number of the insured population.

Government is better equipped to insure against social risks. It has the ability to go into debt during recessions and to spread the burden of a disaster over wide geographical areas or over long periods of time. During recessions government can provide aid to the unemployed. It can guarantee health care to the poor. During wartime, government can finance the allocation of resources to the war effort. It can also spread some of the burden of the war over several generations of taxpayers.

We simply cannot expect private insurance companies to insure against social risks. Society's response to the plight of the elderly during the Great Depression of the 1930s was our Social Security program. Its introduction solved the social-risk problem but required that other efficiency and fairness questions be addressed. What are our social goals? What should be the schedule of Social Security benefits? Should the benefits be based more on a participant's contribution to the program or more on her or his needs? How should we pay for Social Security?

To summarize, various types of social risks require various types of government intervention into insurance markets. In each case, questions of efficiency and fairness arise.

Moral Hazard

Paradoxically, insurance may lead to changes in behavior that increase risks. This phenomenon has been termed *moral hazard*. Of course, the whole point of some insurance is to allow for a change in behavior. It is not surprising that a person who insures his or her jewelry will then wear it in public instead of keeping it locked in a safe. Similarly, we expect people with health insurance to go to the doctor more often. The problem is that insurance can also lead to behavior that is undesirable and counterproductive. Fire insurance leads to more cases of arson and perhaps to less attention to preventive measures. It has been claimed that seat belts and other automobile safety features encourage faster driving and more accidents. Welfare programs aimed at aiding children in poverty may discourage marriage and encourage illegitimacy.

> **Moral hazard** in insurance markets may occur when a person buys insurance against some risk and subsequently behaves in ways that increase that risk.

As we consider social issues and the programs designed to address them, we must pay attention to the inherent incentives and disincentives. These phenomena—asymmetric information, adverse selection, incomplete market, social risks, and moral hazard—may give insight into solutions as well as causes.

PUBLIC GOODS AND EXTERNALITIES

Public Goods

A final necessary condition for perfect competition states that all goods must be *private goods*; all associated benefits and costs must be included in market price. If there is a good or service that some people desire and are able and willing to pay for, we can rest assured that some individual or firm will provide it for them. A private good has the characteristics that it can be assigned to and consumed by the buyer. A *public good*, by contrast, creates benefits that are spread among the community and are not exhausted in consumption. The benefits need not be demanded or paid for by any given individual. For example, the public health campaign that conquered polio benefitted everyone, not just those who took the vaccines and those who paid the necessary taxes.

> A **public good** has the characteristics of nonexcludability and inexhaustability in consumption. National defense exhibits these characteristics.

National defense is a classic example of a pure public good. The benefits of national defense are enjoyed by all citizens. One person's "consumption" of defense does not diminish the benefits enjoyed by others. At the same time no one can be excluded from enjoying those benefits. This brings us to a related phenomenon, the *free-rider problem.*

> The **free-rider** problem occurs when it is difficult or impossible to exclude consumers from enjoying the benefits of a good. Since it is possible to "free ride," the good cannot be efficiently financed without coercion.

The "lighthouse case" is a familiar way of illustrating the difficulty. The story opens at a fishing village where rocks near the harbor make navigation treacherous at evening during bad weather. It is not feasible for one fisherman to build and maintain a lighthouse. Instead, each would choose to take the risks. If, however, someone were to build and operate a lighthouse, then all would benefit. The problem, of course, is that any fisherman who chooses not to contribute can still see the beams emanating from the lighthouse. The question is whether or not enough fishermen would voluntarily contribute to building and operating the lighthouse. In some communities, a system of voluntary contributions would be sufficient; but if the incentive to free ride is followed by a sufficient number, the lighthouse will never be built.

The obvious solution is to have the village government finance the lighthouse through taxes. The free rider problem can easily be overcome by the government's ability to compel citizens to pay taxes. The next question is one of fairness rather than efficiency. Can the village government find a fair way to tax its citizens? The fairest solution may be to tax the fishermen, say with a license fee, since they are the most direct beneficiaries.

Externalities

> **Externalities** are benefits or costs that are caused by economic transactions but that are external to those transactions. Since these benefits or costs are not priced, they are not taken into account by the parties involved in the transactions. They are also known as *spillover* or *third-party* effects.

When market prices fail to capture all of the benefits and costs of economic transactions, resources will be misallocated. These benefits and costs become *external* to the incentives that guide market transactions.

The water pollution caused by a paper mill is a familiar example. The firm has a multitude of prices to consider on both the sales and production sides of its operations; but the costs its pollution imposes on others are not reflected either in its costs or in the final prices it charges its customers. The final prices are too low since they do not reflect all of the costs of making the paper products. In most cases adjustments that improve efficiency will involve a higher final price and a lower output of the good in question.

Let us assume that users of the water downriver include fishermen, swimmers, individual homeowners, and farmers. An interesting part of the question is whether or not these groups can organize and bargain with the paper mill. It also matters whether or not the law specifies liabilities. If the mill has no liability, one possible outcome would be that the fishermen, swimmers, homeowners, and farmers form a coalition and bribe the paper mill to reduce pollution. If the mill does have liability, these groups may be able to use legal action.

Interestingly enough, the most *efficient* solution does not depend on the question of who should pay. Let us suppose that the most efficient solution is that the mill install settling tanks. If the use of settling tanks is the best possible allocation of resources, it does not matter where the liability lies. The mill's being liable simply means that, if required by the courts or some other authority, it will pay for the settling tanks to be built. If it is not liable and the affected groups can organize, they will bribe the mill to build the settling tanks.

Ronald Coase has made the point that negotiations among the affected parties will lead to an efficient resolution of externalities. What is required is that property rights and liabilities be made clear and that the transactions costs be sufficiently low.[5] Thus the "efficiency" and "fairness" questions are quite distinct.

The Smokestack and the Washerwoman

Although it is maudlin and politically incorrect, the familiar "smokestack case" makes a strong point. The story opens with a widow washerwoman who dries her customers' clothes the old-fashioned way, in the fresh air. An expansion by the factory next door creates smoke that blackens the air and the poor washerwoman's laundry. Although it had been an important factor in the widow's business, the pure air of the neighborhood had no price. Now by treating the air as costless, the firm has imposed a negative externality.

According to Coase it does not matter who has the liability; an efficient solution will be found. Suppose the efficient solution is for the firm to install a filter that costs one thousand dollars. The widow digs into her meager savings and subsidizes the firm's installation of the filter. If the firm were liable, it would pay for the filter.

Now suppose that the most efficient solution is for the washerwoman to stop doing laundry. Say that the required filter would

> The **Coase theorem** is an argument put forward by Ronald Coase that externalities will be resolved efficiently if transactions costs are low. Governments can facilitate this process by establishing rights to the use of resources.

cost one million dollars. The washerwoman's business earns less than the return on the cost of the filter. If the firm is not liable, the widow is left to her cruel fate. If the firm is liable, it must compensate the widow. Either way the filter is not installed.

The first point of the story, Coase's point, is that the efficient solution will always be reached. The second point of major concern is that moral judgments, although separate, are still there.

For many important externalities the *transactions costs* problem is decisive. Many cases of pollution involve large numbers of affected parties. They may also involve large numbers of persons or firms who are causing the pollution. In the paper mill case the question arises as to whether or not the fishermen, swimmers, homeowners, and farmers can in fact organize to press their case. If we assume that the mill is not liable, the coalition would also face the problem of collecting from its members if it is to pay for the settling tanks. Even if the mill is liable, the injured parties may have difficulty organizing in order to pursue their case in the courts or in some other venue.

Air pollution in Los Angeles has many sources: automobiles, trucks, buses, small and large firms, and public agencies. There are also many affected parties. In fact, since almost all of the inhabitants are both perpetrator and victim, it would seem that all have incentive to change their behavior. In a smaller-number situation such voluntary adjustments might be effective. With larger numbers a free-rider problem arises. It is difficult for the individual to see how driving her or his car less will make a difference. The problem of air pollution in Los Angeles and other cities has been addressed in a number of ways. In large-number situations such as this, some sort of government intervention is usually required.

Corrective Taxes or Subsidies

When negative externalities exist, the real costs of production have not been fully captured. A basic approach is to impose a tax designed to reflect those costs. Unless marginal costs reflect all costs, production will be carried too far. Consumers, we recall, carry purchases to the point at which the extra benefits (marginal benefits) are equal to the extra costs (marginal costs). A tax added to the product's cost will cause an increase in the price and cause consumers to reduce purchases. For example, taxes could be placed on the effluents that industrial plants make into a river. Alternatively, a subsidy may be paid to buyers of goods with a positive externality. For example, a subsidy could be paid to homeowners who install solar heating units if increased use is deemed to have social benefits such as causing less pollution and conserving depletable energy resources.

Corrective taxes or subsidies will not be practical in many cases. Mandated standards and regulatory agencies may be required to monitor pollution and to prosecute offenders. Automobiles have been required to be equipped with catalytic converters and other means to reduce pollution. In some cities special traffic lanes are set aside for vehicles carrying passengers. The reduction in traffic reduces pollution and congestion in traffic and parking. The point to be made here is that taxes, subsidies, standards, or some combination may be used to improve efficiency and fairness when externalities are present.

If we think of education as a private good with substantial social benefits, we observe that there are a number of ways it could be subsidized. Students could be given vouchers to be used at a school of their choice. Parents could be given tax breaks on educational expenditures. Students could be given low-interest loans. Or, as in the case of public schools, the state may simply assume the entire responsibility and become the producer of education.

Whatever methods are used to attain improved efficiency will, at the same time, affect the welfare and opportunities of the various parties. As those methods are used, they may or may not be consistent with our ethical principles and social goals. For example, when we focus on education as a social issue, we will consider what ethical principles are involved. How does education affect aggregate social welfare? How does the education issue relate to moral principles based on a respect for each individual? Is there a social responsibility to provide individuals with a fair start and an array of economic opportunities? How do these principles relate to the methods used to produce this good? How does a voucher system compare with a public school system in terms of efficiency and fairness?

In many cases efficiency and fairness considerations are difficult to distinguish. Consider the case in which a developer builds new homes near an existing airport. The new homeowners become annoyed with the noise made by the airplanes and decide to sue. There are a multitude of efficiency and fairness norms that could be brought into play. Presumably the building of the airport reduced the property values of the original owners. Were they appropriately compensated? We might ask whether or not the developer purchased the land at a low price that reflected the noise problem. We might ask whether or not the new homeowners were informed about the noise by the developer. The time sequence of externality creation and resolution may complicate the fairness question. Ideally, the original owners were compensated. We can assume that when the airport was built the lower value of the land was immediately reflected in its price. The lower cost of land was also reflected in the price paid by the new homeowners. It is often the case that what started as an external benefit or cost becomes *capitalized*, that is, the stream of future benefits and costs becomes reflected in a good's current market value.

It may well be that the new homeowners deserve no compensation, but the case of the original landowners is stronger. If they were never compensated, they should be paid for their original loss plus interest. We can easily construct complicated cases of externalities that become more and more difficult to resolve at later dates.

PRIVATE AND PUBLIC ACTIVITIES IN A MIXED ECONOMIC SYSTEM

Making Social Choices: Public Goods

Let us return to the more general question of how society's resources should be allocated to public goods. Let us assume that allocation will be determined through democratic political processes. The final decision on how much will be spent on national defense will be made within the legislative and administrative processes of the public sector. Will these processes result in an allocation of resources that is efficient and fair?

The idea of allocative efficiency applies to the public, as well as to the private, sector. This standard, we recall, has two requirements. First, that resources be allocated so that the combination of goods and services produced is the one that provides the most welfare. And second, that each good and service is produced at the least cost possible.

For reasons similar to the choice of free market capitalism as the preferred economic system, we would expect our nation's founders to choose representative democracy as the preferred political system. The attributes of democracy and free competitive markets are similar. Individuals, as citizens, are generally free from coercion and exploitation. While the powers of government officials vis-à-vis an individual are substantial, the system includes safeguards and various avenues of appeal. Certain rights of individuals are guaranteed. In most Western democracies governmental powers are separated, and there are checks and balances to their abuse. Indeed, within our own legislative processes at the federal, state, and local levels, it often seems that the checks on power are so effective that they impede progress toward efficient resource allocation.

Just as we can imagine an economy in which firms have incentive to provide those private goods most desired by consumers, we can imagine a political system in which representatives and administrators have incentive to provide those public goods most desired by voters. In free markets each individual votes with his or her dollars. Given his or her purchasing power and prices established through competition, each chooses that combination of private goods that gives him or her the most satisfaction. In a democracy individuals vote for those representatives or referenda that promise to deliver the most preferred combination of public goods.

Of course, private and public goods are different in kind. Private goods can be purchased and consumed by different people in different amounts. With public goods only one amount is produced and that quantity is consumed jointly by all. Once tax legislation is passed, the individual has no choice as to whether or not she or he will contribute. From certain perspectives, it is certainly appropriate to think of taxes as a voluntary contribution. They can be considered voluntary even though, once tax legislation has been passed, the coercive powers of government will be used to require payment.

The Lindahl Equilibrium

There is an interesting solution to the question of how welfare can be maximized even though all citizens have to "consume" the same amounts of public goods. The answer is that the *tax burden* of each taxpayer can be adjusted so that his or her marginal cost is equal to the marginal benefit enjoyed.

With private goods, the market price is the same, but consumers are free to adjust the amounts they consume, so as to equate marginal benefits and costs. With public goods, the amount produced is fixed but the tax bill (the marginal cost) can be adjusted so that marginal benefits equal marginal costs.

The Swedish economist Erik Lindahl proposed that members of a small community could discover what each would be willing to contribute to the production of a public good.[6] Such a solution is known as a *Lindahl equilibrium*. The point of the concept is not that such an equilibrium is likely through voluntary contributions. The point is that tax rates could be adjusted to benefits, that is MC = MB, for every taxpayer. If we assume that dollars mean more to the poor than to the rich, the Lindahl equilibrium would require that the poor pay lower rates.

Returning to the more general question of allocation, one challenge is to invent a set of political institutions that will allow citizens to voice their preferences for public goods. Theoretically, there is some best allocation of resources that balances the production of private and public goods. The general rule, we recall, is to increase the production of a public good to the point at which marginal benefits are equal to marginal costs. The question is not whether we think national defense is important. The question is about marginal benefits: What additional benefits will we get from extra dollars spent on national defense? We can think of the marginal costs of defense as "opportunity costs," or rather, what benefits we must give up elsewhere. Those resources could be used to produce other private or public goods. While it may be difficult to estimate marginal costs in terms of sacrificed benefits, a rough estimate may be obtained simply from the monetary costs of the extra defense projects. This is true because the prices of the inputs being used already reflect the contribution they would make in producing other goods. Therefore, their prices reflect the "value of their marginal product" not only in the defense industry, but in other industries as well.

In practice, of course, the political, legislative, and administrative processes of government do not always achieve allocative efficiency. Just as we use the term *market failure* to refer to inefficiency and unfairness caused by imperfections in our economic system, we use the term *government failure* to

> **Government failure**, the counterpart to market failure, occurs when government fails to produce public goods efficiently and fairly. More specifically, government failures also refer to the failure to address (1) any of the various market failures, (2) the macroeconomic policy goals of full employment and price stability, and (3) the social goals of fair distribution of wealth, income, and economic opportunity.

refer to inefficiency and unfairness caused by imperfections in our political system. The imperfections can occur at several points in the decision-making process. There can be (1) insufficient information for public officials to make calculations of the marginal benefits and costs of public goods, (2) insufficient information as to the preferences of voters, (3) imperfections in the administrative process that allow for the immediate incentives of bureaucrats to take precedence over the preferences of voters, and (4) imperfections in the legislative process that allow special-interest groups to have undue influence. Before turning to these problems, let us consider another requirement of private–public balance.

Allocating Resources through Time

Government uses two methods to finance its spending: taxes and borrowing. Spending comes in a variety of forms that include *transfers* such as Social Security and welfare payments and *exhaustive spending* such as national defense and education. Exhaustive spending uses up or "exhausts" the economy's resources, whereas transfers merely shift funds from one person to another. We can further categorize government exhaustive expenditure as public consumption and investment. Consumption goods and investment goods deliver their benefits on different time schedules. The benefits of private consumption goods such as food, clothing, automobiles, television sets, and ice cream cones are used up as the goods are consumed. Private investment in plant and equipment, home building, and inventory provides benefits over longer periods of time. The benefits of public consumption goods are also used up when purchased. These include the services of members of the armed forces, social workers, policemen, judges, and legislators. By contrast, public investment goods such as highways, school buildings, and aircraft carriers give benefits over a number of years.

Ideally there is some best balance among the four categories: private consumption or investment and public consumption or investment. Either taxes or debt can be used to shift spending power from the private to the public sector. Generally the balance between private and public consumption should be financed using taxes, while the balance between public and private investment should be financed using debt. Over time, the size of the public debt should reflect public investment that has taken place, the stock of public capital.

Query: How Can an Increase in Public Debt Be Fair and Efficient?

Consider the decision of a community to build a new public school. It would be unfair for the present taxpayer population to have to pay for the school building out of current taxes. Over time, the makeup of the taxpayer population changes, some younger people joining and some elderly people passing away. People move in and people leave. Moreover, the benefits of the investment cover many years. To make the finance schedule fair and efficient, bonds should be issued and paid off in such a way that the benefits and costs each year are approximately equal. Theoretically, the end of the school building's usefulness should coincide with the final payment on the bonds. At that time other bonds are issued to finance a new school and the process continues.

This idea of debt rationality makes sense only if we think of debt broadly as "claims." In the private sector a firm will have assets that have been built up over time and it will have debt, say loans from banks. The net worth of the company will be reflected in the value of its stock. These claims, stock and debt, should be equal to the firm's assets. Individuals also invest in houses, real estate, and of course "human capital," their own education and health. Their net worth can also be calculated by subtracting their liabilities from their assets. Over most of our history the value of public investment has increased much faster than our public debt, leaving each generation with "stocks" growing in net worth.

Just how the public debt relates to future social benefits raises some interesting questions of intergenerational justice. These and other intergenerational considerations are important to social issues such as health, education, social security, and the environment. We will be returning to the idea of relating investment to debt and other types of claims.

Social Preferences and Voting as a Source of Government Failure

When our nation's founders laid the foundations for our democracy, they addressed the question of how citizens could make known their preferences. This question has continued to receive a great deal of attention over the years. We observe that our democratic system relies primarily on the majority vote. Kenneth Arrow studied the question of whether or not majority voting can give an unambiguous result.[7]

Arrow presented the problem succinctly in the form of a paradox of voting. Suppose there are three voters and three budget alternatives as follows:

	Budget in Order of Preference		
	First	**Second**	**Third**
Voter A	low	medium	high
Voter B	medium	high	low
Voter C	high	low	medium

When votes are taken comparing two alternatives the results are ambiguous. If the low budget is compared to the medium budget, the low budget will win (both A and C prefer the low budget to the medium budget). If the low budget is compared to the high budget, the high budget will win, being preferred by A and C. Finally, when the high budget is compared to the medium budget, the medium budget will win, and so the cycle continues with no definitive winner. According to Arrow there is

The **Arrow impossibility theorem** states that all democratic voting schemes are subject to the paradox of voting.

no voting scheme that can avoid the voting paradox. Moreover, other voting schemes present us with some additional questions of rationality and fairness.

We are left with a problem in determining community preferences. We cannot expect a budget process to work unless the voting system used will give unambiguous results. We are left with the question of how often voting paradoxes occur.

Notice that the voting paradox occurred because voter C's preferences were for high, low, and medium budgets in that order. We can assume that few voters would have such an arrangement of preferences. If C's preferences had been high to medium to low, the paradox would not have occurred. The medium budget would win. Generally, if voters use the same standards for evaluating the issues, then voting paradoxes will not occur. Even in situations in which voting paradoxes are likely to occur there may be alternatives. If other issues and tradeoffs can be brought into play, unambiguous results may still be achieved.

Social Choices and Moral Principles

The question of whether or not voting procedures or other political processes can adequately resolve and order social preferences becomes more complicated when we consider the nature of social issues. Unlike the question of the preferred quantity of a public good such as defense or highways, most social issues contain moral issues.

Can we assume that the individuals who make up our society agree on what moral principles are relevant to a given social issue? Since we are taking a pluralist approach, we are not relying on one pure consistent moral theory. It is assumed that our moral intuitions respond to perspectives from several theories and that moral principles will have different weight according to the issue. The task then is to see how much agreement can be reached on principles and the weight to be given each principle.

Arrow has made an interesting comparison between theories of choice and political philosophy. According to idealist political philosophers, all members of society share a general will that may or may not be revealed and implemented through social political institutions. Rousseau, Kant, T. H. Green, and others argued that we share a general conception of what should be society's goals. According to Kant, individuals order preferences according to three imperatives: the pragmatic, the technical, and the moral. The pragmatic is the individual's motive to seek her or his own happiness. The technical is the necessity to know the practical means to an end. These are contingent in nature, while a moral imperative is categorical. Moreover, the moral imperative is valid for all persons.

Arrow argues that the moral imperative can be thought of as a social ordering that is also an individual ordering found in every individual. The idealist doctrine says that individuals have two orderings, one that is relevant to everyday decisions and one that is broader and truer and relevant to social choice, especially the moral content of social choice. This ordering can be revealed under ideal conditions. If that is accomplished, there will be complete unanimity over the ordering of social choices.[8] Arrow goes on to quote

Rousseau as advocating the majority rule as a means for revealing the general will: "The principle of majority rule must be taken ethically as a means of ascertaining a real general will; not as a mechanism by which one set of interests is made subservient to another set. Political discussion must be assumed to represent a quest for an objectively ideal or best policy, not a contest between interests."[9]

Self-Interested Officials and Government Failure

A basic behavioral model used by political and economic theorists assumes that government officials; that is, politicians and bureaucrats, follow their own narrow interests at the expense of their social responsibilities. Politicians are motivated to increase the chances of getting themselves and other members of their party elected. When they can pass legislation favoring large contributors to their campaign, they do so, taking care not to offend other constituents. Government workers are assumed to favor increasing the scope of their own agencies so as to justify higher rank, power, and salary. Although analyses that rely solely on this behavioral model are unrealistic and are prone to error, these motives certainly play a part in resource allocation. As we look more closely at particular social issues, we will consider the roles such motives may play in government failures.

Economic Rents and Rent Seeking

A related government failure arises from high transactions costs. A given public policy may have a small effect on a large number of unorganized individuals and a large impact on a small number of organized groups. For example, there may be a small but well-organized group of firms that imports a product that is consumed by many; or there may be a small but well-organized group of producers who would benefit from protection from foreign competition. Since the harmful effects of tariffs, import quotas, and subsidies are usually diffused over a large number of unorganized buyers, those most directly affected are willing to expend time and money to influence legislation.

The concepts of *rent* and *rent seeking* are relevant here. Within the legislative process there may be opportunities to obtain rents in the forms of licenses, franchises, quotas, and other rights and privileges. The lobbying for rights and privileges is termed rent seeking. The time and money spent in rent seeking is nonproductive, a waste.

To offset these tendencies, budget procedures can be organized so that agencies must fully justify new programs in competition with those of other agencies. As budgetary estimates are compiled at various levels, further comparisons and choices must be made. This process of competing within

> **Economic rent** is the return to an input that is fixed; for example, a skilled worker who can only work at one firm. The point is that the input's contribution is available even though he may be paid less. **Rent seeking** is the behavior of individuals, firms, or special-interest groups who seek to obtain and exploit economic rents.

larger and larger budget categories improves the rationality of the whole budget.

Greater efficiency and fairness can be achieved by reducing the transactions
costs of the otherwise disenfranchised. Laws can require disclosure of campaign
contributions and personal gifts. The legislative procedures can be changed so
that voters are better informed when legislation unfairly favors a special interest. It may be possible to avoid rents and rent seeking by encouraging competition, say by competitive bidding for government projects.

As we consider social issues such as tax fairness, education, health, social
security, and the environment, we must be concerned with government failures as well as market failures. The government failures may lead to too much
spending in some areas and too little spending in others. The failure of initiatives over the years to provide national health insurance must be regarded as
government failure. Our political and legislative processes seem ill-suited to address many of our most pressing social issues even when it is clearly the will of
most citizens that they be addressed.

THREE WORLD VIEWS

When we turn our attention to public discussion on specific social issues, we
will attempt to sort out the inherent moral principles and the assumptions as
to how the economic and political systems work. We will find that ideologies
sometimes make good points of departure. The beauty of an ideology is that
it provides continuity between values and beliefs. Every ideology is built upon
a set of values and related moral principles. These, along with certain assumptions about the political and economic systems, provide answers to a wide range
of questions that include the social issues of this study.

With most social issues, an analysis of the answers given by different ideologies will help clarify the ways moral principles and economic analyses are related. As our study proceeds, we will make use of many ideologies for this purpose. We begin here by describing two, individualism and egalitarianism, and
contrasting them with a position attributed to "the rest of us." The values of
most Americans include those from *both* individualism and egalitarianism. Thus
we are pluralists rather than ideologues. We believe that neither these two nor
any other "ism" has all the answers. Ideally, the rest of us are able to look at
the ideologies dispassionately. This is consistent with our pluralistic approach,
which seeks to evaluate the arguments of all sides of a social issue.

Individualism

The ideology of individualism places great value on the autonomy and liberty
of the individual. Many of its ethical arguments are drawn from libertarianism
but are not as extreme. The individual has the right to self-preservation and,
from that right, to any property that has been fairly acquired. Claims and
responsibilities are the products of voluntary agreements.

The economic assumptions are similar to those of the laissez-faire model, which features perfect competition in every market. Relationships are competitive and adversarial. Like the economy, the political system is competitive in nature.

To the question of how the distribution of income is to be justified, the individualist would evoke the principle "to each according to contribution." The rules of the game in competitive markets are fair because they rely on voluntary contracts. Thus, the results of the game can be considered fair.

To the question of the proper role of government, the answer is that it should be limited to guaranteeing property rights, enforcing contracts, and providing for national defense. Few social programs are justified since competitive market forces guarantee the efficient allocation of resources. Competitive forces also insure against the accumulation of monopoly power in the private sector. What is to be feared is government power. There is little need for income redistribution of other welfare programs since there is ample opportunity for those willing to work. Education, health, and social security are more efficiently provided by the private sector. Only those with severe disabilities need to be provided a safety net.

Finally, nature, or rather, the environment is to be manipulated. It can, at times, be perverse; but that too is part of the game. Individuals and firms have the right to exploit nature.

Egalitarianism

The ideology of egalitarianism takes seriously the idea that all men and women are created equal. Ideal relationships are cooperative and harmonious. The purposes of society are to promote equality and the well-being of all. All members of society are responsible to each other and to society as a whole. The economy is seen as a joint venture. All goods and services produced in the economy require a cooperative effort; therefore, the fairest distribution formula is "to each an equal share."

Government is required to right the wrongs that occur in the economic system. The role of hierarchy in government is problematical. Egalitarians see the necessity of having government use coercive powers to carry out its social programs. But they oppose the idea of one person enjoying more power and prestige than another. While not perfect, the best form of government is a participatory democracy with appropriate checks and balances.

Egalitarians support social programs to redistribute income and benefits such as food, clothing, housing, education, and health care. They see nature as benign. Egalitarians believe we should preserve and live in harmony with the environment.

The Rest of Us

The rest of us includes all Americans who have some degree of objectivity. The problem with an ideology is that it acts as a filter. Facts that do not fit the ideology's paradigm are either ignored or interpreted in a way that fits the prescribed view of the world. The beauty of an ideology is that everything can be made to fit. The "answer" is always clear and certain.

All of us are prone to the ideological syndrome. We recognize from time to time that we are deceiving ourselves in order to hold on to a comfortable set of beliefs. It is always easier to see self-deception in others, but even that demonstrates the point. Ideologies encourage those of like mind to purposefully distort arguments so as to reinforce the commonly held worldview.

Usually persons of good will *can* come to agreement on the best strategy for dealing with a social issue. But everyone must look at the facts objectively and reach some agreement on what moral principles are at stake. The weight each participant gives his or her principles does not always have to be identical for compromise to be reached.

But ideologies get in the way of civil, well-reasoned discussion. We must be prepared to lay ideology aside and explore other ways of looking at the issue, to have an open mind rather than a closed mind.

In contrast to individualism or egalitarianism, the rest of us believe that human nature is complex. In some situations, people are adversarial, and in others, cooperative. We believe strongly in individual liberty, but we also see ourselves as members of a community with responsibilities to others. We are, at times, narrowly self-interested, but at other times, altruistic.

The economic system is made up of markets with varying degrees of competitiveness. We generally rely on competitive markets to allocate resources, but we are aware of a number of ways that markets fail. We generally believe in our democratic form of government, but we are aware of its shortcomings.

Our approach to social issues is eclectic; at times, we ask what policy would be best for society as a whole; at times, we ask what the rights of the least-well-off are. We do not blame big government for every social ill, nor do we blame big business. Instead, we worry about concentrations of power in either sector.

On the issue of income distribution, most Americans are pluralistic. All of the commonly held principles seem to have merit. We agree that it is just to reward effort and contribution to the welfare of others; however, there are limits to the inequality we will accept, particularly if the basic needs of some of our fellow citizens are not being met.

On the issue of welfare reform, most Americans agree on which moral principles are at stake. We argue that adults, particularly parents, have primary responsibility for their own well-being and the well-being of their children. At the same time, society is responsible for there being economic opportunity in the form of decent jobs. Moreover, we agree that society must insure that the basic needs of children are being met. The challenge to states, as they reform their welfare systems, is to develop programs that meet all of these social responsibilities.

On the issue of education, there is widespread agreement that responsibility should be shared among parents, local communities, and society as a whole. To use the fair-game analogy, children have a right to a fair start.

On the issue of health care, most Americans agree that health care is a basic right. There are some forty million Americans without health care insurance. We recognize that we have a social responsibility to make health care insurance available to all. There is less agreement on the best political and economic strategy for meeting that responsibility.

On the issue of social security, most Americans recognize a responsibility to insure that the elderly can afford the basic necessities of life. The program also provides a base upon which most Americans build for a more comfortable retirement. There is some disagreement on what principles should be used to distribute benefits. The individualist would argue that benefits should better reflect an individual's lifetime contribution to the plan. The egalitarian would distribute benefits more on the basis of need. Due to the demography of the baby-boomer generation, there is also a question of intergenerational justice. Will the trust funds be adequate when the baby boomers begin to retire in the year 2010? Interestingly enough, a strategy to preserve intergenerational justice was put in place in 1983. Given the present political climate, which favors tax cuts over social responsibilities, there is some question that these commitments will be honored.

On environmental issues, the values of individualism and egalitarianism are quite different. The rest of us take a pluralistic approach. We appreciate the view that humans and economic opportunity should come first, but we also share the egalitarian view that we have a responsibility to the environment and to future generations.

In all of these issues, the application of ethics and economic analysis will help bring clarity to public debate and to the formulation of policy. We do not expect to always find *the answer*, but this approach may help to narrow perceived differences and to suggest strategies upon which agreement can be reached.

SUGGESTIONS FOR FURTHER READING

Market Failures, Externalities

James M. Buchanan, *Demand and Supply of Public Goods* (Chicago: Rand McNally, 1968). A classic study of externalities and collective goods.

Ronald Coase, "The Problem of Social Cost," *Journal of Law and Economics* (3) (1960), pp. 1–44. The classic exposition of the Coase Theorem argument.

Carl Dahlman, "The Problems of Externality," *Journal of Law and Economics* (22) (1979), pp. 141–68. Analysis of the effects transactions costs have on the resolution of externalities.

The Idea of a Mixed System, Democratic Government and Free Markets

Kenneth Arrow, *Social Choice and Individual Values* 2d ed. (New York: Wiley, 1963). A seminal work on social choice theory. Chapter 3 sets out the Arrow Impossibility Theorem. Arrow uses mathematics to present the argument.

Anthony Downs, *An Economic Theory of Democracy* (New York: Harper, 1957). Downs examines the proposition that voters can use the political process to voice their preferences for public goods, much as consumers voice their preferences in private markets.

ENDNOTES

1. The term *laissez-faire*, introduced in the last chapter, means "hands off." In this context it means for government to keep hands off and let the free market operate on its own.
2. From a lecture given by the classical economist Adam Smith in 1749. Cited in John Rae, *Life of Adam Smith* (New York: A. M. Kelly, 1965), p. 62.
3. Adam Smith, *The Wealth of Nations* (New York: Modern Library, 1937).
4. We must differentiate between the laissez-faire utopian model and Smith's much more realistic assessment of markets in the economic system of his day. While competitive markets were the rule, collusion was, at times, possible. As Smith humorously put it:
   > People of the same trade seldom meet together, even for merriment and diversion, but the conversation ends in a conspiracy against the public, or in some contrivance to raise prices. (*Wealth of Nations*, bk. I, chap. X, part II, par. 27).
5. Ronald Coase, "The Problem of Social Cost," *Journal of Law and Economics* (3) (1960), pp. 1–44.
6. See Erik Lindahl, "Just Taxation: A Positive Solution," in *Classics in the Theory of Public Finance*, eds. Richard A. Musgrave and Alan T. Peacock (New York: Cromwell-Collier, 1958), pp. 168–77.
7. Arrow set out his conditions for a rational voting system in chapter three of his *Social Choice and Individual Values* (New York: Wiley, 1951).
8. Ibid., pp. 81–82.
9. J. J. Rousseau, *The Social Contract*, English translation by Rose M. Harrington, 2nd. ed. (New York: Putnam, 1906), pp. 165–166, as quoted in Arrow, ibid., p. 85.

3

Taxes, the Budget, and Welfare Reform

Issues of taxes and welfare reform evoke deep and sometimes conflicting feelings among Americans. The issue of the Boston Tea Party was one of taxation without representation. With or without representation, Americans still resent taxes. As every candidate for political office knows, running on a platform of raising taxes would be suicide. As voters, we always seem willing to suspend our disbelief when politicians promise to cut taxes, balance the budget, and protect defense spending, Social Security, and Medicare. The fact that every candidate knows such promises to be patently absurd does not seem to matter. The candidate who makes the story more believable will be elected.

Much the same can be said for welfare reform. A basic assumption behind the 1996 reform of welfare was that most of those on welfare were employable and could readily find jobs. All that was required was for voters to say no. Supposedly, once the work disincentives caused by welfare payments were removed, welfare would no longer act as a trap to the poor. As voters we seem determined to ignore the fact that the overwhelming majority of those on welfare were unfit and unable to work; 40 percent were children.

Let us begin by considering issues of taxes and tax reform. Underneath the political rhetoric, there are real issues of fairness and efficiency. Questions of tax fairness are inherent in all of the social issues we will study. Our social programs in welfare, health, education, Social Security, and the environment all require taxes. The fairness of a tax depends in part on how the revenue will be spent. Thus taxes and tax reform must be evaluated in the context of government budgets. Paying taxes is always painful; the whole point is to withdraw spending power from the private sector. The idea is to minimize the pain. A related idea is to make taxes fair. Our general approach, then, is to ask whether or not taxes are efficient and fair. In chapters one and two we developed useful perspectives for both questions.

Taxes: Who Actually Pays?

It is easy enough to identify the initial impact of a tax: personal income taxes are paid by individual persons; corporation income taxes are paid by corporations; businesses collect payroll taxes and general sales taxes and remit them to the federal and state governments; and local governments collect property taxes directly from homeowners, farmers, and businesses. Knowing who writes the check to government does not answer the question of who actually pays. In many cases the *incidence* of the tax, who actually pays, may be *shifted* from the *initial impact*, who writes the check to government, to someone else. Since taxes are borne by people, not businesses, the question of incidence refers to the real burdens placed on individuals. The answer is . . . well, it depends.

> The **initial impact** of a tax refers to the individual or organization responsible for paying government. The **shifting** of a tax refers to transferring the burden from the initial impact to someone else. The **incidence** of a tax refers to who bears the final burden.

Taxes initially falling on businesses must all eventually be shifted to individuals. The final burden may fall on consumers (in the form of higher prices), on employees (in the form of lower wages), on suppliers of other inputs (in the form of lower prices or rent), or on stockholders (in the form of lower dividends or stock values).

How do we predict who will bear the final burden? Obviously all of the potential candidates would prefer not to pay; but, just as in a game of musical chairs, someone will be left without an alternative. The answer to who ultimately bears the tax depends on the relative flexibility of the potential candidates. Do they have other alternatives available? How can they change behavior so as to avoid the tax? Economists use the term *elasticity* to refer to the flexibility of buyers or sellers to vary the amounts they buy or sell. Let us describe the possible outcomes in terms of an excise tax imposed on a good in a competitive market. The excise tax is a tax-per-unit that raises the cost of the good by the amount of the tax. Although the tax raises the cost of the good it may or may not be passed on to the buyers in the form of higher prices. The answer depends on the elasticities.

Tax Shifting with Different Elasticities of Supply

When we say that supply is relatively *elastic* we mean that the suppliers are flexible. They have other options; thus they can change their behavior to avoid the tax. Say, for example, that a firm produces a number of products and only one is taxed. Assume further that the firm has enough flexibility that it can shift to the production of the other products at no great expense. If most firms in this particular industry have similar flexibility, the market supply will be relatively elastic, and most of the burden of the tax will be passed forward to the buyers in the form of higher prices.

By contrast, there are industries where production processes and specialization leave individual firms little flexibility. Here the market supply is relatively inelastic and the burden of the tax is more likely to remain with the firms.

Tax Shifting with Different Elasticities of Demand

Similar results hold on the demand side. Those buyers with more flexibility; that is, more options, are less likely to bear the tax's incidence. If there are good substitutes for the taxed good, any increase in price will lead buyers to shift to other goods. It follows that the sellers will have less ability to raise prices.

If, on the other hand, there are few substitutes; that is, the market demand is relatively inelastic, suppliers will find that they can raise prices and suffer with only small reductions in sales. Buyers will bear the incidence of the tax in the form of higher prices. The mechanics of tax shifting also hold for input markets. Tax shifting in labor markets, for example, depends importantly on the job options open to workers. Here employers represent the demand side and workers represent the supply side. If a firm is taxed, it may be successful in passing some of the burden to its employees in the form of lower wages. This would not happen if the labor market were composed of many potential employers who kept up their wages. The more options open to the workers, the less likely the burden will be passed to them. By contrast, when workers have few options, the labor supply is, by definition, inelastic, and workers are more susceptible to tax shifting.

> **Elasticity of demand** measures the change in purchases caused by changes in price. We ask how much buyers reduce purchases in response to higher prices. Or alternatively, how much do they increase purchases in response to lower prices? More formally, price elasticity of demand is the percentage of change in quantity demanded divided by the percentage of change in the price for that good. **Elasticity of supply** measures the change in quantities offered for sale in response to changes in price. We ask how much sellers will increase the quantities offered in response to higher prices. Or alternatively, how much do they reduce quantities offered in response to lower prices? More formally, the price elasticity of supply is the percentage of change in the quantity offered divided by the percentage of change in the price of the good.

Some Generalizations on Tax Incidence

The incidence may differ according to the time frame. Obviously buyers and sellers are more flexible the more time they have to make adjustments. What matters to the final incidence of a tax is what flexibility buyers and sellers have in the long run. Recall the mechanics of competitive markets outlined in chapter two. The short-run flexibility of firms is quite different from the long-run. The short-run is simply *defined* as a time frame in which the firm has limited flexibility. It differs from industry to industry according to the technology involved. If an important means of production (say plant and machinery) is fixed, firms have little flexibility; they must bear the most of an excise tax's incidence.

The description of the mechanics of competitive markets also takes the long run into account. In this time frame, which again differs from industry to industry, firms have the flexibility to increase or decrease plant and machinery or to quit producing the good altogether.

It follows from this description of the mechanics of competitive markets that, in the long run, firms will have sufficient flexibility to avoid the tax. It will be passed forward to buyers in the form of higher prices. Firms may bear part of the burden in the short run, but these losses will induce enough firms to leave, so that prices will rise by the amount of the tax.

In theory, then, the long-run supply in competitive markets is completely elastic. Since competition requires that firms produce at the lowest cost possible, no additional costs can be borne, and the entire burden must eventually be shifted to buyers. In reality no markets meet the theoretical description of the perfectly competitive market. Recall that in chapter two we outlined a wide range of competitive conditions. As we might expect, the incidence of taxes has to do with the relative market power enjoyed by buyers and sellers. Monopolists typically enjoy an inelastic demand for their product. We would expect them to pass along most of the incidence of taxes they are required to pay.

In markets where there are a small number of competitors, that is, an oligopoly, the results are uncertain. Final tax incidence depends importantly on the ability of the firms to collude with each other. In cases of successful collusion, such as OPEC, we would expect a significant part of any new cost to be passed forward to buyers in the form of higher prices. In cases of cutthroat competition, such as in certain markets in the airline industry, firms find it difficult to shift the incidence of a new tax.

THOUGHTS ON THE FAIRNESS OF TAX SHIFTING AND INCIDENCE

As we trace the incidence of taxes it seems appropriate to ask: Who is intended to bear the burden and why? In some cases the answer to both questions is obvious. The personal income tax is intended to be borne by individuals on the basis of their incomes. Similarly, the sales tax, although collected by businesses, is intended to be borne by consumers on the basis of how much they consume. Both are broad taxes that are difficult to avoid. The funds go to general revenues to be used for a wide range of government activities. Excise taxes are directed at the consumers of specific goods. They are usually imposed on goods with inelastic demands. This strategy follows from our previous analysis. Taxes on goods that have no good substitutes (an inelastic demand) cannot be easily avoided.

From all of this, two rules emerge for raising revenues through taxes: "Depend on taxes so broad that they are difficult to avoid." Alternatively, "tax a good with an inelastic demand."

Although important, a tax's revenue-raising potential is only one of several criteria and may not be the deciding factor in imposing the tax. We ask not only who bears the burden but whether or not they *should* bear the burden. The tax on cigarettes scores well on efficiency grounds. There are no good substitutes; that is to say, the demand is inelastic. Thus, the tax raises revenue and causes little change in behavior and resource allocation. Yet, in the case of tobacco, changing behavior would be an attribute not an inefficiency. If discouraging smoking is one of our social goals, as it appears to be, it would be better if taxes on cigarettes had a larger impact on sales. Instead the tax acts more like a tax on incomes of smokers. Unfortunately a disproportionate number of those who smoke come from the lower-income levels and the poor. While taxing cigarettes does little to inhibit smoking, it requires poor families to reduce spending on other things.

Tax Incidence on Different Income Levels

Tax incidence is often discussed in terms of the impact different taxes have on the different income levels. While the importance of this criterion depends on a number of factors, other things being equal, we would generally be concerned if income inequality were increased as a result of a tax. This leads us to the concepts of progressive, proportional, and regressive taxes. In one sense, they are defined in terms of the personal income tax, where the base is income. *Progressive taxes* are defined as taking a higher proportion of income as income increases. A *proportional tax* would maintain the same rate for all income levels. A *regressive tax* takes a smaller proportion from higher incomes.

> For a **progressive tax** the amount an individual pays *increases* as a proportion of income as the individual's income increases. For a **proportional tax** the individual pays an amount that is a *constant* proportion of income as the person's income increases. For a **regressive tax** the proportion paid *decreases* as income increases. Notice that, while we may apply the criterion to all types of taxes, such as sales taxes and property taxes, the principle relates taxes paid to one's income level.

Although other taxes apply rates to other bases, they are still evaluated in terms of their impact on income distribution. For example, sales taxes are usually specified as a proportional rate that is applied to sales. Although the tax is proportional with respect to sales, its incidence is evaluated in terms of its impact on income distribution. Thus a sales tax of a given rate, say 6 percent, would still be considered regressive. This is because higher-income individuals and families save more and consume less as a percentage of income. Since sales taxes focus on consumption, the higher-income individuals pay a smaller percentage of their income. If the sales tax were increased, everyone's purchasing power would be reduced; but the differences among income levels, that is, income inequality, would be increased. Again, this is only one of several criteria to be used in evaluating taxes. The weight it is given depends on the context. Indeed the largest source of federal revenue, the payroll tax, is quite regressive; but it must be evaluated in terms of the programs it finances.

Incidence of the Major Taxes: Who Actually Pays?

The incidence of the personal income tax and the sales tax follows the rule that broad taxes are difficult to avoid. It is generally agreed that the targeted individuals, income earners and consumers, respectively, actually pay the two taxes. While specifications of the income tax code contain a number of exemptions, deductions, and other preferences, the incidence generally remains on the income of the individual.

Unlike an excise tax, which can be avoided by switching to other goods, the general sales tax can be avoided only by reducing the consumption of all goods and increasing one's saving. Therefore, it is agreed that it is paid by its intended victims. Although its initial impact is on businesses that collect it for the states and localities, it is successfully shifted to consumers. In actual practice, not all consumption is taxed. Every state excludes spending on housing and health care. Another large category excluded by over half of the states is food, that is, food purchased for home consumption. These exemptions reduce by half the consumption spending subject to the tax. It follows that the price differentials caused by these exclusions have some effect on buying habits and income distribution.

The federal personal income tax is progressive. After all exemptions, deductions, and other provisions are accounted for, the effective tax rate for those in the lowest 10 percent income level is only about 1 percent. This compares to rates around 5.5 percent for the middle levels. Those with incomes in the top 10 percent pay an effective tax rate of 12 percent.

Although it is widely assumed that employers and employees both pay their designated parts of the payroll tax, economists are nearly unanimous in their belief that employees bear the entire burden. The supply of labor in most markets and in the nation as a whole is quite inelastic. Workers have few job opportunities that escape the tax. Thus employers are able to shift their part of the tax to employees in the form of lower wages.

As noted, sales and excise taxes are generally assumed to be effective in finding their intended marks: consumers. The general sales tax is so broad it is difficult to avoid, and the excise taxes are usually imposed on goods with very inelastic demand. Their impacts on income distribution are only slightly regressive throughout the middle-income levels. The very poor pay a disproportionate amount; the combined effect of sales and excise taxes is over 17 percent of income. At the other end of the scale, those with incomes over five hundred thousand dollars pay less than 1 percent of income.[1] As explained, the regressivity of the general sales tax occurs because individuals and families with higher incomes tend to consume a smaller percentage of their income. The exemption of food and drugs in many states reduces the regressivity of the general sales tax; however, most of the excise taxes (especially those on gasoline, alcohol, and tobacco) are quite regressive.

If, as is generally assumed, the corporation income tax were borne by the firms' owners, that is, its stockholders, the tax would be progressive. There is wide disagreement among economists as to who actually bears the burden. Some studies claim that most of the corporation income tax is passed on to consumers in the form of higher prices. This would indicate that the tax is regressive (and it would also indicate that increases would add to inflation). Other studies claim that corporations have not raised prices in response to tax increases, and therefore, the burden must reside with the owners.

The incidence of property taxes is also disputed. It is generally held that homeowners bear their part of the tax but that owners of rental housing are able to pass their burdens on in the form of higher rents. With rental housing, the idea is that, since investors have other options, they would be able to avoid the tax simply by investing elsewhere. For property owned by corporations the arguments follow those of the corporation income tax. If they are borne by the owners, the effects are progressive; if they are passed on to consumers, the effects are regressive.

For the economy as a whole, the net effect of the federal, state, and local taxes on income distribution is not substantial. If we accept the arguments that the corporation and property taxes are progressive, the incidence of taxes overall is slightly progressive. Under other assumptions, the incidence of all taxes combined is roughly proportional but regressive for the very poor and the very rich. As we shall see, the major government impact on income distribution comes from the expenditure side, not the revenue side. Our welfare programs have had a major impact on poverty.

Taxes and Efficiency: The Attribute of Neutrality

Another basis for evaluating taxes is in terms of their effects on market prices. We recall the idea of allocative efficiency. In competitive markets, firms are forced to produce those goods consumers want most at the lowest cost possible. Market prices play an important part in the allocative process, and, ideally, they reflect each good's marginal costs. Taxes that unnecessarily change price ratios create not only a tax burden but also an excess burden. The *excess burden* occurs because choices made on the basis of the new price ratios lead to inefficient resource allocation; the new price does not reflect the true opportunity costs of the good. The effect is similar to the case in which a monopoly sets a good's price higher than its real costs, with the result that less of the good is produced. In terms of resources, fewer resources are allocated to that good; presumably they are used to produce other goods that generate fewer benefits.

> **Neutral taxes** have no effect on price ratios. They withdraw purchasing power (the income effect) but have no effect on the relative attractiveness of goods (i.e., they have no substitution effect). **Nonneutral taxes**, by contrast, withdraw purchasing power (income effect) but also affect the relative attractiveness of goods (the substitution effect).

> The **excess burden** of a tax is the difference between the revenue raised and the welfare lost by the taxpayers. Assuming price ratios accurately reflect opportunity costs, a neutral tax would cause no excess burden.

Income and Substitution Effects

To fully appreciate the concepts of *neutrality* and *nonneutrality* we need to consider the two effects a price change has on the choices made by consumers, workers, and firms. These are the *substitution effect* and the *income effect*. When we think of how we respond to a price change, we usually focus on the substitution effect. If the price of a good goes down, we choose to buy more because it is now a better value. It now looks better than its substitutes because it gives more value per dollar. At the same time, the price change affects the purchasing power of our income. Theoretically we could buy more of the good in question and still have money left to buy other goods.

The **substitution effect** refers to the tendency of consumers to respond to changes in price ratios by buying more of the lower-priced goods and less of the higher-priced goods. Consumers compare the relative attractiveness of goods, that is, the additional "welfare per dollar." They substitute in favor of lower priced goods and away from the higher priced goods. The **income effect** refers to changes in purchasing power. The income effect of a price change refers to the impact of a price change on purchasing power: a higher price reduces the consumer's ability to purchase not only the good in question but other goods as well; a lower price increases the consumer's ability to purchase other goods. A price change includes both an income effect and a substitution effect.

The response to a price change always includes an income effect and a substitution effect. In some cases the two effects work in the same direction; in other cases they work in opposite directions. The substitution effect is always predictable. It works in the direction of buying more of a good whose price is lowered and less of a good whose price is raised. Again, it is a simple matter of comparing price ratios and going for the bargain that now offers greater benefits-per-dollar. It is the income effect that may give surprising results. For most goods, that is, *normal goods*, people buy more as their income increases.

We generally spend more on food, clothing, shelter, transportation, and vacations as our income increases. However, there are *inferior goods* on which we spend less as our income increases. We might switch from hamburger to steak or from inferior wines to superior wines as our income increases.

Normal goods and **inferior goods** are defined in terms of consumer response to changes in income. Consumers buy more of normal goods and less of inferior goods as their income increases.

With substitution and income effects working in opposite directions, the net result is not always predictable. Usually we would expect lower prices for inferior goods such as hamburger to result in greater sales. Similarly, reducing the price of an inferior wine usually has the expected result. However, lower prices do not always result in more being purchased, and correspondingly higher prices do not always result in less. For example, a change in the price ratio between income and leisure may affect different people in different ways. An increase in the wage rate has both an income and a substitution effect. The substitution effect of a higher wage clearly favors working more hours. However, at higher-income levels many people prefer to take more leisure time. For some people, the net effect of the two opposing influences will be to work more hours, for others it will be to work fewer hours.

As we consider and evaluate our major forms of taxation, the question of their effects on such things as allocative efficiency, work effort, savings and investment is obviously very important. In each case the results depend on the relative strengths of the income and substitution effects.

Now let us reconsider the attribute of neutrality. We observe that those taxes that affect income directly and have no substitution effects are by definition neutral. The classic example is the *lump-sum tax*. When firms are assessed a lump-sum tax, say a license fee, the tax has no effect on the relative costs of inputs. We expect no shifts in input usage to occur. Similarly, a version of the lump-sum tax imposed on individuals, the so-called head tax, has no effect on price ratios. Once paid, each person still faces the same market prices. To iterate, the lump sum tax is neutral with respect to market price ratios. There is no excess burden.

Margaret Thatcher's Lump-Sum Tax

In the 1980s the Tory government of Margaret Thatcher in Britain introduced a lump-sum tax called the *community charge*. The experience with this tax is an interesting example of the tradeoff between efficiency and fairness. As we have argued, the lump-sum tax is the epitome of efficiency. The price ratios set by the market remain unchanged so that, presumably, resource allocation remains efficient.

The Thatcher tax replaced a local property tax and was designed to enable localities to finance schools, streets, and other local programs. Local governments decided upon the tax levels, and there were considerable differences among localities. Within a locality, however, every citizen paid the same tax.

While the lump-sum tax scores well on efficiency criteria, it is generally considered to be unfair. Since all income levels pay the same amount, there is greater income inequality after the tax is paid. The tax is regressive.

Public reaction caused riots in Trafalgar Square, and many people actually refused to pay. The widespread disapproval of the tax played some part in the eventual fall of the Thatcher government. In 1991 it was replaced by increases in sales taxes and greater financial participation by the central government. The attribute of the lump-sum tax's neutrality toward market prices was of little consequence in the public's perception of the proper balance between efficiency and fairness.

Taxes and Fairness: The Income Tax as a Norm

The personal income tax is similar to the lump-sum tax in terms of efficiency but also ranks high in terms of fairness. Most of the various exemptions and deductions are designed to make the tax more fair by accounting for the particular situations of individuals and families. More generally, the rate structure is designed to spread the tax burden fairly among income levels.

The income tax, like the lump-sum tax, is neutral with respect to price ratios set by the market, and thus it ranks high on efficiency grounds. Of course, a tax on income does change the relative prices of income and leisure. We would expect higher income taxes to reduce work effort and saving. If this were true, its ranking with respect to efficiency could be questioned. However, we observed in chapter two that any price change involves both an income and a substitution effect. For most studies, the two effects seem to offset each other, so that no change in work effort is observed. Suppose, for example, that I am determined to maintain a certain standard of living but am faced with higher income taxes. My response may be to work more, rather than less. Similarly, I may have savings goals that require that I work more in the face of higher income taxes.

This does not mean that we cannot imagine tax rates so high as to discourage work and savings. But most studies indicate tax rates in the United States do not approach such levels.

To summarize, we expect some taxpayers to respond one way and others to respond another way. The net effect seems to be that there is no net effect. Although the substitution and income effects offset each other, there remains a small substitution effect and thus a small excess burden. Even so, the personal income tax ranks very high in terms of efficiency.

Query: Just What Is Income?

The standard definition of income was developed by Robert M. Haig and Henry Simons.[2] It sees income as the *flow* of purchasing power to the individual during the year. It includes *realized income* such as wages, transfers, gifts, and dividends, as well as increases in wealth that have the potential of being realized as purchasing power. The latter includes increased values of capital assets such as real estate and of personal property such as jewelry, stocks, and bonds. The taxing of some increases in wealth would be awkward and expensive. It would not be difficult to assess the value of one's stock holdings at the beginning and end of the year, but assessing the values of assets where market prices are not readily available may be impossible.

The Haig-Simons definition would also include benefits from work outside the market such as do-it-yourself projects, additions to the home, cooking, cleaning, and sewing. Benefits accruing from past investments should also be included, but here again a market transaction may not be involved. For example, buying a house creates benefits year after year, just as do other investments. Thus the imputed rent on the house should also be considered income.

What the Haig-Simons definition offers is an appropriately comprehensive description of income. The idea is to include all income and other increases in wealth that occur during the year. Since the comprehensive definition includes both realized and unrealized income, it becomes impractical to tax several of the income sources. Although possible, it would be awkward to collect taxes on unrealized capital gains; therefore, they are not taxed until realized. The treatment given capital gains is a subject of continued debate. The benefits created by work that is never priced are not taxed. Moreover, no attempt is made to tax the "income" gained by living in one's own home rather than having to rent.

Income as Consumption

It has been argued that income can be considered the utility an individual derives from consuming goods and services. Instead of taxing economic power as it accrues, we could tax it when it is used to purchase and consume final goods and services. From this view *double taxation* occurs when one is taxed on income, say from wages, and then taxed again when an investment pays dividends. Again the argument is that only consumption should be taxed.[3]

Two Principles of Tax Fairness

There are two broad principles of tax fairness that have developed over the years: the *benefit principle* and the *ability-to-pay principle*. The *benefit* approach suggests that we consider benefits, as well as costs, of public programs. When programs have direct private benefits as well as social benefits it seems fair for those who benefit more to pay more. The ability-to-pay approach focuses on the cost side, assuming that all citizens benefit equally as they consume public goods. The problem becomes how to fairly apportion the burden.

> The **benefit principle of taxation** states that the burden of taxes paid should be related to the benefits enjoyed from the spending program.

The benefit approach has developed over the years as part of the theory of welfare economics, especially by welfare economists Antonio de Viti de Marco and Knut Wicksell, and, more recently, the voluntary exchange theory of Eric Lindahl.[4] The basic idea is that resources should be allocated for every good up to the point where marginal benefits (both private and social) are equal to marginal costs

> The **ability-to-pay principle of taxation** is the argument that those with greater income or wealth should pay more taxes than those with less.

(both private and social). Since consuming extra units of any good creates declining (marginal) benefits and rising (marginal) costs, there will be some level of output where they are exactly equal (i.e., MB = MC).

Adam Smith explained tax fairness in the following way:

> The subjects of every state ought to contribute toward the support of the government, as nearly as possible, in proportion to their respective abilities; that is, in proportion to the revenue which they respectively enjoy under the protection of the state. The expense of government to the individuals of a nation is like the expense of management to the joint tenants of a great estate, who are obliged to contribute in proportion to their respective interests in the es-

tate. In the observation or neglect of this maxim consists what is called the equality or inequality of taxation.[5]

He adroitly linked the benefit and the ability-to-pay principles. An individual's ability to pay is reflected in the revenue she or he enjoys under the protection of the state. The expense of this joint venture should be borne in proportion to its respective benefits. Both approaches are useful for evaluating spending and taxing in terms of moral principles; both are vulnerable to competing considerations.

Since it relates taxes to spending, the benefit approach must cope with the difficulties of estimating private and public benefits and costs. The basic presumption is that the benefits and costs of purely private goods are accounted for by market prices. However, when goods create social benefits and costs, no such approximations are available. As noted in chapter two, we must rely on various *ad hoc* devices such as cost-benefit analysis.

The ability-to-pay approach must also deal with the problem of somehow quantifying welfare, but only on the revenue side. This argument appears in the earliest discussions of tax fairness. With the invention of taxes, no doubt, came the realization that it is fair as well as efficacious to tax more heavily those with greater ability to pay. As the argument has developed, a more refined moral principle has been introduced: the principle of equal sacrifice. We start with the idea that society has a tax burden to be spread fairly among its citizens. Unless some individuals are due special treatment, say they have meritorious exemptions, simple justice would seem to demand that the burden be shared equally. Since a dollar means less to wealthy persons than poor persons, equalizing burdens requires that more dollars be taken from the former than the latter. The reasoning is fundamentally deontological in that it assumes every person deserves equal respect and in this case equal pain.

However, a utilitarian argument can yield the same result. Now the goal is to maximize the total welfare of society. More pertinent to the problem at hand, we want to minimize the total burden of the tax. It would be a simple matter to equalize burdens if we could assume that each person's evaluation of additions to income follows the same path. In other words, the diminishing marginal utility of income is the same for all. If we employ an income tax to raise the revenue, we simply adjust the tax rate so that the same burden is exacted from each person. Under these assumptions, equalizing burdens also minimizes the total disutility of the tax. Theoretically, utility functions can differ among individuals, so that equal burdens will not minimize the total burden. But the utilitarian approach is generally taken to suggest that equal burdens will minimize society's tax burden.

John Stuart Mill refined the case of Smith and other classical economists for the ability-to-pay principle and the *equal-sacrifice argu-*

> The **equal-sacrifice principle** applies to taxes with which the goal is to spread the burden equally. Since dollars mean less to those with greater wealth or income, this implies that they should pay more.

ment. To Mill the equal treatment guaranteed under the law meant that taxes should be evaluated on the basis of whether they impose equal sacrifice.[6]

Even if we agree that the equal-sacrifice principle seems fair, the choice of a tax rate is not obvious. Let us assume that the extra dollar is worth less to the wealthy than to the poor and that equal sacrifice requires that the wealthy pay more. But how much more? We assume a "diminishing marginal utility of income," but just how rapidly does it diminish? If a progressive rate structure is called for, just how progressive? An extreme version of the utilitarian argument would call for complete progression. Everyone's final income would be identical, and thus everyone's sacrifice of the last (marginal) dollar would have been equal. Thus, total sacrifice would be minimized and total welfare maximized.[7]

The more traditional approach is to consider each person's sacrifice. Equality is achieved when each taxpayer suffers the same total amount of pain. Here again the rate schedule depends on the utility each person gets from extra income.

The personal income tax can be structured to spread tax burdens evenly. As we have seen, it fares well on all of the criteria used to judge efficiency and fairness. In most comparisons it provides the benchmark upon which other taxes are evaluated.

TAXES AND EXPENDITURES

Market Failures Again

Just as it is appropriate to ask What social needs can government provide? it is appropriate to ask How will we pay for the necessary government activities? We have described the marvels of the free market: how competitive markets organize production efficiently to produce those goods we prefer at the lowest cost possible. But the market is not infallible. Market imperfections of various kinds result in a failure to provide for some of our more important needs.

The point is that the special characteristics of certain goods and the nature of market imperfections offer clues as to how government may best proceed. We have observed that government programs differ widely in nature, ranging from public goods (such as national defense) to not-so-public goods (such as health care). The nature of the good and the associated market failure should tell us something about the fairness and efficiency of possible sources of tax revenue.

The budgets of federal, state, and local governments illustrate the responses made to different types of market failures. Markets fail to allocate resources to public goods such as national defense and basic research. Until very recently defense spending was the largest category of the federal budget. Other goods such as education, although not pure public goods, have important social benefits. Public spending on education is concentrated at the state and local levels.

Now consider the nature of the benefits of these pure and not-so-pure public goods. The benefits of national defense, a pure public good, are shared equally by all and no one's "consumption" reduces the benefits left to others. Education also produces social benefits but creates private benefits as well. So how should we pay for these two goods? Assuming we pay for defense with a broad general tax, how should the burden be spread? And given that education has direct as well as social benefits, should those who benefit directly pay more?

Several public programs are responses to negative or positive externalities with which the market cannot cope. Air and water pollution can be addressed by a number of means: regulations, assignment of property and other legal rights, or corrective taxes and subsidies. Other types of failures occur in markets featuring monopolies or oligopolies. Here again regulations, subsidies, and taxes may be employed. In some cases, the ideal solution is for government to encourage more competition.

In chapter two we also observed how misallocation may occur when the availability of information is flawed. The list of possible imperfections includes asymmetric information, adverse selection, moral hazard, social risks, and incomplete markets. These problems call forth a wide range of government responses.

As we shall see, the link between taxes and spending is at times obvious; some taxes for example, are linked with specific government services. In other cases the benefits are more general, and the appropriate funding would be general revenues.

Tables 3.1 and 3.3 outline the most important expenditures at the federal, state, and local levels. Tables 3.2 and 3.4 outline the revenue sources. In recent years Social Security and Medicare have assumed a larger and larger share of federal spending. Correspondingly, the payroll taxes have become the largest source of revenue.

National defense had always been the most significant expenditure in the federal budget. During World War II federal expenditures were made up pri-

TABLE 3.1
FEDERAL EXPENDITURES
(Approximate Percentages in Recent Budgets)

	Percentage
1. Social Security (24%) and Medicare (12%)	36.0
2. National Defense, Veterans, and International Affairs	19.0
3. Income Security (14%) and Health (8%)	22.0
4. Net Interest on the Debt	14.0
5. Education	3.5
6. Transportation	2.5
7. Commerce and Housing	1.5
8. Other	1.5
Total	100.0

Sources: Averages are taken from data of recent federal budgets.

TABLE 3.2
FEDERAL RECEIPTS
(Approximate Percentages in Recent Budgets)

	Percentage
1. Payroll Taxes	41.0
2. Income Taxes	40.0
3. Corporate Income Taxes	11.0
4. Excise Taxes	4.0
5. Estate and Gift Taxes	1.5
6. Customs Duties	1.0
7. Other	1.5
Total	100.0

Sources: Averages are taken from data of recent federal budgets.

TABLE 3.3
STATE AND LOCAL EXPENDITURES
(Approximate Percentages in Recent Budgets)

	Percentage
1. Education	37.0
2. Income Support, Welfare, Social Security, Housing, and Community Services	26.0
3. Transportation	10.0
4. Civilian Safety	10.0
5. Health and Hospitals	3.5
6. Recreation and Cultural Activities	1.5
7. Other	12.0
Total	100.0

Sources: Averages are taken from data of recent state and local budgets.

TABLE 3.4
STATE AND LOCAL RECEIPTS
(Approximate Percentages in Recent Budgets)

	Percentages
1. Sales Taxes	24.0
2. Property Taxes	21.0
3. Federal Grants	21.0
4. Income Taxes	14.0
5. Payroll Taxes	8.0
6. Corporate Profit Taxes	3.5
7. Other	8.5
Total	100.0

Sources: Averages are taken from data of recent state and local budgets.

marily of defense spending and accounted for over 40 percent of the gross domestic product (GDP). During the late 1960s and early 1970s defense spending at times accounted for over half of the federal budget. Again, during the early years of the Reagan administration, spending on defense was increased dramatically. Recent easing of cold war tensions has reduced defense spending in real terms, especially during the Clinton administration. At the same time the Social Security and Medicare programs have expanded rapidly and now account for over a third of the budget.

Correspondingly, payroll taxes, which fund the Social Security and Medicare programs, have become a larger component of the budget, now providing around 40 percent of federal revenues. Although the Reagan administration accomplished massive cuts in the personal income tax, it remains the main source of general revenues at the federal level.

Education makes up the largest expenditure item at the state and local levels; however, income support and welfare are a rapidly growing share. This share will grow substantially in the next few years, since the new welfare reform proposals require states to take a larger role in raising revenues. Accordingly, the related federal grants will also assume a larger role on the revenue side of state budgets. States rely primarily on sales taxes and personal income taxes for general revenues, while localities are left to depend on property taxes.

Are these revenue sources the most appropriate ways to fund the various functions of the federal, state, and local governments? Let us consider each of the major spending categories in turn.

Funding National Defense—Query: Is the Income Tax Appropriate?

Government production of national defense is necessitated because of its two public-good characteristics: no one can be excluded, and its benefits are not diminished by greater numbers of consumers. Since the benefits are consumed and enjoyed equally by all, a broad general tax is appropriate, a tax whose burden is borne by all. In the United States there are two taxes of this nature, the personal income tax and the general sales tax. Since the income tax can be used to distribute burdens more equally, it seems the appropriate choice.

By contrast, excise taxes, that is taxes on specific private goods, would be less appropriate for funding the collective benefits we enjoy from public goods. A tax on cigarettes, for example, may have several attributes, but it does not share burdens equally. In fact, as we have noted, the cigarette tax hits the poor especially hard.

We will also argue that the income redistribution component inherent in several of our welfare and retirement programs has public-good "characteristics." The benefits from knowing that the poor are receiving aid are collectively shared by all of us. Surprisingly, the free-rider problem arises with income redistribution programs. While it may seem odd that redistribution, which is essentially benevolent, would encourage free riding, consider the fact that, while most of us have sympathy for the poor, we would prefer that the necessary revenues be contributed by our fellow citizens. It follows that we should fund redistribution programs with a broad tax such as the personal income tax.

We have been using the term *redistribution* in its broad sense: transferring income from some groups to others; that is, from those with more income to those with less. The points made pertain to both cash and in-kind transfers. We would argue, then, that all welfare programs, from food stamps and school lunches to cash transfers to the poor or disabled, should be funded by broad, general taxes that spread the burdens evenly.

The personal income tax provides the basis for general revenues at the federal level and has grown in importance at the state level. Its importance in funding national defense and redistribution efforts, such as our welfare programs, seems justified.

Funding Social Security and Medicare—Query: Are Payroll Taxes Appropriate?

We will devote considerable attention to the issues of Social Security and Medicare in later chapters. To anticipate, we observe that there are a number of market failures requiring government intervention. In the depression of the 1930s, for example, the savings of the elderly and indeed all age groups were decimated. There had been very few organized retirement programs and fewer still survived the depression. It is an understatement to characterize the market for retirement plans in the 1930s as an incomplete market. Obviously, depressions and recessions are social risks that by definition cannot be borne entirely by private retirement plans. As part of Roosevelt's New Deal the government initiated the Social Security program. It guaranteed that the basic needs of the elderly poor would be met.

The Medicare program was added in the 1960s. Here again the market was incomplete. The types of market failure in health care markets range from noncompetitive markets to asymmetric information and adverse selection. Many retirees had difficulty securing health care insurance once they left their employer-based plans. At the same time the health care needs of the elderly were growing as life expectancies increased and new, expensive treatments became available. To the extent that Social Security and Medicare promise direct private-good type benefits to individual participants, it can be argued that funding by payroll taxes is fair.

Social Security is similar in some respects to retirement plans in the private sector; individual benefits partially reflect the contributions made. Although the analogy cannot be stretched too far, since benefits only roughly reflect contributions, the "purchase" of social security can be compared to the purchase of a private good. In the private sector no consideration is given the income level of the buyer when prices are set. It depends on the fairness criteria we have applied to the free market system. Ideally, we, as workers, input owners, and so on, are rewarded according to our productivity. To the extent that Social Security has private-good characteristics, the payroll tax need not be evaluated in terms of its obvious regressivity.

The Social Security program provides a base upon which all can build their preferred retirement programs. If it is to maintain wide public support, it seems important that all contributors be able to expect an acceptable return. Social Security also has a second function: to provide the elderly poor with benefits adequate to support themselves at some socially acceptable level. It is this second function, the guarantee of a social minimum, that may involve redistribution.

There are many of the elderly poor whose contributions to the system reflect the fact that they had periods of unemployment and low-paying jobs during their working careers. Although the benefits they receive represent only the social minimum, there is still an element of redistribution required. This raises the next question.

Query: Is It Appropriate to Use the Payroll Tax to Finance the Redistribution Component of Social Security?

For reasons similar to the more general arguments regarding redistribution, the answer to the above query is no. Redistribution is a public good; for financing public goods, the personal income tax is clearly the weapon of choice. The redistribution component of the Social Security program insures that the elderly poor receive a social minimum, even though it may not have been justified by the contributions they made during their working years. But those direct benefits to the elderly poor have social benefits for all of society. These social benefits are collective, nonexcludable, and subject to the free-rider problem. It is appropriate that they be paid for by a tax that distributes the burden equally. The payroll tax may be appropriate for the private-good component, that is, to provide a base upon which all Americans can build their retirement plans. But it is unfair as a revenue source for the redistribution component.

Medicare, the health care insurance for the elderly, is also financed by the payroll tax. It is a two-part program of covering hospitalization (Part A) and doctors' services (Part B). The hospital insurance is financed through the payroll tax. The insurance to pay for doctors' services is voluntary. It is financed through monthly premiums and heavily subsidized (two-thirds of the cost) through general funds. Since there are elements of redistribution in the administration of Part A, it raises questions similar to Social Security financing.

These programs will be analyzed and evaluated in some detail in chapters five and six. Both Social Security and Medicare raise important questions of intergenerational justice. The demography of the baby-boomer generation necessitates that taxes not simply be used to finance benefits on a pay-as-you-go basis. The existing trust funds must be increased dramatically through tax increases if the tax burdens are to be fairly distributed among the generations.

Funding Public Education—Query: Are Sales Taxes and Property Taxes Appropriate?

When we consider economic opportunity in terms of the fair-game analogy, education is seen as an important element in promoting a fair start. As a society, we do not attempt to give everyone an equal start. Instead, public debates on education usually focus on what is an "acceptable level" of educational opportunity. Our standards for educational opportunities are closely connected with how they affect social and economic opportunities.

Since education creates social as well as private benefits, it is not clear just how it should be financed. One proposal advanced in recent years is that government should issue education vouchers to families with school-age children. Presumably the vouchers would account for the social benefits. The net cost to families would reflect only the private benefits. Since families demand education for its private benefits we would expect them to also use their own resources. They would be free to purchase the type and the quality they prefer for their children.

While such a plan would get high marks on the criterion of allocative efficiency, it scores less well in terms of fairness. As a society we have been reluctant to rely too heavily on family income to determine the quality of educational opportunity open to children. On the other hand, we allow families to purchase education from private schools if they are willing and able to do so.

Our society uses the public school system to provide educational opportunity to children from all family-income levels. What is clear is that all schools should provide a socially acceptable level of educational opportunity. In chapter four we will question whether or not our schools do, in fact, provide that minimum.

Public education is financed jointly by states and localities. States rely on general revenues, primarily sales and income taxes. These two taxes rank well in terms of fairness and efficiency. However, localities also play a large role and must depend heavily on property taxes. Reliance on the property tax is more difficult to justify. In the first place we are not clear as to who bears the tax's final burden. Second, there are great differences among localities in wealth and therefore in their ability to raise tax revenues. The revenue capacity of poorer localities often tends to be inadequate to fund an acceptable level of educational opportunity.

Should the educational opportunities open to children depend on the ability of their locality to fund education? If the result is that some children have opportunities clearly below what is socially acceptable, the answer is no; and that is now the situation in many states. Roughly half of the states do not adequately compensate for differences in the wealth of different school districts.

Query: When Is Issuing Government Debt Justified?

Our present focus is on taxes, but recall that governments have another means of extracting spending power from the private sector: they can issue public debt. We have argued that in the ideal mix of government and market allocation, public-sector debt should reflect the public investment that has taken place.

Public investment and debt should be arranged so that during each time period the debt costs borne by taxpayers are balanced by the benefits received from past investments. In actual practice this balance is seldom achieved. In periods of recession, when the economy needs stimulus and the ranks of the poor and unemployed are temporarily swelled, it may be quite appropriate for the public debt to grow faster than public investment. It may also be appropriate for government debt to grow during times of war.

Putting a figure on public investment is difficult for a number of reasons. It is not always clear what parts of public spending should be considered investment. Moreover, because of their public-good character, the benefits of many public investments are not easily priced. We can, however, make some generalizations. It can be safely concluded that the dramatic increase in public debt in the 1980s was not matched by public investment.

All of this raises questions of intergenerational fairness. Again the appropriate starting point for such discussions is the principle that debt costs should reflect the stream of benefits from public investment. As we turn to other social issues we will have occasion to look more closely at the relationships among taxes, debt, and the benefits from public programs.

Query: Should We Adopt the Flat Tax?

In recent political campaigns, several candidates have advocated that a *flat tax* be substituted for our present income tax. Its major appeal is its simplicity. It is also touted as being more fair than other taxes. As is the case with other tax schemes that are generous to the wealthy, its advocates claim that it would foster savings, investment, and greater economic prosperity.

> The **flat tax**, or rather, the flat rate income tax features a flat, proportional rate on income. Most versions exempt several sources of income, for example, dividends and capital gains.

The flat tax would eliminate all tax preferences and have one low tax rate for all. If, as is argued, the present tax code creates incentives that lower efficiency, a simple code would increase efficiency. Moreover, a simpler tax would save hours and expense for all who must now fill out complicated tax forms every year.

However, the issues are much more complicated than flat tax proponents claim. How does the flat tax rank in terms of traditional tax criteria? The most appealing attribute of the flat tax is its simplicity. This is achieved not by introducing a single, proportional rate but by doing away with all of the present tax preferences: the exemptions, deductions, loopholes, and so on. At least for salaried workers, no receipts would have to be kept for the various deductions. But when we tax income derived from running one's own business, the procedure becomes more problematical, since presumably business expenses would be deducted in calculating taxable income.

The perception that a flat rate in and of itself would simplify the calculation of one's tax is illusionary. As most Americans know from figuring out their own taxes, the reading of the tax tables is the easy part. Whether or not the table reflects a proportional rate or a progressive rate is immaterial.

The argument that ending all exemptions and deductions would improve fairness and efficiency is also illusionary. We should recall that, for the most part, the present exemptions and deductions have been adopted for the purpose of increasing the tax's horizontal and vertical efficiency. It is very unlikely that an administration and congress, no matter how composed, would eliminate all of the tax preferences, say the contributions to health care and retirement insurance or the preferences given to home ownership.

The favorable treatment given home ownership is certainly nonneutral with regard to market prices and allocation. Thus, it could be argued to be inefficient. But it is clear that encouraging home ownership, particularly among young people entering the workforce, is a "nonneutrality" that enjoys wide public support. Indeed, it has been proposed that one-time grants be awarded to first-time home buyers to enhance this social goal. Arguments can be made on behalf of the fairness and efficiency of other tax preferences as well. This is not to say that all of the specifics of the present tax code can be so justified. It is certainly appropriate to subject all present and proposed tax laws to scrutiny. For example, the present exemption of "tax-free" bonds has little justification on the basis of fairness or efficiency. Although some of the projects so funded may warrant subsidization, others clearly do not. There are better methods of subsidization. More important, the favoritism given income earned by tax-free bonds allows wealthy taxpayers to lower their tax bills. Very simply, this means that they do not pay their fair share. It follows that there is little justification for this particular tax preference.

The flat tax could be made progressive, and thus more fair, by giving an exemption for the lowest levels of income. Thus, the flat rate would be applied only after a certain income level had been attained. The range of progressivity would reflect the exemption being averaged out. But no flat tax scheme can maintain progressivity into the higher-income levels. Although much less progressive than that in other industrialized countries, the highest marginal income tax rate is close to 40 percent (the marginal rate for the U.S. federal income tax reaches 39.6 percent for income over $250,000). A flat tax, say of 20 percent, would substantially reduce the tax burden of the wealthy. The current approach, based on the idea of imposing equal burdens, would necessarily be abandoned. The use of the equal-sacrifice principle seems to require a progressive rate schedule.

Most of the flat tax plans exempt all income except that earned in the workplace. Thus, interest, dividends, and capital gains—income that accounts for a significant part of the incomes of the wealthy—would simply not be counted. Obviously, this would represent a radical departure from the traditional meaning of income as it is understood by most Americans. It would tax the income from labor but not from capital.

This new focus would create strong incentives against earning labor income and in favor of earning capital income. We have already questioned the argument that redistributing income in favor of the wealthy leads to more real investment. Much depends on one's analysis of what policies will lead to better job opportunities for those at the bottom of the scale. The advocates of the flat tax, and other policies favoring the wealthy, argue that there is a shortage of funds for investment. With greater savings and investment, there will be greater job opportunities for all. Opponents of this line of reasoning argue that the economic policies and events of the 1980s lend little support to this argument and, thus, little support to the radical redistribution inherent in the flat tax.

In the next section, we will consider what changes in institutions and incentives give the most promise of raising the expectations of the poor. Should we depend on policies that give the wealthy incentive to save and invest or should we attempt more direct means of creating jobs?

In summary, the idea of tax simplification is appealing to most Americans. But the idea of redefining income to exclude everything but wages goes against most people's sense of fair play. The flat tax definition is fundamentally different from what most Americans consider to be income. Once given serious attention, the tax's outcome, which would leave many of the most wealthy Americans paying no tax at all, will have little support.

Some Recent History of Macroeconomic Policy

Ideally the impact of fiscal policy (the budget) and monetary policy (the money supply and interest rates) would be coordinated so that spending by consumers, business, and the government would just match our economy's productive capacity. The recent record, especially during the 1980s, has been extremely disappointing. Part of the problem is that decision making is separated. Fiscal policy is the combined effect of government spending, taxes, and transfers on aggregate spending. Increases in aggregate spending are said to be *expansionary*, while decreases are *contractionary*. Fiscal policy must be coordinated by the president and Congress, but, as we know, American voters seem to get a perverse satisfaction from creating a dysfunctional budget process.

Monetary policy is carried out by the Federal Reserve system. By manipulating the money supply, the Fed can affect interest rates and, in turn, investment and consumption. Here again, an expansionary policy would feature monetary ease, lower rates of interest, and increased aggregate spending. Contractionary macroeconomic policy would feature tighter money, higher interest rates, and reduced aggregate spending.

Much has to do with estimates of where we stand relative to the economy's productive capacity. Ideally aggregate spending can be matched to that level of employment (usually termed *full employment*) that realizes our full capacity without causing inflation. Assuming that those responsible for fiscal and monetary policy share the same assessment of how much spending is required, the two sets of macroeconomic tools can be successfully coordinated. If it is determined that too much spending threatens to ignite inflation; a coordinated policy would feature a monetary policy of tighter money and higher rates of interest. The appropriate fiscal policy would feature less government spending and higher taxes.

This familiar recitation of the basics of macroeconomic policy is necessary if we are to fully appreciate the perversity of policy in the 1980s. The familiar analogy of the economy as an automobile is useful. Monetary and fiscal policy can be used as gas pedal (expansionary) or brake (contractionary). Alternatively they can be used against each other. That is, the gas pedal and the brake can be applied at the same time. During the 1980s, fiscal policy was excessively expansionary (the gas pedal) and monetary policy was very contractionary (the brake). The Reagan budget featured substantial increases in defense spending and massive tax cuts. The Fed (chaired by Paul Volcker), fearing a renewal of inflation, applied the brakes to the economy. The contest was clearly won by the brake. The economy was plunged into the deepest recession since the 1930s.

To say that macroeconomic policy in the 1980s represents a government failure is to understate the case. Consider, for example, how this policy mix affected the national debt. Expansionary fiscal policy naturally creates debt as spending exceeds revenues. But this tendency was exacerbated by the recession; in recession tax revenues automatically fall and spending on unemployment benefits, welfare, and so on automatically rise. This unhappy policy mix could not have been designed better to maximize the federal debt.

Returning to the automobile analogy, it is possible to chug forward with your foot on both the gas pedal and the brake but the process is very inefficient. With respect to our economy, it created huge, unnecessary deficits. The record of the 1980s and 1990s has been an expansionary fiscal policy being restrained by a tight monetary policy. Coordinated policy could have achieved equal or better results without the huge deficits.

Rational criteria for managing the public debt follow the general arguments for equating marginal benefits and costs. An example we used earlier featured a community building a new school. It is appropriate to arrange financing so that the costs will be spread among current and future taxpayers in accordance with the benefits the building will convey over the years. More generally, at the state and national levels, it is appropriate that public debt expand as public capital expands. A somewhat conflicting short-run macroeconomic policy criterion treats the debt as a by-product of fiscal policy. As noted, fiscal policy may be required to help stimulate aggregate spending. Lower taxes and greater transfers and government spending naturally lead to a short-term deficit. But neither of these criteria can be used to justify the enormous deficits incurred during the 1980s and 1990s. A case can be made for a small deficit in the early 1980s when the economy was at less than full employment. A case can also be made for a small deficit in every year when public capital is growing. When we turn our attention to social security, we will return to the question of how debt should be related to investment and in turn related to the question of taxpayer burdens and benefits through time.

Obviously, the Social Security program has criteria of its own, which should determine the management of the Social Security Trust Fund. Very simply, the baby-boomer generation is contributing to a huge trust fund which will in turn be brought down in 2020s and 2030s. This will allow for the burdens for then current taxpayers to be fair.

In the next several years, we will continue to debate what it means to balance the budget and how this relates the trust funds for Social Security and

Medicare. Obviously the two questions are separate—the size each year's deficit should relate to each year's public investment. More generally, public debt should relate to public capital. For our generation to improve the lot of the next, public capital should increase more than the public debt. Interest payments on the debt would be lower relative to benefits from past investment. It is safe to say that that was the case for all generations prior to the 1980s; but during the 1980s and 1990s increases in the debt far exceeded increases in public investment.

Tax Cuts and Political Rhetoric—Query: Should We Simultaneously Cut Taxes, Maintain Defense Spending and Social Programs, and Balance the Budget?

Why not? Indeed. The recent epidemic of tax cutting arose in California in the late 1970s and quickly spread across the nation. In California the tax revolt occurred in response to rapidly escalating real estate values and accompanying property tax liabilities. Politicians at every level soon began to promise lower taxes while at the same time claiming that the quality of existing social programs could be maintained. This was supposed to be possible by making government more streamlined and efficient.

When Jimmy Carter ran for reelection against Ronald Reagan in 1980, both candidates promised tax cuts in order to stimulate the economy. But Reagan promised more. Citizens elected Reagan, who proceeded to cut income taxes by 30 percent. The rather dubious claim by Reagan supply-siders that these tax cuts would raise, rather than lower, revenues proved to be false. Nevertheless Reagan was reelected in a landslide. His successor, George Bush, added a classic phrase to the annals of political rhetoric when he proclaimed "Read my lips, no new taxes!" This promise was made in the face of record budget deficits. Bush failed to keep his promise and that failure contributed to his defeat in 1992.

Overriding Republican opposition, Bill Clinton was able to raise tax rates on upper-income taxpayers as part of his 1993 deficit-reduction plan. The next year Republicans destroyed Democrats at the polls and gained majorities in the House and in the Senate. This set the stage for a rude awakening of public awareness of what tradeoffs are actually possible.

The new Republican majorities in Congress did, in fact, fashion sharp cuts in social programs such as Social Security, Medicare, Medicaid, and Head Start. They assumed they would maintain wide public support for carrying out their mandate. However, it was President Clinton's vetoes of these measures that gained wide public support.

Finally, after a number of serious episodes of gridlock, bargaining, and political posturing on both sides, several pieces of significant legislation were passed. Although President Clinton proclaimed the new welfare legislation to be his long promised "end of welfare as we know it," both parties deserve the credit. And of course, for those parts that will most certainly turn out badly, both parties deserve the discredit.

The 1996 presidential campaign once again muddied the waters with unrealistic promises. The Dole economic plan closely followed the promises made by the Reagan campaign of 1980: large tax cuts, increases in defense spending, and maintenance of the integrity of Social Security and Medicare. Again, in an echo of the promises of Reagan supply-sider rhetoric, all of this was to be accomplished while balancing the budget.

Not all the blame should be placed on politicians; as we observed earlier the voting public seems intent on suspending its disbelief. Although the public insists that the budget be balanced and social programs be maintained, no politician can afford to advocate the necessary increase in taxes.

How Fast Has Government Been Growing?

Another rather widespread misconception concerns the resources allocated to private and public goods. It is generally assumed that increased taxes have been financing an ever-increasing transfer from taxpayers to government. Actually federal, state, and local taxes have held steady at around 18–20 percent of GDP since the early 1950s. Moreover, transfers make up an increasing part of the budget. This means that smaller percentages of the economy's resources are being allocated to the production of public goods. The increase in Social Security payments relative to defense spending means proportionately more resources devoted to private goods, say automobiles, than to public goods, say military aircraft. Shifts in funds from working-age individuals to retirees via Social Security may do little to the total spent on private goods. Indeed, in many families it merely replaces some intergenerational transfers that otherwise would have taken place. The point is that, as the proportion of spending on public goods (such as defense) has been reduced, the proportion of resources being devoted to private goods has increased.

Some Observations on Income Inequality

There is no guarantee that incomes in an economy that features free markets will be equal. Indeed, since rewards differ with efficiency and the ability to satisfy consumer tastes, wide variations can be expected. Some causes of income inequality are: differences in innate ability such as intelligence, artistic and athletic talents, and inventiveness; differences in effort and perseverance; differences in willingness to take risks; differences in educational opportunity; differences in job opportunity; differences in family wealth; and finally, differences in pure luck. Most of us approve of the idea that individuals are rewarded for using their talents to increase the welfare of others. We also approve of rewards for diligence, hard work, and the willingness to assume risks.

We have mixed feelings about the role of luck in economic success, as well as its role in life in general. Chance obviously plays an important part in the success or failure of individuals and economic enterprises. We generally do not begrudge a person's striking it rich. At the same time we support the availability of "safety nets" for those who suffer misfortune; certainly where those who are unlucky are not at fault. Of course income inequalities arising from such things as illegal business practices, cheating, or unfair discrimination on such bases as race, religion, or gender are considered unacceptable.

Our social goals regarding the distribution of income are derived from a number of moral principles. Along with "to each an equal share," we include "to each according to need, effort, contribution, rights, and merit." Our official definition of poverty is based on the lack of what we consider the *necessities of life*. There is widespread acceptance of the social obligation to provide a social minimum for all. Until the recent welfare reform, income redistribution and in-kind programs were designed to guarantee that families would be able to meet their basic needs.

The rule that income should reflect one's contribution breaks down in cases of unfair competition such as monopoly power or oligopolistic collusion. Usually the results are both inefficient and unfair. In such cases, corrective action may be required by a government agency.

Many people are uneasy with the role inherited wealth plays in the inequality of income. Here the inheritors often have no claims on the bases of effort or contribution. It is the person making the bequest who has a right: a right to give to others. Does this right have limitations? According to arguments made by some libertarians, property rights are sacrosanct and individuals should have few limitations to the use of fairly accumulated wealth. Other schools of thought see property rights as social inventions. The various privileges within this bundle of rights should reflect our broad social goals. Property rights are necessarily limited in various ways and the right to transfer wealth to others can also be limited. Estates and gifts are taxed when they exceed certain levels. According to most studies, increasing gift and estate taxes would negatively affect work and saving incentives. But the right to bestow or bequeath wealth is not based on efficiency arguments; it is an extension of the argument that at some point the wealth was "earned." Along with that original justification came the privilege of leaving it to others at death. It follows that, although one has the right to give gifts and leave bequests, that right is not without limits.

In a similar vein the other distributive principles are also subject to limitation. The idea that income should be distributed according to contribution does not specify the level at which contribution should be rewarded. Americans seem to enjoy asking themselves whether the salaries of certain professional athletes can be justified on any grounds.

In the ideal model of the economy, allocative efficiency and fairness are enhanced as inputs are rewarded according to their contributions (marginal products). In the real world the rewards bestowed by the market are much more contingent. While the principle of rewarding according to contribution carries great weight, there is ample room for balancing it against other principles.

John Stuart Mill discussed the balancing of principles in the following way:

> In a co-operative industrial association, is it just or not that talent or skill should give a title to superior remuneration? On the negative side of the question, it

is argued that whoever does the best he can deserves equally well and ought not in justice be put in a position of inferiority for no fault of his own. . . . On the contrary side, it is contended that society receives more from the more efficient laborer; that his services being more useful, society owes him a larger return for them; that a greater share of the joint result is actually his work, . . . Justice has in this case two sides to it, which it is impossible to bring into harmony.[8]

According to Mill, any such conflict among principles could always be resolved by reference to the Utilitarian Rule: "Social utility alone can decide the preference."[9]

Tax Cuts for the Wealthy: Is the Tradeoff between Efficiency and Equality a False Issue?

For the moment let us assume that we can ignore all of the income distribution principles except the principle of maximizing total utility. We are now card-carrying utilitarians. Let us further assume that income redistribution will have no effect on economic incentives and that utility functions are identical. The welfare maximizing solution would be to distribute income equally. Redistribution would take dollars from the wealthy (whose marginal utility of income is lower) and give them to the poor (whose marginal utility of income is higher) until incomes were equal and total welfare maximized.

Now if we keep the total welfare goal but consider the effects of economic incentives, we are faced with a tradeoff. In a market economy, some inequality is necessary to furnish incentives to work, save, invest, and take risks in economic activity. We must ask what incentives and what level of inequality are necessary to attain the greatest total welfare.

This line of reasoning, the so-called tradeoff between efficiency and equality, appears frequently in economic literature. Upon reflection, however, the tradeoff between efficiency and equality is a false issue. Equality, or rather, exact equality of income has never been one of our social goals. It is true that incentives are important, but the tradeoffs between efficiency and fairness are more complex than the idea of equality.

The point is that the tradeoff between efficiency and equality may not be as clear-cut as it is purported to be. Even when it is phrased in more sensible terms as a "tradeoff between efficiency and equity," we may still be facing a false issue.

It is certainly true that some disparity in income is a necessary part of a market system. But once we accept the idea that equity requires a balance among several distribution principles, such as "to each according to contribution" and "to each an equal share," our definition of equity has already been modified. It already includes the incentives to work, save, and invest. The interesting question becomes: Do our ideas of distributional fairness include enough incentives so that efficiency and fairness can be achieved simultaneously? In the public debate on what policies are conducive to economic growth, those who favor more tax cuts for the wealthy argue for them on grounds of efficiency. It is argued that greater disparities may seem unfair, but they are necessary to achieve greater economic growth. Tax cuts for the wealthy will increase saving, investment, and jobs. Thus the greater income disparities will lead to everyone's being made better off. Again, it is not argued that the disparities in income and wealth are fair in and of themselves. It is generally acknowledged that they can be justified only in the tradeoff between efficiency and equity.

The obvious counterargument is not that we should be willing to give up some efficiency for more fairness. The counterargument questions the validity of the purported tradeoff. According to this argument, there are already more than enough incentives built into the rules of the game to insure efficiency. In fact, it is likely that a more equitable distribution would lead to greater efficiency. There is a tenuous chain of logic that claims tax cuts favoring the wealthy will increase economic activity, and will eventually increase the prospects of the least-well-off. While the argument has strong advocates, it is certainly not the majority view. Indeed, as was true in the early 1980s, there is widespread agreement among economists that such policies would do great harm. Here again we see that the economic assumptions underlying many social issues should be an integral part of the public debate.

Summary: The Shape of a Just Revenue System

The political rhetoric notwithstanding, the social choices Americans most favor require that taxes be raised rather than lowered. Of course, we remember that for political candidates to advocate such a policy would insure their defeat. It is not difficult to explain this seeming flaw in the character of American politicians and voters. There is not a close link between government expenditures and taxes. As voters, Americans are eager to believe that the benefits they enjoy will still be available even if their own tax bills are reduced. There is always the possibility that government revenue can be found by eliminating bureaucratic waste and inefficiency. There is always the possibility that someone else's taxes will be raised. In this way, the wish by voters for a free ride evolves into a prisoners' dilemma in which we are all worse off. In focusing on our own tax bill, we follow a strategy that makes everyone worse off.

There are a number of good reasons why taxes should be raised, and these will become more clear in the succeeding chapters. As we turn to the question of welfare reform, for example, it becomes immediately obvious that, in the short run, breaking the cycle of poverty will cost more money than the former system. In the short run, it is much less expensive to meet the immediate needs of families with dependent children than to provide the training, subsidized jobs, day care, and other services necessary to turn their lives around. It will be interesting to see how many states will be willing to raise the revenues necessary for the task. As a nation, we are embarking on a very exciting but dangerous experiment.

Taxes also need to be raised to restore solvency to the Social Security and Medicare trust funds. The revenue requirements are no mystery; the standards of solvency are already in place. There are even some sound proposals that would make the existing trust funds more productive. The missing component is sufficient political will to raise the necessary taxes.

A final reason for raising taxes is the most obvious: to balance the budget. Balancing the budget has become the most hackneyed phrase in our political jargon. It seems incredulous that our politicians could propose budgets that seem designed to maximize deficits and at the same time support constitutional amendments requiring that the budget be balanced. This is not to say that the commitment to balance the budget every year is a good idea; it clearly is not. Even so, the use of this rallying cry to bring us closer to fiscal rationality seems efficacious for the foreseeable future.

The deficits that accrued in the 1980s were a result of unwise expansionary fiscal policy featuring large tax cuts and increases in defense spending. At the same time, tight monetary policy created a severe recession that was followed by a period of sustained but disappointing growth. This unhappy blend of macroeconomic policies seemed designed to maximize the debt with no accompanying benefit. The federal debt increased from $906 billion, or 26 percent of GDP, in 1980 to $2.6 trillion, or over 50 percent of GDP, in 1988. It was not until taxes were raised in the early 1990s that the ratio of debt to GDP began to fall. Public investment was, in fact, reduced. The point to be made here is that, although it is appropriate to finance public investment by creating debt, the 1980s and the early 1990s were clearly years when the debts passed on to future generations were not matched with investment. It follows that higher taxes and continued deficit reductions are needed to restore intergenerational justice.

Our brief survey of the federal, state, and local budgets raised a number of questions as to whether or not the taxes used are fair and efficient. The question of whether or not a particular tax is fair can be answered only in terms of how it fits with other revenue sources and the social programs they fund.

Does the Tax Fit the Benefit?

In Gilbert and Sullivan's opera the *Mikado*, the Lord High Executioner's idea of fairness is to "Let the punishment fit the crime." We could paraphrase the benefit principle of taxation as "Let the tax fit the benefit." The links between taxes and benefits are not always as direct as we would like. However, it is still possible to associate particular taxes with particular programs.

We can loosely associate the personal income tax with the public goods: defense and income redistribution. Very generally, public goods provide collective benefits enjoyed by all. It seems appropriate that they be funded by general taxes such as the personal income tax. When benefits are enjoyed by all, we can shift attention to the revenue side. Using the ability-to-pay approach, the central question becomes: How do we divide the burden fairly? The answer offered by the equal sacrifice principle is to divide the burden equally. The income tax offers an efficient means of apportioning burdens according to some socially chosen rule of fairness.

As we observed, the personal income tax fares well when subjected to efficiency and fairness criteria. However, that does not mean that it has no problems or is free from controversy. Accepting the Haig-Simons definition of income raises the question of how unrealized income such as capital gains, owner-occupied housing, and housework are to be treated. Moreover, the claim that the tax has significant impact on work effort, savings, and investments will remain a mainstay of political rhetoric.

In evaluating the payroll tax as a means for funding Social Security and Medicare, we observed that the tax is quite regressive. This regressivity is greater than generally perceived since both parts are actually paid by the employee. Nevertheless, it was argued that it was not an inappropriate method of finance, since both programs provide private benefits to the participants. Each Social Security participant is promised a retirement base, and each Medicare participant is promised medical care.

Although the tax-benefit comparison seems appropriate, two important questions of fairness were raised. First, we noted that both programs have a redistributive component, in that the elderly poor generally receive greater benefits than their former contributions warrant. It is not appropriate to fund that component with a regressive tax; the programs should be augmented with general funds. Second, we observed that, although designed to maintain intergenerational fairness, the trust funds are not being maintained according to the guidelines established in 1983.

There are a number of excise taxes that raise questions of fairness. The gasoline tax has the attribute of being a "user charge." Its purpose is to finance roads; thus, the more one travels, the more tax one pays. On the other hand, the tax is quite regressive. Lower-income families pay a higher percentage of their income in taxes. Similarly, the excise taxes on cigarettes and alcohol rank high on efficiency criteria. Since they are imposed on goods with an inelastic demand, the taxes have little effect on resource allocation. Like the gasoline tax, however, they are quite regressive. The point is that the evaluation of excise taxes usually requires balancing a number of fairness and efficiency considerations, as it does with other taxes.

The funding of education depends on a number of taxes, the primary sources being income and sales taxes at the state level and property taxes at the local level. Since the benefits are both private and public, it would seem appropriate to have joint funding, say using a voucher approach. In chapter four, we will consider a number of arguments for various funding arrangements. One widely held social concern, that all students be given a fair start to educational opportunity, is compromised in those states where local spending must depend on the property tax base of the locality.

ISSUES OF POVERTY AND WELFARE REFORM

An historic turning point occurred in late July, 1996, when President Clinton and the Republican Congress finally agreed on how to "end welfare as we know it." Although Clinton had made that promise in 1992 and had approved reform initiatives in forty-three states, the new legislation represented a dramatic shift in our society's commitment to the poor. The basic dilemma can be phrased in terms of a question.

Query: How Can We, as a Society, Encourage Welfare Recipients to Be Responsible but also Guarantee That Their Basic Needs Will Be Met?

The answer implicit in the new legislation is that the federal government will no longer guarantee that basic needs will be met. Welfare recipients no longer qualify for aid simply on the basis of need; they must demonstrate a willingness to work.

Within certain parameters, welfare was turned over to state governments. The specific work requirements to be determined by each state are expected to be strict. The idea that families with dependent children automatically qualify for aid was replaced by the idea of aid to meet short term emergencies. Whether or not suitable jobs will always be available and how many of the former welfare recipients are, in fact, capable of holding jobs are judgements that a whole new set of state agencies will have to determine. But the point agreed to by the president and the Congress is that our national policy will be to hold individuals, specifically heads of families, responsible for caring for themselves and their families. Government, at least at the federal level, will no longer be responsible for insuring that the children of the poor are provided with the necessities of life: food, shelter, clothing, and health care.

This ended a long-standing social commitment undertaken during the Great Depression of the 1930s as part of President Franklin Roosevelt's New Deal. The commitment was expanded in the 1960s when President Johnson declared a War on Poverty.

Some History

The noble experiment to end poverty began in the early 1960s. The issue was brought to the American consciousness in the 1962 book by Michael Harrington, *The Other America*. His point was that, while most of us lived in relative comfort, there was a growing underclass about whom we seldom thought. While most Americans had overstuffed closets and tended towards obesity, the poor had inadequate clothing, housing, and nourishment. While most young people faced almost unlimited opportunity, the children of the poor were caught in a "cycle of poverty." All of this was occurring in the wealthiest nation in the world.

Many Americans, shocked and embarrassed by these revelations, believed that we, as a society, could do and should do better. Now, after decades of government bashing, the faith Americans of the early 1960s had in social action seems naive; but at that time the obvious answer seemed to be government action. This culminated in President Johnson's declaration of a War on Poverty in 1964. From some perspectives the War on Poverty was a failure; poverty is still with us. However, if we momentarily ignore the current political rhetoric and look at the facts, we see that poverty, which ran between 24 and 22 percent in the late 1950s and early 1960s, was cut in half by the early 1970s (11 percent in 1972). Moreover, these figures only refer to the monetary income of the poor. Since many of the programs featured in-kind benefits, the poverty measurements substantially understate the effectiveness of the War on Poverty. Changes in Social Security retirement benefits and Medicare have virtually eliminated poverty among the elderly.

Over the decades, our perceptions of poverty and what can be done about it have changed. As the late 1960s and early 1970s proceeded, the assassinations of John F. Kennedy, Martin Luther King, and Robert Kennedy; the war in Vietnam; and violent and nonviolent civil rights protests had demoralizing effects on social attitudes. Moreover, in the mid-1970s economic growth slowed from the 3.5 percent rate of the previous thirty years to barely over 2 percent. Four major recessions and ill-advised fiscal and monetary policies kept unemployment at over 6 percent for most of that period. The huge national debt created during the Reagan and Bush administrations has greatly reduced the possibility of new spending initiatives. There is wide public support for the effort to get welfare recipients "off welfare and back to work"; but, except in a few states, there may be insufficient support for the tax increases that will be required in the short run. We are left with unrealistic public perceptions of what is possible.

As part of the War on Poverty initiatives, the government developed a definition of poverty. In 1964 the poor were defined as families with incomes below three thousand dollars. The idea is that a family's income must be sufficient for a "nutritionally adequate diet" and other basic necessities. The poverty threshold is raised each year to account for inflation. The original goal, to raise all Americans above the poverty line by 1976, was not reached.

Just what are the characteristics of the poor? About 40 percent are children. There is very high unemployment among black teenagers. A small but worrisome percentage of the poor are families headed by teenage mothers. Obviously many of these heads of families should be in school. For families headed by females who need some combination of schooling and work, there is the additional requirement of day care for the children.

The official poverty level is defined in terms of family size, where the family lives (on a farm or in the city), and whether or not the head of household is sixty-five or over. The definition only counts the cash income available to the family. By this definition, some forty million Americans live below the poverty line. In one sense this is a measure of the challenge our poverty programs face. Prior to the new welfare reform, most of these people were guaranteed aid to help them meet their basic needs.

To say that President Johnson's War on Poverty and subsequent efforts have "failed" is to miss the point, or rather, two points. There are two aims to antipoverty initiatives. The first and more immediate aim is to provide poor families with their basic needs. The second, more complicated goal is to make families self-sufficient. By providing food, shelter, clothing, and health care, as well as educational and employment opportunities, it becomes possible for some of the poor to break the cycle of poverty. In our economic system, we cannot expect all individuals and families to be self-sufficient, so in that sense we will never be able to conquer poverty. One important social responsibility is to provide for those who, for various reasons, are unable to meet their own needs. Another is to enable and encourage those now in poverty to break out of that condition. Over 14 percent of the U.S. population and over 20 percent of the children are classified as poor. Many live in substandard housing, lack sufficient nourishment, and have difficult access to medical care. The economic opportunities open to the poor are often limited. The adults have few skills and few employment opportunities, while the children have limited educational opportunities.

The former system evolved in spurts as our government attempted to respond to crises as they arose. Some important programs were begun in Roosevelt's New Deal, others immediately following World War II, and a new wave in Johnson's War on Poverty.

Welfare Programs in the 1990s

The welfare system at the federal, state, and local levels will be fundamentally restructured in the 1990s. Some programs will be abolished, some will be restructured, and entirely new initiatives will appear. The old edifice contains some programs that will be continued, at least for now. The Social Security program, Old Age, Survivors, and Disability Insurance (OASDI), provides income security in several ways to a number of groups, as the name indicates. In its major role as retirement insurance, it not only furnishes a base on which to build a retirement plan, it helps to provide a social minimum for the elderly. Medicare, like Social Security, is an insurance program designed to meet the needs of the elderly. Both have the character of private insurance plans and are financed by payroll taxes. In chapters five and six, we will analyze these programs in some detail.

Medicaid, Head Start, and Food Stamps, like Medicare, are in-kind programs. Medicaid is an in-kind program that pays for health care for the poor. Although it was not designated to do so, it also pays for long-term health care for the elderly. (Since Medicare has no provisions for long-term care, the elderly must "spend down" their wealth in order to become poor and eligible for the Medicaid program.)

Head Start is an in-kind, means-tested program that fits our analogy of trying to provide a fair start. Since the children of the poor are so often disadvantaged when starting to school, Head Start provides day care and nursery school training. Its purpose is to increase the chances that children from poor families will be closer to the level of others when they enter elementary school.

The economic analysis of in-kind transfers is similar to that of excise taxes. There is usually an income effect and a substitution effect. The income effect simply means that the purchasing power of the family has been increased. While they may consume more of the subsidized good, they can also buy more of other goods. For example, a housing allowance will allow the family to rent a better house or apartment and also have more money to spend elsewhere.

The Food Stamp program affected almost 10 percent of our population. Its role in the future is not clear. It exemplifies the in-kind approach to insuring that families receive the necessities of life. It is paternalistic, in that families are given incentives to purchase food. In one sense it is nonneutral. Although market prices may not be altered, the choices families make with respect to food and other purchases are affected. Economic theory can be used to argue that these families would be better off if left to make their own choices; that is, they would attain a higher level of welfare if simply given cash. The point is that with food stamps society is being paternalistic; we as society's citizens and taxpayers want to insure that all family members, especially the children, receive adequate nourishment.

In another sense, the program is neutral. For most families, the food stamp bonus does not affect the choice between food and other goods. The same amount of food is purchased as would be purchased without the stamps. Thus, the program has the same effect as a cash grant. At its peak, the program not only reached those below the poverty line, but any low-income and temporarily unemployed families immediately above the line were also eligible.

Sadly, there are some parents who are irresponsible, some who have addictions such as gambling, drugs, alcohol, or tobacco who would sacrifice nourishment for their children if they received cash instead of food stamps. Moreover, poor families are prone to financial emergencies. Crises also occur randomly, as when an old car breaks down and must be replaced. The point of the food stamp program is that nourishment, especially for the children of poor families, must be assured regardless of what preferences the family may have or what emergencies they may encounter.

Welfare Programs and Disincentives

Almost all of the federal programs created work disincentives. Those finding work had their benefits reduced. A poor, single-parent family that qualified for Aid to Families with Dependent Children (AFDC), food stamps, housing assistance, and Medicaid would have all of these reduced as income increased. The rate at which benefits were reduced as income increased, the *transfer reduction rate*, could be quite large. For some families the rate was over 100 percent.

> The **transfer reduction rate** is the rate at which welfare recipients lose benefits as their income increases.

> A **welfare notch** can occur at a certain income level where welfare recipients lose benefits at a faster rate than their increase in work income.

A more extreme case of transfer reduction is the so-called welfare notch in which added income produces a net loss. If a new job means the family's income goes well beyond the notch, then the disincentive is not important; but for jobs with incomes near the notch, there is a strong disincentive effect.

Although the major purpose of reorganizing welfare is to restructure incentives, most states will not be able to avoid the tradeoff between incentives and basic needs. Most will still search for ways to meet the needs of those children whose mothers no longer qualify for aid. Let us assume that the state provides such a family with vouchers designed to provide children with food, clothing, diapers, and so on. The state still must calculate the program's transfer reduction rate. Just how fast are benefits to be reduced as the mother earns more money? We must recognize that the income-earning prospects of former welfare recipients are limited. Many who find steady work will remain in poverty. If we assume that the states supplement their wages in some way, there must be some rate at which the supplement is reduced as earnings increase.

It is true that the 1996 welfare legislation signals a radical departure from the federal government's guarantee that the family's basic needs would be met. It is also true that work disincentives will be greatly reduced under programs that evolve in the states. However, the basic tradeoffs cannot easily be avoided. It is unlikely that we, as a society, will allow innocent children to starve due to the unwillingness or the inability of their parents to earn a sufficient income.

The largest of the cash transfers, AFDC, made cash payments to some fourteen million people. As the name implies, its focus was on the children of poor families. This and other welfare programs were *means tested*. In order to qualify, a family had to have an income below a certain level. The monthly payments differed according to how much each state was willing to add to the federal contribution. Some state governments had additional assistance programs that attempted to fill in holes left by the federal programs. These covered the poor who did not pass the status and means tests of Social Security Insurance or AFDC. There was a very wide range among the programs administered by the states. In 1990, for example, the average monthly benefit for AFDC families ranged from $114 in Alabama to $651 in Alaska.[10]

In one sense AFDC was a quick fix in reducing poverty. Families with young children but no income earner were given direct cash grants. The grants were intended to provide for the basic necessities.

The AFDC program received widespread criticism for a number of reasons. Although it had few defenders, it remained central to the welfare reform debate. What had been lacking in the debate until recently were acceptable alternative proposals. In a climate of spending reductions and aversion to taxes, there are no easy answers. As welfare reform progresses, the simplistic argument that former welfare recipients will be better off when forced to rely on their own initiatives will be seen to be in error. Government will be required to take a larger role, not a smaller role.

The AFDC program was a classic case of creating poor incentives. If the family consisted of a mother with several young children, there was a great disincentive for her to work. Additional earnings reduced benefits on a dollar-for-dollar basis once a small exemption was passed. The family was thus subjected to a 100 percent marginal tax rate. Moreover, a host of other benefits were reduced as more income was earned. The effective transfer reduction rate was well over 200 percent.

Another source of criticism lay in eligibility requirements that encouraged out-of-wedlock births and the breakup of existing families. Welfare benefits were not paid if there was an unemployed father. In most of the new proposals, benefits are paid if the father is temporarily unemployed. A related charge was that the eligibility requirements encouraged unwed mothers to have even more children since more children meant additional benefits. Actually there was little evidence that the small increase in benefits encouraged having additional children. Most new proposals by the states contain much better work, marriage, and other incentives; but, as noted, such programs will be much more expensive in the short run. States, it is argued, are in a much better position to design programs to meet the special needs of their citizens. Some who make this argument also add the rather unrealistic assumption that these programs will be accomplished at much lower costs. There well may be some success stories as greater reliance is placed upon state governments. The criticisms of the AFDC programs are valid, and better approaches are required. Moreover, some states will be willing and able to finance new initiatives; at the same time there will be costly failures.

Under the old system there were great disparities among the states. The disparity in benefits will increase now that states have been given the responsibility to invent their own welfare programs. Those states that are willing to try innovative and necessarily expensive programs may achieve some new breakthroughs. Those states that showed an inability to meet the most basic requirements of the AFDC program can hardly be expected to finance new, more expensive approaches. Along with some successes there will be widespread failures, and the poor, especially the children, will suffer. The immediate future will offer hard choices to state governments. How will they balance conflicting social responsibilities? It seems likely that the future will also provide examples of what happens when hard choices are *not* taken; when we simply choose to ignore our most fundamental social responsibilities.

The Public Debate and the New Legislation

The public debate and bargaining that have accompanied recent legislative welfare reform efforts are informative. Many of the concerns voiced during the process have not been satisfactorily resolved. It will be interesting to see which of the various predictions will be accurate.

In 1992, President Clinton had come to office promising, as noted, to "end welfare as we know it." His initial proposals included a two-year limit on aid to welfare mothers, followed by work requirements. Whether or not a workable plan would have emerged became a moot point. Like most of his initiatives, including his ill-fated attempt at national health insurance, Clinton was unable to break the gridlock achieved by the Republicans in the Senate. After their 1994 landslide, Republican leadership in the House and Senate raised the stakes considerably beyond those originally proposed by Clinton. During 1995, Congress played fiscal brinkmanship with the White House with periodic threats to close down government. Although the blame for prior legislative failures had been shifted to Clinton, the public now blamed the Republican Congress. Clinton was successful in portraying the Republican reform initiatives as too draconian. His vetoes gained wide public support. Two of these vetoes had already been aimed at welfare legislation and a third was threatened in the summer of 1996. This was to be the last serious effort before party conventions and the November elections. This fact was not lost on President Clinton nor on the Republicans in Congress, all of whom had promised radical welfare reform.

Congress had removed several provisions that had prompted the two previous vetoes. House leader Newt Gingrich and most of the new House members had insisted on including Medicaid reform as part of the bill. In June, a meeting in the Republican ranks led to Medicaid being removed. There remained several other key issues including the fate of the Food Stamp program and the eligibility of legal immigrants for social benefits. Perhaps the most important question concerned the fate of children when welfare benefits were ended. Republicans in the House had softened cuts in foster care, school lunches, and care for disabled children.

The Senate defeated two Democratic attempts to soften the bill. One would have restored assistance to legal immigrants and the other would have provided vouchers to obtain diapers, clothing, medical supplies, school supplies, and other basic services for children after their cash assistance had been cut off. Although the Food Stamp program was not terminated, its eligibility requirements were tightened. Adults without children are limited to three months during any five-year period.

The most fundamental tenet of the new approach is that aid is to be temporary, very temporary. There is to be a two-year limit for any one stretch of time and a five-year lifetime limit. If the recipient is not employed at the end of two years, aid will be cut off. The challenge to the states is to insure that the individual succeeds in getting a job that will provide the necessities of life. For heads of families, the challenge is to find a job adequate to support the family.

Within the two-year parameters, states are designing their own programs. They must determine what procedures will be followed in applying for and accepting jobs. The states will decide how much will be allowed for such expenses as rent, food, and transportation. Each state will be responsible for insuring that day care is available for children of mothers who are required to work. The federal law allows states to make exceptions to the two-year limitation not to exceed 20 percent of its cases.

Although the federal government will give states block grants and considerable freedom in their use, a token effort is made toward equalizing benefits. Recall that, under the old program, basic monthly payments for a family ranged from $114 in Alabama to $651 in Alaska. Under the new legislation, states are required to maintain their welfare spending at 80 percent of 1994 levels. Increased federal funding is made available to states with high unemployment or rapidly growing populations.

Many critics of the cuts demanded by Republicans argue that many of the states are ill-equipped to meet the challenge of welfare reform. In the short run, providing the support necessary to enable families to break the cycle of poverty will surely be more expensive than in the former system. For example, teenage mothers need to finish school and prepare for full-time work upon graduation. More, rather than fewer, social services will be required for the children. Yet the federal government originally anticipated saving some sixty billion dollars, primarily from reductions in the Food Stamp program.

The level of effort required of states depends importantly on how many jobs there are waiting for former welfare participants. While predictions based on solid evidence are scarce, there is no shortage of pronouncements by the ideologically pure. Those who believe in the unlimited abundance of the market are certain that any responsible person will be able to find a good job. It follows that all that is required is to rescind the work disincentives. At the other end of the ideological spectrum, egalitarians argue that, if decent jobs had been available, few families would have chosen to rely on welfare payments.

The rest of us, presumably, see the problem more objectively. The former system did, in fact, create significant disincentives, especially when compared to low paying and sporadic job opportunities. On the other hand, breaking the cycle of poverty in which many families, indeed many communities, find themselves will require both ingenuity and commitment on the part of local and state organizations.

While some states and local communities will succeed, others will undoubtedly fail. The failures will increase the suffering of the most vulnerable. That is the tradeoff we are making.

Some Promising Strategies

As states design and redesign their welfare programs, they can observe and compare notes with other states. Some pilot programs were started well before the final legislation was passed. President Clinton had been liberal in granting waivers to the old law; some forty-three states had already begun designing their programs, and several had gained valuable experience through pilot programs. Many states were well on their way to developing the necessary institutional framework.

As anticipated, the states are taking a variety of paths to welfare reform. While some approaches will fail and cause suffering, others will succeed. The law allows states to use money formerly going to benefits to provide subsidies to wages. Employers are encouraged in these and other ways to hire welfare recipients.

Welfare caseworkers largely abandoned home visits in the 1970s, when they were viewed as an invasion of privacy. But now closer consideration of the home situation and job prospects of each recipient must be undertaken if the new initiatives are to succeed.

In most states "diversion programs" are being instituted that attempt to meet the short-term emergency needs of families. In the past, short-term emergencies such as illness or transportation problems could force a family to go on welfare. In many cases, temporary help is all that is required.

A welfare recipient's job prospects can be improved with greater mobility. Several states are assisting families in moving to communities with better job opportunities. If this means relocating a family to another state, so much the better. More generally, states with more generous programs must face the problem of attracting former welfare recipients from other states. This problem is not new but will be exacerbated under the new reforms. Some states are experimenting with a two-tier system that gives lower benefits to newcomers.

An early reform model in Wisconsin takes the funds formerly used to pay welfare recipients and subsidizes the wages employers pay when they hire former welfare clients. The state plans to increase its own spending by more than 13 percent, which will be required to fund large increases in the number of children in day-care centers. It is also expected that many former welfare recipients will not be able to find jobs. Thus the state must invent large numbers of community-service or transition jobs. The success or failure of the program hangs on whether or not social workers can transform themselves into employment agents.

As the Wisconsin welfare experiment was being put in place, a very public exchange took place between two good Wisconsin Catholics, Governor Thompson and Milwaukee Archbishop Rembert Weakland. Writing in the *Washington Post*, Weakland appealed to society not to end our sixty-year "covenant" to insure a minimal level of assistance for food, clothing, and shelter for the children of the poor. "Catholic social teaching holds that the poor, especially children, have a moral claim on the resources of the community to secure the necessities of life. We cannot afflict these children with hunger in order to infuse their parents with virtue."[11]

Thompson replied that, under the Wisconsin program, families would be better off. The AFDC program "had done nothing but harm children for the past 60 years. It is the padlock that has closed the gate, trapping families in a well of dependency and despair. And the people harmed most severely by the AFDC 'entitlement' have clearly been the children."[12]

Query: Does Irresponsible Behavior Cause Poverty or Does Poverty Cause Irresponsible Behavior?

These two questions reflect two theories of behavior. The theory that irresponsible behavior causes poverty is fundamental to the ideology of individualism. Most Americans subscribe to the idea that we, as individuals, are responsible for our own destiny. At the same time, we know that life can be terribly unfair. Even the most conservative of us believes that, as a society, we need to insure that everyone gets a fair start and that the rules of the game are fair. Moreover, all Americans agree that since bad luck and miscalculations can bring disaster to even the most well-intentioned of us, our social institutions should include safety nets and even second chances. Within those parameters, our individualistic values hold that each person has much to do with his or her own destiny, success, or failure. It is obvious that many of those in poverty have no one to blame but themselves. For an unmarried teenager to conceive and bear a child is clearly irresponsible. The difficulties she may have in supporting herself and her child are her own doing. The new welfare law, the "Personal Responsibility and Work Opportunity Act of 1996," makes these values abundantly clear.

The ideology of egalitarianism rests on another theory of behavior: we are responsible for each other. Society is a joint venture to which all of us contribute in our own way. Our income and wealth should be shared according to need. We should be sympathetic to those who are not successful, since their failure is more the fault of the system than of themselves. Teenage mothers in poor communities view caring for children as the one thing they can do that is socially responsible. It gives meaning to their lives and creates possibilities for the future. Society has an obligation to share in the upbringing of its children.

The rest of us claim to be more objective. We share values with a number of the ideologies, but we see that at times these values must be balanced against each other. As individualists, we believe that each person is responsible for her or his own success or failure. Moreover, families have the primary responsibility for raising their own children. A family should only have children when reasonably certain that they can provide for the children's needs. On the other hand our egalitarian values emphasize our social responsibilities, especially to the children. We are responsible for the plight of those caught in a cycle of poverty. We certainly have a social responsibility toward the children. The plight of the children caught in poverty presents us with a moral dilemma. It is not easy for us to balance the values and related moral principles.

The new approach to welfare reflects a new balance among our social values. In implementing this new approach one "efficiency consideration" should be clear. From a macro point of view, at least, it is poverty that causes irresponsible behavior and not the other way around. If we want to lift families out of poverty, we must not only instruct them in the proper social virtues, but we must also give them hope and dignity. For example, if more young women were given economic opportunity, we would see a dramatic drop in childbearing by teenage mothers. In some communities welfare reform can focus on creating more job opportunities. In others a more concerted approach must be taken. The entire community must be restructured. Not only are increased job opportunities and training required, but improvements must be made in child day care, transportation, health care, crime prevention, and, of course, education.

SUGGESTIONS FOR FURTHER READING

Taxes

Barry Bosworth and Gary Burtless, "Effects of Tax Reform on Labor Supply, Investment, and Saving," *Journal of Economic Perspectives* (6)1 (1992), pp. 3–25. An analysis of the incidence and behavioral effects of changes in taxes during the 1980s.

Peter Mieszkowski, "Tax Incidence Theory: The Effect of Taxes on the Distribution of Income," *Journal of Economic Literature* (7) 4 (1969). A survey of tax incidence theory.

Joseph Pechman, ed., *Comprehensive Taxation* (Washington, D.C.: The Brookings Institution, 1977). Essays concerning the idea of comprehensive income and problems of taxation.

————, *Who Paid the Taxes: 1966–1985?* (Washington, D.C.: The Brookings Institution, 1985). A survey of the entire system of taxes and their incidence.

Joel Slemrod "Optimal Taxation and Optimal Tax Systems," *Journal of Economic Perspectives* (4)1 (1990), pp. 157–78. A survey of tax criteria and difficulties of application.

Public Debt

Charles L. Schultze, "Of Wolves, Termites, and Pussycats or, Why We Should Worry about the Budget Deficit," *The Brookings Review* (7) 3 (1989), pp. 26–33. A summary of the various arguments concerning the size of the budget deficit.

Janet L. Yellen, "Symposium on the Budget Deficit," *Journal of Economic Perspectives* (3)2 (1989), pp. 17–21. A summary of the several budget deficit articles contained in the symposium issue.

The Budget

Robert H. Haveman and Julius Margolis, eds., *Public Expenditures and Policy Analysis*, 3d ed. (Boston: Houghton Mifflin, 1983). Articles on various methods for analyzing public expenditure policies.

Welfare Reform

Gary Burtless, "The Economist's Lament: Public Assistance in America," *Journal of Economic Perspectives* (4)1 (1990). An overview of the welfare programs prior to the reforms of 1996 and 1997. Proposals for reform.

Robert Moffitt, "Incentive Effects of the U.S. Welfare System: A Review," *Journal of Economic Literature* (30)1 (1992), pp. 1–61. A survey of analyses of welfare programs and their incentive effects prior to the 1996 reforms.

Demetra Smith Nightingale and Robert Haveman, eds., *The Work Alternative* (Washington, D.C.: The Urban Institute Press, 1995). Analyses of the problems of replacing welfare with work.

ENDNOTES

1. See Joseph A. Pechman, *Who Paid the Taxes: 1966–1985?* (Washington, D.C.: The Brookings Institution, 1985), p. 56. See also U.S. Congress, Congressional Budget Office, *The Changing Distribution of Federal Taxes: 1975–1990* (Washington, D.C.: Congress of the United States, October, 1987).

2. See Henry Simons, *Personal Income Taxation* (Chicago: University of Chicago Press, 1938); and Robert Murray Haig, "The Concept of Income: Economic and Legal Aspects," in *The Federal Income Tax*, ed. Robert Murray Haig (New York: Columbia University Press, 1921). Also see U.S. Department of the Treasury, *Blue-*

prints for Basic Tax Reform (Washington, D.C.: U.S. Government Printing Office, 1977), chap. 3.

3. See Nicholas Kalder, *An Expenditure Tax* (London: Allen and Unwin, 1955), chap. 1.

4. See Antonio de Viti de Marco, *First Principles of Public Finance*, trans. Edith Paolo Marget (New York: Harcourt Brace, 1936); Knut Wicksell, "A New Principle of Just Taxation" in *Classics in the Theory of Public Finance*, eds. Richard A. Musgrave and Alan Peacock (London: Macmillan, 1958); and Erik Lindahl, *Just Taxation*. See also R. A. Musgrave, *The Theory of Public Finance* (New York: McGraw-Hill, 1959), pp. 73–78.

5. Adam Smith, *The Wealth of Nations* (New York: Modern Library, 1937), p. 777.

6. See John Stuart Mill, *Principles of Political Economy*, in *Collected Works of John Stuart Mill*, ed. F. E. L. Priestley (Toronto: University of Toronto Press, 1969).

7. Several concepts of equal sacrifice were outlined by A. G. Cohen-Stuart and F. Y. Edgeworth. See a discussion of their work in Musgrave, *Theory of Public Finance*, pp. 95–102.

8. Mill, *Utilitarianism* (1861), in Priestley *Collected Works*, pp. 253–54.

9. Ibid., p. 254.

10. *Statistical Abstract of the United States*, (Washington, D.C.: U.S. Government Printing Office, 1993).

11. See the *Washington Post*, editorial pages, July 4, 1996.

12. Ibid, editorial pages, July 14, 1996.

4

Education, Fair Starts, and Economic Opportunity

As parents and citizens we have many goals for education. We firmly believe that a good education is necessary if children are to have a fair start in life. Americans of every political persuasion believe that every child deserves a fair start.

For the decades following World War II, the paintings of Norman Rockwell have helped Americans shape their visions of society. In Rockwell paintings of schoolrooms, we see teachers lovingly imparting solid American values to eager, receptive children. Their hopes and expectations run high.

More recently this picture of society and education is being challenged. In the competing vision, social institutions are depicted as having failed. Visions from an age of optimism and social responsibility are being replaced by those of an age of pessimism and adversarial greed. We are left with two diametrically opposed pictures of American society and education.

Has the original vision been lost completely? Certainly the image has been tarnished. In most communities the vision not only continues, but continues to be fulfilled. Most of our communities take great pride in their schools. Oddly enough, the great majority of Americans perceive their own local schools as doing very well, even though they have come to accept the conventional wisdom that our schools have failed.

Before any balanced judgement can be made, we need to realistically assess the successes and failures of American education. The educational opportunities provided most American children are of high and improving quality; however, there are some communities and some schools that must be improved.

Public Support for Improving Our Schools

President Clinton used his 1997 State of the Union address to declare a *national crusade* to improve public education. Public opinion surveys consistently

rank this social issue higher than all others. Clinton's and others' proposals reflect the general perception that students are not being adequately prepared,
especially in the fundamentals of English grammar, reading comprehension,
and math. We can expect bipartisan support at the federal, state, and local levels. These proposals also reflect the ideas of educators and social scientists. There
is support for establishing national standards of student performance. This idea
is closely related to the curriculum question—what subjects and skills should
be mastered at the various grades. Generally, the approach has been to move
teaching of the basic skills (reading, grammar, and math) to earlier grades. Obviously, the standards used will reflect society's new priorities and expectations.
They are based in part on assumptions of the skills required to be successful in
an increasingly dynamic and competitive economy.

Clinton would encourage all school districts to administer standardized
reading tests at the fourth grade. All eighth grades would be given a standardized test on math.

Other proposals include expanding the 1993 Family and Medical Leave
Act to include time from work for parent-teacher conferences; school curfews;
and income tax incentives for college education.

The idea of increasing educational opportunities beyond the high school
level has always had wide support among Americans, far exceeding other countries. The particular tax breaks in the Clinton proposal would help lower- and
middle-income families meet the rising cost of tuition. Here again, however, it
is appropriate to sort out the implicit social goals and match them with the
available policy tools. One purpose, clearly, is to reduce some of the burden
on lower- and middle-income families and their college-age children. Another
is to enable more students to attend advanced technical schools or colleges.
With respect to lower-income families two market failures are involved. First,
credit markets are imperfect. Most students will increase earnings significantly
over their working years; but at the time they need loans to attend college,
they have insufficient collateral and credit ratings. Second, as with the elementary and secondary schools, there are positive externalities. As various proposals, including Clinton's, proceed along the legislative processes at the federal and state levels, the various goals, market failures, and remedies will be
compared. More direct approaches such as increased loan subsidies (to offset
credit market failures) and greater public monetary support for lower tuition
at community colleges and state universities (to compensate for the inherent
social benefits) will be considered.

The public's level of anxiety about education and jobs began to build during the social strife of the late 1960s and early 1970s and during the recessions
of the mid-1970s and early 1980s. During the 1980s economic institutions experienced rapid change. The pace of technological change accelerated. Deregulation allowed for cutthroat competition, leveraged buyouts, widespread bankruptcies, and massive downsizing within the surviving business firms. The
severity of competition was also increased by foreign companies taking advantage of lower barriers to international trade. These developments combined to
undermine job security. Parents who worried about their own job security be-

came equally concerned about future prospects for their children. A frequently asked question has become: Are our schools preparing our young people for the new realities of the global economy?

A related question concerns the distribution of educational opportunity—Is it fair? While most of our children are being well educated, others are falling behind and will experience great difficulty responding to changing technology and competition in the job market. As we consider our educational goals, we must differentiate between two distinct issues. First, given the rapid changes in technology and competition, how do we change curricula so that the great majority of students enjoy economic success? Second, how can we provide adequate educational and economic opportunity for our most disadvantaged school districts? The most flagrant cases involve the urban ghettos of our large cities. The disintegration of families and family values, high crime rates, the drug culture, underfunded schools, and poor job opportunities make the challenge of providing opportunity to those young people almost impossible. These two issues must not be conflated. They require initiatives that are different in kind.

Query: Do Fair Starts Mean Equal Starts?

At several points in this study we have asked whether or not the social goal of fair starts should be interpreted to mean equal starts. We observe that equality is usually dismissed as a naive egalitarian concept. Realistically, there can be no such thing as an equal start. After all, we are born with different mental and physical talents. We are born into various family situations, into various neighborhoods, and into various cultures. It seems more reasonable to define a fair start as an acceptable range of opportunities.

We have used the idea of a social minimum in several contexts; for example, welfare, job opportunities, and social security. We certainly do not expect the results of a fair game to be exactly equal. To the extent that we use the perfectly competitive market as a fair-game analogy, we expect the results to be unequal; correspondingly, we do not expect distribution "according to contribution" to be equal.

With education perhaps the idea of fair starts as equal starts deserves to be reconsidered. We must agree that children and young people could never face exactly equal starts, but what types of inequality should we accept as fair?

In comparing our two strawmen ideologies, we have criticized the egalitarian's emphasis on equal results and the individualist's emphasis on winnings. The egalitarian has a much stronger case for equality when we focus on starts rather than results. It is one thing to argue that playing a fair game under fair rules justifies the unequal results, but educational opportunity is about fair *starts* not fair results. How can we justify differences in starting points?

It is too simplistic to argue that exact equality is impossible. We know that life is not fair. The question is what efficiency and fairness considerations can be brought to bear against the argument for *equal* educational opportunity.

The utilitarian goal of maximizing social welfare does not require equality of starts. From society's point of view, the most efficient approach is to give opportunity on the basis of what social contribution is anticipated. The educational systems in most European countries are much more selective than in the United States. In one sense, this selectivity is a question of fitting the opportunity to those best equipped to take advantage of it, but in another real sense, opportunities are organized on the basis of what will contribute most to society. By contrast, American education is much more egalitarian, and we are proud of that attribute. Compared to European education, the barriers to further achievement are not as high. There is ample room given to late bloomers and to slow-but-determined students. In philosophical terms, the moral principles inherent in the design of our system are more deontological in the sense that the rights of each person to follow his or her own life plan are given weight. Thus the focus on maximizing social welfare is given less weight. Of course, it is often proposed that the two educational goals are complementary.

Our strawman individualist, like the egalitarian, appreciates the social goal of insuring that each child gets a fair start but does not believe that an equal start is required. Determined individuals can overcome whatever challenges they may face. Moreover, our educational and economic systems offer unlimited opportunities to those who are willing to work. On the other hand, our individualist has little faith in efforts by the state to equalize opportunity. Such efforts are doomed to failure.

The individualist's primary argument against an equal-start focus is similar to the one used to justify inequality of income and wealth. The free market economy requires a system of property rights. For parents, these rights include the right to give to their children and the right to purchase a higher-quality education.

It is frequently argued that these rights extend to our roles as taxpayers. Just as parents have the right to send their children to private schools, taxpayers in wealthy communities have the right to improve the quality of their public schools. Surely the egalitarian would object to this right. Is it fair to let parents in a wealthy school district purchase a higher quality of education for their children? Should the children in poor communities, who are already disadvantaged, be further penalized by unequal educational opportunities? Does the state government have an obligation to equalize educational opportunity, say, by redistributing funds on a per-pupil basis?

Is there some middle ground between the individualist and egalitarian positions? How are the values and moral principles to be balanced? Recall that, unlike with other social issues, the distance between the two extremes is not so large. The individualist and the egalitarian, like most Americans, share the belief in fair starts. Most of us favor an institutional arrangement where parents take pride in their communities and take an active part in their children's education, but we also acknowledge the argument for equality. The right of a young person to have a fair start in pursuit of his or her life plan seems fundamental. The special character of education is that it helps prepare children for life.

As parents and citizens, we see our individual and social responsibility not simply as providing a social minimum or a safety net. On the contrary, we must feel pride in the level of educational opportunity that we are able to provide our children. Our perception of education carries with it the question of what values and possibilities we leave for the next generation. We want it to emulate the vision of a Norman Rockwell painting.

The Real Concerns

As with many social issues, political rhetoric tends to obfuscate real problems and concerns. Before tracing the history of recent public debate, it is appropriate to make a list of what should be our real concerns.

We first need to recognize that most Americans have not lost their visions of what roles education can and should play. Some commentators are justifiably concerned about the degradation of life taking place in some areas, especially in the poverty-stricken ghettos of some of our cities. In most of our communities, however, education needs to be improved, not reformed. In most communities, we need to build on what we have. By contrast, our poorest communities need radical change not only in the school, but in *all* aspects of the community. In the previous chapter, we examined the challenge we face in transforming the cycles of poverty that trap families in some of our inner cities. Education reform must be viewed as part of welfare reform. The reforms initiated by states are aimed at providing jobs for parents and day care for children. They also expanded Head Start programs and educational opportunities. In short, the building of viable communities requires a coordinated effort.

Within this context, what should be our priorities in education?

1. *Financial Resources.* We need to ask what our goals are in education and what levels of spending will be required. An assessment of the revenue requirements will depend in part on demography. How many students do we expect at various grade levels? What will be the demand and supply for teachers?

2. *Quality Education for All.* There are great disparities in expenditures per pupil. A more serious aspect of the problem is that the quality of educational opportunity for some of our poorer areas is far below established standards.

3. *The Role of Education in Local Communities.* Americans expect a great deal from our public schools, perhaps more than can be delivered. The role of schools in local communities has always been important and many-faceted. As our communities change and face new challenges, the schools will play important roles in the community response.

4. *Preparing Students for Economic Success.* A major concern in recent years is whether or not our students are being adequately prepared for the new demands of the job market. This is one area where the public debate has generated more heat than light. The real concern here should be to teach the *basics* such as math, science, economics, and computer skills. These are more essential than skills applicable to a particular job. The international nature

of competition will require adaptability and mobility on the part of every successful participant.

5. *Preparing the Well-Rounded Person for the Full Life.* The major function of education is not to supply productive workers to industry; it is to enable our children to realize their full potential in every facet of life.

This balancing of social goals introduces yet another philosophical question. Are we to focus on increasing the productivity of our workforce or are we to focus on preparing our students for a rich, satisfying life?

Education and Public Expectations: Some History

The thirty years following World War II were remarkable in terms of economic growth and the democratization of education. The goal was to extend educational opportunity to every citizen. Enrollments in high schools increased over 50 percent. The percentage of those completing high school rose dramatically, from one-third of Americans in 1950 to three-fourths by 1985.

The states assumed the important role of making college education affordable to all those who qualified. World War II veterans were granted federal support under the GI Bill. College and university enrollments more than doubled.

These decades saw public expectations rebound from the Great Depression. People gradually gained confidence that their standard of living would continue to improve. Although we experienced some periods of recession and slower growth, the overall growth rate was a remarkable 3.5 percent. Economic growth allowed for upward social mobility and for confidence that discrimination against minorities and women could be overcome. The role of public education in fulfilling these expectations was seen as crucial.

Attitudes towards education in the early 1960s reflected the optimism of rising living standards and expectations. John F. Kennedy, a bright, young, charismatic president, personified this optimism as he launched the effort to travel to the moon: "But why, some say, the moon? . . . And they may well ask, why climb the highest mountain? . . . We choose to go to the moon . . . and do the other things, not because they are easy but because they are hard; because that goal will serve to organize and measure the best of our energies and skills. . . ."[1] Kennedy spoke to a rising sense of social responsibility when, in his inaugural address, he challenged Americans to "Ask not what your country can do for you, but what you can do for your country."

In the previous chapter, we described the contrast in public attitudes between the early and late 1960s. Starting with Kennedy's assassination in 1963, a series of events dampened the American spirit and created social unrest. Later, the civil rights leader, Martin Luther King, and the presidential candidate, Robert Kennedy, were assassinated. Actually the liberal dream of solving our social problems did not end with the assassination of President Kennedy. Many new initiatives in welfare, health, and education were begun under the leadership of Lyndon Johnson. The War on Poverty reduced the number of families in poverty by half by the early 1970s. Federal spending on education increased from $1.3 billion in 1964 to almost $10 billion by 1972. The liberal agenda for education included new and innovative approaches to learning. Partly in response to the youth movement, less emphasis was placed on the basics such as English, math, science, and foreign languages, and more emphasis was put on making courses interesting and relevant. Many of these reforms were hotly debated; in retrospect, there is general agreement that the curriculum was weakened.

The Vietnam War was the final blow to the age of social optimism. The alienation between the generations was widened into what became known as the "generation gap." Many leaders of the youth movement adopted the political rhetoric of the New Left. On the economic sphere, two severe "cost-push" recessions occurred in the mid and late 1970s. These featured both inflation and unemployment. This combination proved very difficult to combat with traditional macroeconomic policies. Later the fear of inflation led Paul Volcker, chairman of the Federal Reserve, to engineer the sharp recession of 1981–1982 and, following that, to continue to restrain economic growth. Whether or not by design, the most effective constraint on social programs since the early 1980s has been the public debt; it was the creation of recessions, tax cuts, increased spending on defense, and a slower rate of economic growth.

A Reappraisal of Education

The drastic decrease in the rate of growth in the mid 1970s set the stage for a reappraisal of all social programs, education included. During the period between the end of World War II and the mid-1960s, education was heralded as an important factor in our growing economic prosperity and social mobility. Schools promised to provide opportunity to minorities and to women, to end racial prejudice, and to build community pride. A faith had developed that science and technology could solve all our problems and usher in a golden age. Institutions of higher learning enjoyed this approbation.

As the economy slowed, however, wages and job security faltered. The funding of education began to lag behind other Western countries. During the recessions, other financial demands such as unemployment benefits, medical care, and welfare entitlements competed for government funds.

During the early 1970s, Presidents Nixon and Ford were able to curtail many of the programs begun as parts of the War on Poverty. At the same time, unfortunately, the recessions exacerbated many social problems: violence, drug use, and teenage pregnancies. Urban flight led to decay and growing pockets of poverty in most cities.

At a time when social expectations were being disappointed, the schools were having to cope with greater challenges and tighter budgets. During the 1970s, an awareness was growing that American education could not effectively carry out all its missions, especially in those areas hardest hit by economic crises. There were many critics offering various solutions. These general concerns set the stage for the public debate on education in the 1980s.

The critics of public education came from all political persuasions. When Ronald Reagan was elected in 1980, some of the most reactionary critics of public education were suddenly given center stage. Several of these critics wished to abolish public education and to replace it with a voucher system. They had always been critical of public education, but now their criticism was given legitimacy and press coverage.

Other critics supported public education but believed that major reforms needed to be made. On April 26, 1983, a presidential committee published an influential statement entitled *A Nation at Risk*. Although a number of failures in American education were asserted, no actual evidence or studies were cited in the thirty-six page statement.[2] Many of the recommendations were supported by a wide audience. The committee recommended a return to the basics: English, science, and foreign languages (the last to be begun in the elementary grades). It recommended higher standards and salaries for teachers and funds for computers.

While increased federal spending on education would have been welcome, especially in the poorer school districts, it was not forthcoming. The Reagan administration's policy featured reform: higher standards for teachers and students, longer school days and school years, more homework, and fewer "frills" such as the fine arts.

As the public debate has gathered momentum, the more radical critics have attempted to set the stage for the ultimate reform: the abolition of public education. That was unforeseen by many of those who voiced concerns in the early 1980s. The initial call for reform was supported by many different parts of the political spectrum.

THE GREAT DEBATE: REFORM OR PRIVATIZATION?

A Caution: Beware the Political Hyperbole

In recent years, the public debate on education has been so filled with hyperbole that rational thinking about basic questions has been set aside. During the 1996 presidential campaign, Republican candidate Bob Dole called President Clinton the "pliant pet" of the militant teachers unions, currying favor with the very same vested interests who were fighting reform. The Clinton campaign iterated its support of public education and accused Dole of pitting parents against teachers.

The campaign to discredit public education, which began in earnest in the 1980s, has now reached the stage that the shift to a voucher system is taken quite seriously. The change in public perceptions has been dramatic.

The Ideology of Public School Critics

The critics of public education come from all ideological persuasions. We observed that the general discontent of the late 1960s and early 1970s gave way to disillusionment by the late 1970s and the 1980s. This disillusionment embraced all of the social programs that had promised to defeat poverty and racial and gender discrimination, and to usher in an age of greater prosperity for all. Critics on the Left and on the Right offered explanations for why these social ills had not been eradicated.

Within the Reagan and Bush administrations, several ideologies competed for influence: traditional conservatives, libertarians, and the religious right. Two schools of economists also vied for influence: the monetarists and the supply-siders. Both of these schools generally hold to a libertarian view of the world; social problems are a result of government interference in the market. The extremists of these ideologies have a blind faith in free enterprise and the markets. Both schools favor deregulation, tax cuts, welfare cuts, and privatization of most social programs to include social security and education.

The ideological split between the supply-siders and the monetarists appeared immediately over the first Reagan budget. The budget included dramatic increases in defense spending coupled with huge tax cuts. The supply-sider arguments, based on the Laffer curve, claimed that tax cuts favoring the wealthy would actually produce greater revenues. The monetarists in the Reagan administration and, more important, Paul Volcker of the Federal Reserve, believed that the Reagan budgets would be highly inflationary. Consequently, the Federal Reserve responded by tightening the money supply, raising interest rates, and precipitating a severe recession.

The Reagan economists were not split on educational reform. Their approach to education, as to every social program, was to take greater advantage of market incentives—to *privatize*. It is acknowledged that there are some public-good-type benefits in education. However, the most appropriate way to finance education is to (1) use vouchers to cover the public-good benefits, and (2) allow parents the choice of augmenting the vouchers as they see fit. Privatization would then allow the market to allocate resources efficiently in response to family choice. This argument has now become a standard fixture in the public debate. Whether or not it is true that private schools are actually more efficient than public schools is an important question. Privatization would certainly be more efficient in one sense: education would be rationed very efficiently by the market. Privatization would ration education according to a family's purchasing power. Whether or not the market would effectively accomplish our social goals for education is another question.

The support for privatization was not universal within the Reagan administration. Some, including Education Secretary Terrel Bell, wanted to reform, but not abolish, public education. Indeed, the recommendations of *A Nation at Risk* were focused on improving the existing system of public education, but as the reform campaign progressed, the proponents of privatization became ascendant. Presidents Reagan and Bush and, more recently, Bob Dole have argued for the voucher system. At the same time, where Republicans have gained control of state governorships and legislatures, voucher systems have been introduced.

The Voucher Movement—Some History

The voucher movement can be understood only in the context of the more general reform movement begun in the 1970s and gaining momentum in the 1980s. We have already discussed how the various social and educational problems of the 1960s and 1970s evolved.

Initially the reform movement was nonideological and bipartisan. For example, its leaders included Governor Bill Clinton of Arkansas and Republican Governors Thomas Kean of New Jersey and Lamar Alexander of Tennessee. The common themes of reform included tougher standards for students, more rigorous courses and textbooks, higher qualifications and preparation for teachers, longer school days and years, merit pay and leadership roles for outstanding teachers, and increased funding across the board.

There was also a growing realization that schools could not solve all of society's problems. Somehow the prospects of the whole community must be improved. The schools could only play their part in a concerted effort. Of special concern was the deterioration of family values and economic opportunities in the inner cities.

In the late 1980s, this movement was largely co-opted by supporters of private schools and vouchers. Thus, the original goals of reform movements were replaced with a radical new agenda. Ironically, the reforms of the late 1970s and early 1980s were already having significant effect, but the political rhetoric of the voucher movement ignored the new trends.

The Current Debate: School Choice as a Political Issue

The idea of privatization is not new. Libertarian economist Milton Friedman proposed the idea of using vouchers in the late 1950s. The idea has attracted the interest of academics and others from all sides of the political spectrum (Christopher Jencks, Henry Levin, John Coons, Stephen Sugarman, Lamar Alexander, and Diane Ravitch). Recently, the idea has received strong advocacy from a Brookings Institution study by John Chubb and Terry Moe, *Politics, Markets, and America's Schools.* They claim that vouchers are, in fact, a panacea. The choice given parents by vouchers is not like other reforms. They insist that vouchers not be combined with other programs. The various efforts of reformers should be abandoned. The privatization of education will accomplish the goals of reform all by itself.[3]

Although, when elected, President Bush saw vouchers as much too costly for public budgets, by 1991 he made privatization and vouchers the centerpiece of his bid to become known as the "education president." The election of Bill Clinton, a strong supporter of public schools, seemed to ring the death knell for the privatization campaign. But the Republican landslide in 1994, not only in Congress but also in the states and localities, was interpreted by many as a mandate for radical welfare and education reform. Experiments with vouchers and parental choice of schools were introduced in many states. Criticism of public schools intensified during the 1996 political campaign. One of Bob Dole's campaign advisors was voucher advocate Bill Bennett. One somewhat ironic slogan pointed out that the wealthy had always had the choice to send their children to private schools; supposedly a voucher system would extend that choice to all.

The support for vouchers comes from a wide spectrum of voters; some are conservative ideologues and some are not. As expected, many wealthy families whose children attend private schools support vouchers. Those who support church-related schools on the religious right, including some Catholics, also would benefit from vouchers. In some areas, white parents have chosen to establish private schools to avoid sending their children to predominately black schools.

As a political rallying cry, "school choice" has become one of the first issues since communism that can link the Republican party's suburban base to free market ideologues and to fundamentalists of the Christian Right. The issue also solidifies the support of white racists. The more extreme political rhetoric charges that public schools promote atheism, liberalism and socialism.

At the other side of the political spectrum, the strategy of most Democrats has been to support public education. They attempt to counter Republican criticism by publicizing the success stories of recent reform initiatives. Many of these initiatives seek to engage parents and other volunteers in a wide range of school programs from special reading-readiness programs to field trips and other extracurricular activities. One continuing issue will be the role of Head Start, a program President Clinton rescued from extinction.

The present political battle lines will probably remain for several years to come. The effectiveness of the federal government may or may not be revived, but it could potentially play an important role in setting parameters and in funding.

The future of educational reform will depend to a great extent on the states and localities. As noted, a number of states under Republican governors and legislatures have introduced voucher systems and will seek to increase the privatization of schools.

The continued progress of the voucher movement will depend on a number of factors; an important factor will be how the parties fare in elections. So far, the courts have thwarted the efforts of several states to extend the voucher system to religious schools.

Sorting out the Myths from the Real Problems

The international comparisons cited in *A Nation at Risk* and other critiques of American education revealed a number of real problems; they also led to a number of misconceptions.

Here we must consider some important ways American education has always differed from other nations. We bring along a much higher percentage of our students, early bloomers as well as late bloomers, through high school and even on to college. Other countries are much less tolerant of the late bloomer. In some countries, the educational future of twelve-year-olds has been settled; other hurdles must be met later. Only those who excel at tests given at the end of the primary grades are considered for the university track. The others are funneled into trade schools.

International comparisons of scholastic achievement began in 1967 with a study by the International Association for the Evaluation of Educational Achievement (IEA). The tests compared the mathematic achievements of students of the same age in twelve countries. This study was closely followed by tests in other subjects. Surprisingly, the United States did not do well in these comparisons. In many categories American students were last among comparable countries such as Japan and Korea and nations in Western Europe. These studies formed the basis of critical commentary in *A Nation at Risk* and other statements.

The international comparisons cited in *A Nation at Risk* justified the back-to-the-basics movement of the 1980s and 1990s. Unfortunately, these original studies still form the bases for current political rhetoric. A number of the original conclusions were based on unwarranted comparisons, but more important, many of the trends have been reversed. In order to know what our real problems are, it is necessary to look at current results and trends.

It is also important that studies that make international comparisons account for differences in curricula. For example, international comparisons such as the Second Mathematics Study by the IEA from 1980 to 1982 looked at the achievement levels of thirteen-year-olds (eighth graders) and high school seniors. It found that the American eighth graders lagged far behind in algebra. This should not have been surprising, since almost none of the American students had taken algebra. Later, when those American students who had had algebra classes were isolated into a separate category, it was found that their scores were substantially higher than their Japanese counterparts.[4]

In recent years, we have begun to emulate Korea, Japan, and Western European countries and now introduce algebra and other fields of mathematics at earlier grades. The teaching of calculus, which was once reserved for college curricula, has become common in high schools. Other trends that will make international comparisons more relevant are the back-to-the-basics trends at all levels. Many schools are beginning to teach foreign languages in earlier grades. These changes will not be without cost. Coupled with severe funding cuts in the poorer schools, the "luxuries" such as music, art, drama, enrichment extracurricular clubs, and other enrichment courses are being sacrificed.

Trends in Student Achievement

It is claimed that student achievement in our public schools is declining. Figures that purport to show this come from studies made over a quarter of a century ago; they reflected the social turmoil of the late 1960s and early 1970s. Since that time, student achievement has steadily improved; the recent progress among minorities has been remarkable.

It is often suggested that intellectual abilities and abstract problem-solving skills have declined, but again the reverse is true. It has been claimed both that

IQs are fixed and that spending more on public schools would neither improve intelligence nor improve achievement. Again, these statements are simply false. It is also claimed that America spends more on schools than other nations such as Japan and Western European nations. In fact, we spend less than the average of the industrialized nations; we are near the bottom in spending as a percentage of per capita income.[5]

It is common to hear that our teachers are lazy and unprepared, and that our textbooks teach homosexuality and sexual promiscuity. These claims and the inference that most parents have lost faith in their children's teachers and schools have been demonstrated to be false by many studies and surveys.

Dropouts

It is widely believed that a large percentage of the young drop out of school and add to our unemployment. In fact, the percentage of high school dropouts continues to decline. Over 75 percent graduate from high school on time, and this rate increases to 90 percent when high school equivalency diplomas are added.

Back to the Basics

The back-to-the-basics reforms of the 1980s have been highly successful. The comparatively low scores of the 1970s have been offset by progress in the 1980s, and black students have made remarkable gains. A portion of the comparative gains has been the result of beginning science, algebra, and geometry at earlier grades, as is done in Europe and Asia. This trend will continue as curricula changes become more general.

Achieving our goals does not require that education be made a burden. Instead, it is possible to make it more challenging and interesting, and to expect more rigor, sophistication, and imagination. These are strategies for real reform that deserve continued effort. It is generally agreed that the success of educational reform depends to a great extent on our ability to foster a much greater sense of responsibility and integrity among our students.

School Finance: Does Funding Count?

As noted, there is a misconception that the United States spends more on education than our counterparts in other countries. Those who argue that our public education fails badly go on to reason that the money is being wasted. Neither part of the argument is true. The cost per pupil in grades K through 12 in the United States is considerably lower than in Japan and a majority of the Western industrialized countries. For example, the 1985 expenditures (in 1988 exchange rates) were $7,061 in Switzerland and $3,456 in the United States.[6]

These averages hide a more serious problem. Whereas most countries operate a national education system that distributes funds equally, our system is characterized by great inequalities. Some school districts spend five times more per pupil than the poorer districts. Thus, the myth tends to conceal a real problem.

Another interesting myth concerning school finance is that more spending on schools does not really improve educational opportunity. That such nonsense could ever be taken seriously is remarkable. A 1966 study by James Coleman and others, popularly known as *The Coleman Report*, concluded that schools bring little influence to bear on children's achievements either in school or when "they confront life at the end of school."[7] Instead, only family background and neighborhood count. Needless to say these conclusions have been widely disputed.

It is true that school districts with better home environments are invariably those with more funding, smaller class size, and teachers with higher qualifications. It is not an easy matter to separate the correlative effects of inheritance, home environment, and funding on the quality of education. Nevertheless, most studies that attempt to do so find that funding is crucial. Moreover, of the characteristics we would expect of higher-quality education—the pupil–teacher ratio, the length of the school year, the average teacher salary, and the teachers' qualifications—all have significant effects on scholastic achievement, as well as on success after graduation.

IQ and High-Quality Educational Opportunity

We also must deal with the myth that learning abilities are unaffected by the quality of education. In *The Bell Curve*, Richard Hernstein and Charles Murray argued that intelligence is largely inherited.[8] Most psychologists disagree. Each of us knows from our own experience that high-quality schooling has increased our ability to use our mind. Many studies have related increases in IQ to the specific learning abilities fostered in school.[9]

Unfortunately, the reverse is also true; children fail to develop IQ when they miss high-quality education. The comparisons between children who miss the age cutoff for kindergarten and those who barely make it are interesting. Although there is only one month's difference in age, the two groups are substantially different in IQ measurements. Obviously, while inheritance and home environment are important to intelligence, the quality of education is also important.

If we, as a society, wish to promote high levels of intelligence and ingenuity among our youth, we can do so by providing them with high-quality education. On the other hand, those children who experience poor home environments and poor educational opportunity will be disadvantaged for life. And all of society will suffer the consequences.

Working parents are well aware that the quality of day care they provide is important. Parents generally attempt to spend time teaching their children. They also purchase instructional toys, read books to them, play games, and sing songs with them. It would seem preposterous to tell parents that this neither increases their children's knowledge nor their ability to learn. In good schools this process continues.

Education and the Competitiveness of American Workers

There is a generally held perception that the United States is at a competitive disadvantage in certain international markets due to poor education and to low worker productivity. Actually American workers have long been, and continue to be, the most productive in the world. To the extent that there is a link between education and productivity, our present system deserves credit for our nation's economic success. The productivity of workers in Japan and Germany is approximately 80 percent of American workers.[10] A related claim is that America does not produce enough engineers and scientists. In fact, the supply of engineers and scientists continues to increase and far exceeds demand. This is not to say that our economic growth would not be enhanced if our corporations were so organized that these young people could be put to work. Unfortunately, the reorganizations that followed the leveraged buyouts, takeovers, and maximization of corporate debt in the 1980s led to massive cutbacks in research and development. At the macro level, the monetary policies of the Federal Reserve have been designed to keep economic growth well below the rates prior to the mid-1970s.

All of this is not to say that the adaptability and ingenuity of American workers cannot be improved and that that would not improve our competitiveness in the international economy. Indeed, this is one of our most important social goals. But the claim that American industry has been at a competitive disadvantage because of our educational system is false.

BACK TO THE REAL CONCERNS

So let us end this tiresome, but necessary, examination of the political debate and its current myths about education. Let us return to some real concerns. Our brief list included:

1. what financial resources will be needed and where they are to be found;
2. how best to overcome the disparities in educational opportunities and, more important, how to bring the poorer areas up to established standards;
3. what role education can play in the community;
4. how we can best prepare students for the changing job market; and
5. how we can enable students to become well-rounded individuals.

Financial Resources

There are several facets to the question of finances. The demography of education is an important determinant of the required revenues. We need to anticipate what will be the size and character of the student population. What changes will be needed in the way we fund education? Who will be responsible? Let us start with the last question first. We, as a society, determine the institutional structure and the responsibilities within it.

Query: Whose Responsibility Is Education?

Earlier we proposed that every child has a right to an education. If we agree that children have natural or human rights to life, liberty, and the pursuit of happiness, then several things follow. The basic necessities of life such as food, clothing, shelter, and health care must be provided. This leads us to the next question: What range of social and economic opportunities should be available if the individual is to be free to choose and pursue a life plan? While education is not the only factor in shaping the life prospects of children, it is one of the most important. A good education is a necessary condition for a fair start.

If we agree that a good education is every child's right, we are still left with the question: Who has the correlative responsibility? Possessing a right when others have no correlative duties is of little value. Do all of us share a social responsibility that all children receive a good education? Of course we do. Only those who are willing to argue that we have no social responsibility at all could argue that we have no responsibility to provide for education. The most interesting question, one that we encounter in every social issue, is how we, as a society, specify the particular responsibilities of parents, churches, neighborhoods, localities, states, and the federal government. What are the "lines of defense" for insuring that a child is well educated? What are the responsibilities of parents, of teachers, of principals, of school boards?

In the United States, localities are given primary responsibility for financing and running the public schools. The states also play an important role. The division of responsibilities between locality and state government differs from state to state. As observed in chapter three, localities depend heavily on the property tax to fund their contribution, while the states draw from their general funds: sales and income taxes, and in some cases state lotteries, and other earmarked revenue sources. In about half the states, funds from localities are gathered by the states and redistributed to those localities by various formulae—roughly on a per-pupil basis. In other states, more of the funding by localities is retained, so that large differentials in spending-per-pupil arise among wealthier and poorer school districts.

There are also differences among states in the autonomy given to local school boards, but generally they have the major responsibility for school administration. One advantage of this organization is that it allows parents to participate directly in decision making. Most educators and parent groups advocate continuing the effort to get parents and other local citizens more involved in the local schools.

The school systems of other nations are much more centralized with respect to both finance and administration. This has the advantage of making expenditure-per-child much more equitable. We will point out that the present system of financing in the United States is clearly unfair. While it may be argued that it is not unfair for wealthier parents and school districts to add to the quality of their children's education, it is clearly unfair for the quality of education of children from poor families and poor school districts to fall below some recognized social minimum.

Now let us return to the idea that societies organize lines of defense for attending to their individual and social responsibilities. If localities are hard pressed to carry out their responsibilities, then the states are responsible. If states are unable or unwilling to carry out their responsibilities, then the national government should intervene.

The debate over the most efficient and fair way to finance education will no doubt continue. We have stated that the property tax does not score well on the fairness and efficiency criteria. Moreover, the incidence of the tax is uncertain, especially with respect to renters and rentees. Finally, we observe that many localities compete for industry by giving tax breaks and free services to new businesses. This further undercuts the financial capabilities of the communities.

Parents have primary responsibility for their children. They are responsible for bringing them into the world and providing for most of their needs until they are adults. Within our society, there are many institutional layers that have various responsibilities toward children: family, church, school, locality, state, and so on. Since the roles parents play are so important, children of irresponsible parents are greatly disadvantaged. Even though succeeding lines of defense such as social workers, the courts, and various social programs can be brought into play, they can never compensate for the absence of a nurturing, loving family.

Parents are expected to play important roles in the education of their children. Ideally, schools and parents complement each other. Most Americans share the vision of the parents being involved in the Parent Teacher Association (PTA), volunteering for class excursions and athletic events, and participating in the decision making of local school boards.

For children in the public school system, most expenses are financed through local and state taxes. Church-run schools are heavily subsidized by the church. Nonsectarian private schools that depend on endowments and on parents to pay tuition are usually quite expensive. Various forms of vouchers, some of which are already in operation in some states, would change all of that. The new distribution of financial burdens among taxpayers, parents, and churches will depend on the particular voucher system.

THE DEMOGRAPHICS OF EDUCATION

Demographic factors have great impact on the size and shape of our schools. These factors include the size of enrollments, as well as the ethnic and economic characteristics of the families and their children. The current population of the United States is 260 million, with an enrollment in our public and private schools, grades K through 12, of 50 million. The numbers in each grade have been increasing during the 1990s. The total enrollment during the mid 1980s was around 45 million.

The population continues to grow even though the rate of increase has declined in the decades since the 1960 census. That year reflected the full effect of the baby-boomer generation, those born after World War II. The K through 12 enrollments increased from less than 29 million in 1950 to over 50 million in late 1960s. The more recent bulge in enrollments reflects the children of the baby boomers.[11]

The major challenge in financing comes not from the overall increase but from its geographical concentration. The 9.8 percent growth during the 1980s included growth rates of 22.3 percent in the West, 13.4 percent in the South, 3.4 percent in the Northeast, and only 1.4 percent in the Midwest. Growth has been concentrated in California, Florida, and Texas. Much of that growth has been from immigration. A large percentage of the Mexican immigrants have settled in the metropolitan centers of California. This means that, while some school districts will experience little or no increase in enrollments, others will face dramatic increases. Not only are enrollments increasing, but also the communities and the families within them are in a state of flux. The challenge to the educational system is many-faceted.

Currently, there are two population bulges, one in the age group between 35 and 44 and one in the school-age group 5 to 19 years old. Although the population as a whole is aging, a relatively large part of it will be enrolled in the schools.

Recruiting Teachers

Another demographic factor explains the growing difficulty in recruiting teachers: the 20 to 34 age group is relatively small. Moreover, many of those currently teaching are reaching retirement age.

In recent years, many school districts have been able to reduce student–teacher ratios from twenty to one in the mid-1970s to seventeen to one in the early 1990s. The decline in the number of students and the oversupply of teachers kept salary increases low. In the decades of the 1950s and 1960s, teacher salaries had remained depressed due to traditional gender roles. American education attracted some of the best and brightest women. In the late 1970s and 1980s, greater opportunities began opening for women, but, as noted, dropping enrollments and an oversupply of teachers continued to depress salaries. The combination of lower salaries and attractive alternatives persuaded many talented women to choose other professions.

Now the trends that dampened teacher salaries have been reversed. The demand will remain high for a number of years. The supply of teachers has decreased sharply. The pool of teachers is declining as the older generation retires, and the younger generation has had less incentive to enter teaching. Once salaries increase, there will be a delay before they influence young people entering college and choosing majors.

Demographic Impact and Financial Issues

In summary, several issues in educational finance are being exacerbated by demographic change. Since population growth is very uneven among geographical areas, the question of who is responsible. becomes pertinent. Those local school districts that face large increases in population, much of it moving in from other states and countries, are unlikely to have adequate financial resources.

The disparities in wealth among school districts will continue to grow. The average incomes of white families are well over 50 percent higher than those of black families. Non-Hispanic white families also have incomes 50 percent higher than those of Hispanics as a group. By the year 2000, a significant percentage of the children attending school will come from low-income families. The challenges faced by the children's families will directly affect the schools. Some school districts have a heavy concentration of single-parent families living in poverty. Schools must cope with extra financial demands created by the breakdown of families and the increase in teenage pregnancy.

It is important to assess the impact of these demographic trends in the context of the revenue systems now in place. There are great disparities in financial ability and spending among states, and even greater disparities among local school districts. Recall that local revenues depend largely on property taxes. Not surprisingly, those school districts with high concentrations of families living in poverty are generally those that have low tax bases.

In the early 1990s, ten states had per-pupil expenditures of less than $4,000; three states exceeded $8,000. These disparities among school districts are more worrisome because they result in clearly inadequate educational opportunities provided to the children in some school districts. There are two distinct models of education finance. About half of the states redistribute funds largely on a per-pupil basis, and the other half leave the level of spending largely up to the locality.

Our survey of the demographic projections and the current funding arrangements leads to three conclusions. First, more funds will be needed for teacher salaries. Second, the concentrations of population and low-income families require that states change their revenue-sharing practices. States that now depend heavily on localities to determine spending levels must change to more centralized systems. Otherwise, current trends will lead to even greater disparities. Finally, the federal government needs to take a more active role in spreading the financial burdens caused by the demographic trends.

A Real Concern: Education in the Contexts of Communities

Recent demographic changes have made most communities quite fluid; families must be adaptable and mobile. This fluidity threatens the stability of communities. Religious, racial, and cultural diversity must be accommodated.

As noted, the changes in population are very uneven. Hispanics are concentrated in the West and in Florida. Fifty-five percent of Asian Americans live in the West, whereas 54 percent of blacks live in the South. Projections indicate that the total number of births and the number of white births will drop sharply through the 1990s. Meanwhile the black population will increase over 50 percent, and the Asian population will increase over 300 percent. At the turn of the century, many schools in certain areas of the country will have a significant percentage of minority and immigrant children. In the history of American culture (or rather its cultures), change is nothing new, as the portraits of America as a "melting pot" and as a "land of opportunity" attest. Over the centuries, waves of immigrants have been assimilated while adding their own unique contributions.

Our expectations of the roles public education can play are mixed. On the one hand, we are acutely aware that it has not solved some of our more intractable problems: the breakdown of families, the cycles of poverty in many cities, crime, violence, drugs, and AIDS. On the other hand, the vision of education as an important component of the American dream remains alive.

It is still appropriate to use that vision as a norm—to see where it has applicability and where it does not. Ideally, dedicated teachers interact with eager students. The curriculum lays the foundation for a successful life, opening up a vast array of possibilities. Students learn to respect the rights and aspirations of others. Teachers impart the traditional virtues, including individual and social responsibility.

So what are the roles we realistically expect schools to play? It is generally agreed that our society is becoming much too adversarial. One obvious challenge is to foster a spirit of cooperation and of community. As noted earlier the success of our efforts to improve scholastic achievement depends importantly on instilling a greater sense of individual and social responsibility. Just how school curricula or community–school relationships could influence these attitudes is a difficult but important question.

The challenge is much greater in areas of urban blight, where families find themselves in a cycle of poverty. A recent study by the U.S. Department of Education compared poverty levels and student achievement in rural and urban settings. Poor students in rural settings scored higher than their urban counterparts. Poverty levels are not the only factor.

The urban setting features classes with high enrollments, poor discipline, and high absenteeism among teachers as well as students. There is easy access to drugs and lethal weapons. A large percentage of the students come from dysfunctional families. In our discussion of welfare reform, it was argued that any successful restructuring effort in the inner-city ghettos must be many-faceted. There must be a cooperative effort among government welfare agencies, businesses, churches, civic organizations, and the schools. It would be futile for education policy makers to approach the problem single-handedly. For politicians and others to criticize our public schools for not solving the problems of our inner-city ghettos is disingenuous. Our schools can make a vital contribution, but only as part of a concerted effort.

The discussion of the possible roles schools may play in local communities may seem to have a decidedly communitarian ring. As noted, however, support for public schools is broad; it encompasses a wide spectrum of ideologies to include even our strawman versions of the individualist and egalitarian ideologies. The common thread is that schools are viewed as a necessary means of providing all children with fair starts.

There is also wide support for the back-to-the-basics movement of recent years; within that context there is ample room for disagreement. There is public debate on school prayer, on sex education, and on alternative lifestyles. Public discussions on schools are important. *What* schools teach and *how* they teach it are matters of vital concern to parents and to the entire community. We should expect and welcome continued and wide-ranging discussions of the curriculum.

Most Americans share the belief that schools should be managed primarily by the local community. It is necessary that states play a major role in equalizing funding; however, the participation of local citizens is vital to many of the roles schools play in the community.

A Real Concern: The Curricula and What We Should Teach

The back-to-the-basics movement in American education has enjoyed wide support. As noted earlier, it has enjoyed some success in increasing achievement scores. Without getting lost in minutiae, let us briefly consider how our social goals should influence the curriculum. We have outlined the two goals of preparing students for the job market and of producing well-rounded individuals.

In public discussion, the social goal of preparing students for economic success is given great emphasis. School curricula are frequently evaluated on this criterion. Often the language used is utilitarian or some mixture of utilitarian and efficiency criteria. Preparing students for the job market increases social welfare. The implicit standards of social welfare are taken to be gross domestic product, favorable balance of trade, or low unemployment figures.

The alternative focus is on the well-rounded student; that is, being well-rounded for its own sake, not just for economic success. Here the focus of public discussion is more on the opportunities offered students and what curriculum will best enable them to realize their full potential.

The two social goals are to a great degree complementary. Economic success requires not only technical skills but also well-adjusted, well-motivated workers. Economic development is driven by new technology that requires inventiveness and imagination; and these are often the attributes of self-reliant, well-rounded individuals. However, the two goals are not entirely complementary. We are left with a choice of which goal to emphasize when curricula decisions are made.

In summary, the focus on the well-rounded student is more deontological; the moral principles require respect for persons as an end, not a means. Each person is to be provided with an opportunity to choose and pursue her or his own life plan. The focus on productivity and social welfare is utilitarian. We develop curricula that will produce productive workers and in turn maximize social welfare.

Back-to-the-Basics: Some Reservations

There is some evidence that the goals of the back-to-the-basics movement have been misinterpreted. There is always a danger that teaching techniques and the curriculum will focus on quantifiable results. Education standards and achievement tests will perform important roles in the crusade to improve our schools. But they cannot capture important aspects of learning. For example, math and science *skills* are important but it is equally important for the student to discover the role of *deductive reasoning* in these disciplines. In literature, it is important to read widely, but it is also important to read in depth and to become engaged in the creative process. The focus on vocabulary and grammar is not simply to improve scores but to enable students to better express themselves.

Traditionally, Americans have been committed to a broad education. Students are expected to master basics such as grammar, math, and science, as well as a vast array of subjects that include literature and the fine arts. Education is seen as broadening the students' outlook on life. Great emphasis is placed on extracurricular activities such as sports, student government, journalism, and community service. Indeed, colleges and universities seek the well-rounded student, as opposed to the bookworm. To reiterate, in discussions and evaluations of educational curricula, the purposes should not simply be taken as givens. The criteria must be continually reassessed.

PRIVATIZING SCHOOLS: WHAT RESULTS CAN WE EXPECT?

The advocates of privatizing schools, such as Chubb and Moe, predict that competition in the free market will quickly accomplish all of the educational goals reformers have been seeking for years. Let us review the argument: It starts with the familiar notion of allocative efficiency as derived from the utopian model of laissez-faire capitalism. Perfectly competitive markets respond to the preferences of consumers to produce that combination of goods that maximizes welfare. At the same time, competition insures that goods will be produced at the lowest cost possible.

Of course, education has social as well as private benefits, but theoretically, vouchers can be used to account for the social benefits. The income of parents could be augmented by vouchers so that social and private benefits would be correctly represented in effective demand. The market would respond to the various tastes of parents. Private schools would tailor their products to the individual tastes of different families. Schools would compete to offer the best education at the lowest cost. Privatizing schools would end the stultifying effect of public education's bureaucracies and teacher unions. The fresh air of free market competition would bring innovation and a wide variety of choice.

The proponents of public schools predict another scenario. In the first place, they would argue that the social benefits from education are many and varied. These social benefits cannot all be captured by vouchers augmenting the effective demand of parents. Just as we would not expect the kind of defense we need to be produced if individual families were given defense vouchers, we cannot expect private markets to produce the social benefits inherent in public education.

Even if we ignore the many social benefits that cannot be captured by vouchers, there remains the question of whether or not a free market for private education would be as responsive to parental choice as is claimed. Our more exclusive private schools have their choice of students, not the other way around. In some communities, young married couples start campaigning for entrance to certain schools before their children are born. Of course, for children with certain family backgrounds, the battle is lost before it is begun.

Much depends on the role the voucher is expected to play. There are as many voucher plans as there are proponents. Most plans refer to one or more principles of fairness.

One possible model would provide a voucher sufficient to purchase a standard, socially acceptable level of educational opportunity. Another model would feature vouchers of different amounts relative to the family's income, its ability to pay. Theoretically, the vouchers could be arranged so that the family contribution would reflect equal sacrifice; that is, the family's diminishing marginal utility of income would be estimated.

Some plans assume that some communities will maintain their public schools in competition with private schools. Competition would have the desirable effects of making the remaining public schools more responsive to parents and more efficient; that is, they would have to emulate private schools in order to survive.

We would expect two or more tiers to evolve in most communities. The lower tier would provide schooling for those who were unable or unwilling to augment the vouchers. The public schools supported only by vouchers would find it difficult to compete in terms of quality. Eventually, they would fail. In such cases, the community would have to resurrect its public schools or subsidize a private contractor. The higher tier would provide higher quality education for families able and willing to augment the voucher system.

Plans can also differ according to the financial roles played by federal, state, and local governments. The present public school system is largely financed by some combination of state and local revenues. In about half of the states, most revenues are dispersed roughly on a per pupil basis. In the other half, the state plays a smaller role in equalization, and greater variations occur.

Most voucher systems assume that the state will play the major financial role in funding vouchers. Even so, the tension among wealthier and poorer communities with respect to taxes and benefits will remain, especially if property taxes continue as a major source of revenue. Given the political clout wielded by wealthier communities in most states, it seems likely that wide variations will remain in the dispersion of tax revenues.

In the more egalitarian voucher plans, no augmentation is allowed. Equality is assured by making vouchers the same for every student (subject to regional cost differentials). Although such proposals seem idealistic, if not un-American, they answer the charge that vouchers would foster a more elitist system of education. At the same time, some of the promised efficiencies of the market would be realized. Surprisingly, some of the most ardent advocates of privatization would agree that fairness could only be achieved if school revenues are limited to unaugmented vouchers. These advocates include Chubb and Moe, as well as others.[12] Are they naive? Yes, and unforgivably so. It is safe to say that almost none of the present privatization coalitions would support a system entirely financed by equal vouchers.

It is more reasonable to assume that any voucher system will feature vouchers that would support the lowest acceptable level of educational opportunity. Wealthier parents would augment their vouchers in order to send their children to schools that offer higher-quality education and more homogeneous student bodies.

In previous discussions of revenues and fair starts, it has been pointed out that the revenue systems in some states lead to gross disparities; many school districts are so underfunded that they cannot meet state-mandated standards. Under a system of privatization and vouchers, we can expect those disparities to be increased.

What is missing from most privatization discussions is an appreciation of the various social roles that schools play in local communities and the nation as a whole. Even if it were true that a system of vouchers and private schools would be more efficient in giving parents greater choice, these gains should be weighed against the social benefits that would be lost.

SOME FINAL WORDS

The Issues and the Courts

Not surprisingly, many of the issues being addressed in public debate have been argued in the courts. A review of the courts' decisions makes a useful summary.

Since the constitutions of most states commit themselves to providing quality education, the courts have been challenged to decide just what level of education satisfies that criterion. Generally, the criterion amounts to what we have termed a *socially acceptable minimum*. The courts have also been asked to decide on the relative merits of strict equality versus social-minimum principles.

The point in question in most cases is the fairness of the particular state's system of financing schools. While most states have committed themselves to providing quality education, those states with systems that rely heavily on localities result in wide variations. Moreover, the poorer localities claim that their resources are insufficient to fund the required standards of education.

In an important case that holds a state responsible, the Kentucky State Supreme Court in *Rose v. Council for Better Education* (1989) found that the state's educational system violated the guarantees in its constitution. The court required that the state pass legislation to reorganize the entire system of primary and secondary schools, as well as the way schools were to be financed.

Some History of the Courts and School Finance

Court pronouncements on the states' financial responsibility have evolved over a number of years. In 1912, Sawyer, in a state court case *Sawyer v. Gilmore,* argued that the formula of distribution used in Maine's school finances violated the state's constitution. He argued that the formula resulted in an inferior education for the children in the less wealthy towns. The rights of taxpayers to provide the children of their community a higher-quality education had to be balanced against the rights of other children to an acceptable level. The state Supreme Court, in deciding between fairness to taxpayers and fairness to the children, decided in favor of the taxpayers. The court decided the taxation scheme was equal and uniform and satisfied the constitution. It concluded that the benefits arising from a fair scheme of taxation did not necessarily have to be "enjoyed by all the people to an equal degree." Although the court showed consideration for the rights of taxpayers of wealthier towns, it made clear that distribution rules could be on other bases. In a related state court case in South Dakota, *Dean v. Coddington* (1964), a foundation program seeking to equalize funds among school districts was challenged by taxpayers of one district that did not operate its own schools. This court also distinguished between the principles of fairness in taxation and fairness in distribution and concluded that no "equal protection" requirements in either the South Dakota or the U.S. Constitution limited the power of the state to tax one district and to distribute those funds to another.

The U.S. Supreme Court case of *Brown v. Board of Education of Topeka* (1954) is significant in two ways: it applied the equal protection clause of the U.S. Constitution to access in education, and it ruled that public education was a constitutional right.

The Kansas law allowed Topeka to operate segregated schools and thus require a student, Linda Brown, to attend an all-black school even though an all-white school was more convenient. The Court declared that educational opportunity was a right that must be made available "on equal terms." The Court essentially reversed the *Plessy v. Ferguson* (1896) decision that had specified the separate-but-equal doctrine. Segregated schools could never be equal; they deprived the plaintiff of the equal protection of the law guaranteed by the Fourteenth Amendment.

What Are the States' Financial Responsibilities?

In several cases in the 1960s, the courts considered the fairness of state funding schemes; in each case, they deferred to the legislatures. In both *McInnis v. Shapiro* (1968) in Illinois, which was decided by a federal district court and *Burrows v. Wilkerson* (1969), which was decided in the state courts in Virginia, the courts allowed that wide differences in funding could exist among localities. However, in the Virginia case, the court served notice that the state's General Assembly should "undoubtedly" come to the relief of students in underfunded districts.

The equal protection interpretations evolved to another level in the 1970s. In a series of California state court cases known as *Serrano v. Priest* (1971 to 1988) it was argued that heavy reliance on property taxes resulted in wide disparities and violated equal protection under both the U.S. and California Constitutions. Here the state's foundation scheme was aimed at guaranteeing that each district could reach, or exceed, a certain minimum. It is appropriate to phrase this in the language we have developed in our social ethics approach. Thus, we see that the socially acceptable minimum principle was being applied to educational opportunity.

The plaintiffs argued that the quality of education received by a student should not depend on the wealth of the children's parents nor on the geographical accident of the children's residence. The California Supreme Court noted that differences were not simply a function of the tax base but of the willingness of residents in a district to tax themselves. The court approved of the idea of a guaranteed minimum with some differences added by localities. At the same time it imposed a limitation on the maximum per-pupil expenditures.

Is Education a Fundamental Right?

The early Serrano cases implied that education was a fundamental right, but before the series of cases were finally settled, the U.S. Supreme Court had spoken. In *San Antonio Independent School District v. Rodriguez* (1971), the Court held that education was not a fundamental right. It reasoned that education was not specified by the Constitution as one of the rights requiring explicit protection. Moreover, the Court could find no "basis for saying it is implicitly so protected." Needless to say, this goes against a number of the principles and lines of arguments we have pursued in this study.

In the *Rodriguez* case, the U.S. Supreme Court took up the issue of whether or not wealthier school districts could raise additional funds over and above the minimum level required by the state. The Court decided that it could. Equal protection did not require "absolute equality or precisely equal advantages." Thus, again, justice is assumed to be served if students are provided a socially acceptable minimum of educational opportunity.

What Is an Acceptable Minimum of Educational Opportunity?

In a series of cases in New Jersey, the courts considered the questions of unequal local resources and wide disparities in per-pupil expenditures. In *Robinson v. Cahill* (1973 to 1976), the court found that the state did not "effectively equalize." The New Jersey Supreme Court acknowledged that the system did not effectively equalize but cited *Rodriguez* to the effect that strict equalization is not required. It also noted that education had been declared not to be a fundamental right. Nevertheless, the New Jersey Supreme Court decided to focus on its state's own constitution that required that it support a "thorough and efficient" system of free public schools for all children ages five through eighteen. The court determined that the state's system was not "thorough and efficient." Moreover, the state was required to define in some way what the *educational obligation* should be. The local districts could then be compelled to provide that level of opportunity. The court held this minimum level to be "that educational opportunity which is needed in the contemporary setting to equip a child for his role as a citizen and as a competitor in the labor market."

Finally, the court spoke in the lines of defense analogy we have used. If the less-wealthy school districts could not be expected to provide the minimum level, the state had final responsibility. It must reorganize funding in order to meet the "thorough and efficient" standard. The state responded by setting up a process by which local and state educational goals would be established and reviewed. The court later added the stipulation that the "thorough and efficient" standard required at least the setting of a minimum level in terms of dollars spent. Thus, we see that the trend in recent court cases and legislation has been to evaluate state funding in terms of the language of state constitutions rather than the federal equal protection standard. Recently, states, with the encouragement of the courts, have begun to develop funding standards. In addition to New Jersey, California, Kentucky, and Texas, over half of the states have begun the process. But, of course, the language of each state's constitution is different. In Texas the focus has been on the language "a general diffusion of knowledge," while in Montana the standard is "quality public schools." Several states consider the meaning of the term *efficiency* in ways similar to the New Jersey and Kentucky cases.

Subsequent litigation in New Jersey further extended the "thorough and efficient" standard to something well beyond the idea of a social minimum. In a series of cases termed *Abbott v. Burke* (1985, 1990) students from poor districts argued that, although the court had approved the state's funding scheme that resulted from the *Robinson* cases, the final result still failed children in the poorer districts. The New Jersey Supreme Court agreed. Interestingly enough the court declared the overall scheme to be fair but unconstitutional with respect to the poorer district. Special funding arrangements must be made to bring the poorer urban districts up to the "level of property-rich districts." Moreover, the level of funding must be "adequate to provide for the special educational needs of those poorer urban districts in order to redress their extreme disadvantages" (*Abbott v. Burke II*, 1990). The judges did not presume that the social problems of the inner cities could be solved by the schools, but they were sure that greater educational opportunity needed to be part of the answer. Moreover they believed it self-evident that "even if not a cure, money will help."

It is not surprising that the issues that are important in public debate have been contested in the courts. The question of who is responsible for providing education has been clearly resolved: the state.

The question of what moral principles to use in determining the distribution of funds would seem to have been resolved in favor of the idea of a social minimum, with localities free to augment according to their ability and choice. In several recent cases, however, the idea that all students should have "equal educational opportunity" has reemerged.

The courts in several states have insisted that the legislatures clarify what the appropriate level of educational opportunity should be. One interesting observation is that, in the New Jersey cases, the state courts are insisting on a minimum level considerably higher than that found in many other states.

With respect to the question of fairness to taxpayers, two rules have emerged. The states clearly have the right to tax wealthier school districts and to transfer those funds to poorer districts. This is justified as promoting the social good. Moreover, there is a limit to what effort can be expected of the poorer districts in meeting educational standards.

Again, while reference is often given to the idea of *equality* of educational opportunity, the principle of allowing wealthier districts to spend more is also frequently honored. On the other hand, judges assessing the prospects of children in the urban inner cities concluded that greater levels of spending would partially overcome their extreme disadvantages.

Finally, another interesting idea that has emerged in several contexts is that a maximum should be set on how much some wealthier districts should spend. We will not pursue this idea here, but we note in passing that usually the prohibition against spending too much assumes that there are some scarce resources being bid away from those with less financial clout.

Let us end with a word about fair starts. We agree that exactly equal starts are impossible. However, this does not resolve the conflict between the principle of equal starts and the rights of parents to give their children advantages. Neither we nor the courts have been able to resolve the question of how far local taxpayers should be able to go beyond the socially acceptable level. However, the courts indicated that there should be a maximum.

As to the question of how high the acceptable minimum should be, the answer of the New Jersey Supreme Court was: "The educational opportunity needed in the contemporary setting to equip a child for his role as a citizen and as a competitor in the labor market." The fair start here refers to the child's roles in the social, political, and economic spheres. The social minimum is to be much more than a safety net; the fair start includes a wide range of opportunities.

SUGGESTIONS FOR FURTHER READING

David C. Berliner and Bruce J. Biddle, *The Manufactured Crisis* (Reading, Mass.: Addison-Wesley, 1995). A diatribe against what Berliner and Biddle see as a campaign to discredit public schools. An effective antidote to much of the conventional wisdom that our schools have failed.

John Chubb and Terry Moe, *Politics, Markets and America's Schools* (Washington, D.C.: The Brookings Institution, 1990). The argument for privatizing schools. Recall that Chubb and Moe assume that equal vouchers would fund education.

John F. Jennings, ed., *National Issues in Education* (Washington, D.C.: Institute for Educational Leadership, 1993). A collection of readings representing different sides of the reform and funding debates.

K. Forbes Jordan and Teresa S. Lyons, *Financing Public Education in an Era of Change* (Bloomington, In.: Phi Delta Kappa Educational Foundation, 1992). An outline of school funding issues.

National Commission on Excellence in Education, *A Nation at Risk: The Imperative for Educational Reform* (Washington, D.C.: U.S. Department of Education, 1983). The original report of President Reagan's commission to make recommendations on educational reform.

ENDNOTES

1. See Theodore C. Sorensen, *Kennedy* (New York: Harper and Row, 1965), p. 528.
2. National Commission on Excellence in Education, *A Nation at Risk: The Imperative for Educational Reform* (Washington, D.C.: U.S. Department of Education, 1983).
3. John Chubb and Terry Moe, *Politics, Markets, and America's Schools* (Washington, D.C.: The Brookings Institution, 1990).
4. Ian Westbury, "Comparing American and Japanese Achievement," *Educational Researcher* (21) 5 (1992), pp. 18–24.
5. Edith M. Rasell and Lawrence Mishel, *Shortchanging Education* (Washington, D.C.: Economic Policy Institute, 1990).
6. Ibid., Rasell and Mishel used data from the *Statistical Yearbook* (New York: UNESCO, 1988) and the *Digest of Educational Statistics* (Washington D.C.: National Center for Education Statistics, 1988).
7. James Coleman, Ernest Campbell, Carol Hobson, James McPartland, Alexander Mood, Frederick Weinfeld, and Robert York, *Equality of Educational Opportunity*, (Washington, D.C.: U.S. Government Printing Office, 1966), p. 325.
8. Richard Hernstein and Charles Murray, *The Bell Curve* (New York: The Free Press, 1994).
9. See, for example, Stephen Ceci "How Much Does Schooling Influence General Intelligence and Its Cognitive Component? A Reassessment of the Evidence," *Development Psychology* (27) 5 (1991), pp. 703–22.
10. See Table 1.1, Service Sector Productivity (Washington, D.C.: McKinsey Global Institute, 1992).
11. For demographic projections, see U.S. Bureau of the Census, *Projections of the Population by States, by Age, Sex, and Race: 1988 to 2010*, Current Population Reports, Series P-25, No. 1017 (Washington, D.C.: U.S. Government Printing Office, 1989); and U.S. Bureau of the Census, *Projections of the Population of the United States by Age, Sex, and Race: 1988 to 2080*, Current Population Reports, Series P-25, No. 1018 (Washington, D.C.: U.S. Government Printing Office, 1989).
12. See Chubb and Moe, *Politics, Markets*; also J. E. Coons, W. H. Clune, III, and S. D. Sugarman, *Private Wealth and Public Education* (Cambridge, Mass: Harvard University Press, 1970).

5

Moral Choices and Health Care Policies

Recent health care debates feature two broad issues: Should health care be available to all? and How can health care costs be contained? If society has a moral obligation to insure health care for all, what are the difficulties in achieving this goal? How can it best be achieved? Given that increases in health care costs must be curtailed, how are resources to be rationed? What sorts of rationing decisions must be made and who should make them?

Within these two broad issues, coverage and costs, there are many facets. Before focusing on each part let us consider how they fit into the larger picture.

Currently health care insurance coverage in the United States is largely *employer-based*. About 60 percent of Americans are covered by employer-sponsored health insurance, and these policies pay about one-third of all medical expenses. The government provides coverage for the elderly and permanently disabled through Medicare and for the very poor (mainly those receiving welfare benefits) through Medicaid. In August of 1996, the Kennedy-Kassebaum insurance reform bill required insurance companies that provide employer-based policies to arrange for workers who change or lose their jobs to retain coverage. It also included an extensive four-year trial program for some 750,000 individuals who were previously uninsured. They are offered a package of medical savings accounts and insurance policies covering major expenses. There remains a very large gap in coverage. Over forty million low-income Americans are left with little or no access to health care insurance. When insurance is available the costs are often prohibitive. For most Americans this situation is not simply a matter of public debate; it is a national disgrace. The failure to provide universal coverage reveals deficiencies in both our political and our economic systems.

As with other social issues we will begin by asking why we cannot rely on free markets to allocate resources to health care; what are the missing conditions that lead to market failure? What is peculiar about health care markets? Our list will include a number of the conditions described in chapter two. We ask first whether health care is a private or a public good. A related question is whether or not health care is considered a human right. In either case the market cannot be relied upon and government intervention may be appropriate.

The structure of the health care industry is changing rapidly in response to changes in technology. New forms of business organization are evolving: health maintenance organizations (HMOs) and preferred provider organizations (PPOs) are replacing the traditional relationships among doctors, hospitals, and patients. At the same time insurance companies and hospitals, as well as physicians and other health care professionals, are forming new alliances of countervailing economic power. These developments may lead to new forms of competition, monopoly, oligopoly, and collusion that are not in the public's interest. This raises questions as to how government could regulate and set parameters so that the changing market structure would lead to more fairness and efficiency.

Several kinds of information asymmetry affect competition in health care markets. The most obvious asymmetry is between physician and patient. The physician has an informational advantage that he or she could exploit, say by prescribing expensive, but unneeded, treatment. A second type of asymmetry exists among insurance companies and prospective policyholders. Here potential buyers know more about their own health prospects than companies attempting to write policies. Once

> **Health Maintenance Organizations (HMOs)** integrate the finance and delivery of health care. HMOs contract to provide comprehensive medical care on a capitation basis. The HMO's profit depends on keeping costs down. It does so by using leverage over the salaries and fees it pays to physicians, hospitals, pharmacies, drug companies, and other health care providers. The access of patients to specialists is screened. The number of persons covered by HMOs is expanding rapidly.

> **Preferred Provider Organizations (PPOs)** use traditional fee-for-service payments for physicians. Insurance companies contract with PPOs and their physicians to provide services at reduced rates. The patients are free to choose among health care providers, but the coinsurance payments are lower with those health care providers in the PPO.

a health policy is written, the process of *adverse selection* begins. Only those who stand to benefit most from the insurance; that is, those most prone to the illnesses covered, will select that particular policy. This process requires that the company continually raise the premiums. Unless the insurance company can develop efficient, cost-effective screening procedures, no insurance will be offered. This result, when an obvious need draws no response from potential suppliers, is known as an *incomplete market*.

Health insurance, like other types of insurance, encourages the phenomenon we have termed *moral hazard*. In some cases, having insurance causes one to take greater risks. Obviously, health care insurance encourages individuals to take greater advantage of health care services. Some people may even lead lifestyles that put their health at greater risk. Since final payments for health services are made by a third party, neither physician nor patient has incentive to contain costs. A straightforward strategy to reduce the costs associated with moral hazard and *third-party payment* effects is to require that the patient pay part of the bill. This would be in the form of a deductible and/or a copayment. This strategy raises further questions of fairness and efficiency. Although higher rates increase efficiency, they also limit the access of lower-income groups to health care.

The medical savings account approach of the Kennedy-Kassebaum health insurance bill promises to change incentives and overcome the moral hazard and third-party-payment effects. The medical savings accounts, which are tax-deductible, would be used to pay for routine expenses such as visits to the doctor. In theory, individuals will use these services only when necessary and will shop around for the most cost-effective treatment. Competition among doctors and other health care providers will lower their charges. Whether or not the market will respond in these ways remains to be seen. Most people take care in choosing their physicians and are not inclined to shop around. And while economists generally endorse the idea of using insurance only for "big ticket" emergencies, most people would rather have *all* of their health care costs covered. For example, most of the elderly buy supplementary insurance policies for that purpose.

Another, more serious, objection to the medical savings account approach is that some people, particularly poor people, will have greater incentive to forgo doctor visits for minor symptoms and to forgo regular checkups. Currently, many serious illnesses could be avoided by what is termed *preventive medicine*. This unfortunate tendency would be strengthened by the medical savings account approach.

An interesting feature of the large-scale trial program is that it offers an opportunity to test these theories. It will be interesting to see what part, if any, the new payment system will have in curtailing costs. We can also observe how much shopping around and competition among doctors takes place. It will also be interesting to see whether or not the program gains wide public support and what effect, if any, it has on the practice of preventive medicine.

Several other moral conflicts arise from the present system of coverage. One interesting question relates to the *insurance pools* that now exist. Who is to be excluded and why? The exclusion of 40 million persons with low incomes is, of course, indefensible. But that aside, consider the configuration of existing pools. The employer-based pools are essentially an historical accident. The adverse selection phenomenon necessitates pools made up of persons whose freedom to shop around is limited. It is unlikely that a person will change jobs on the basis of a better health care package, and a captive audience is precisely what is required to overcome the adverse selection problem. Employer-based insurance, therefore, evolved by default; no other pooling arrangements were available. The government has encouraged an employer-based system through tax incentives to employers and employees.

Since the Medicare and Medicaid programs provide coverage at low or no cost, respectively, and since the pools' boundaries are straightforward, no adverse selection problems arise.

How we justify the existing pools, especially the employer-based pools, remains an enigma. It has been proposed that the uninsured be offered coverage by assigning them to enlarged employer-based pools. What criteria would be appropriate for such assignments?

The second set of issues running through the health care debate concerns costs. How do we curtail costs? How will health care be rationed? Again, for most goods and services we leave rationing to the market. Consumers, workers, businesses, and others operating within competitive markets have incentives to allocate resources efficiently. While market incentives are important to resource allocation in health care markets, the rationing function is not left to market forces. Somehow the same two questions must be answered: Who is to receive health care and how is it to be financed? Until recently, the system of third-party payment encouraged the introduction of new technology and treatment no matter how expensive. Developers of improved drugs, equipment, and procedures could be sure that they would be adopted regardless of cost. The blank-check era ended in the 1980s, but the question of how best to ration health care is yet to be resolved. The approach we will take assumes that there are several types of rationing and each can be best accomplished at some appropriate stage of the decision-making process. For example, major rationing decisions are made at the federal budget level, others are made at the state or regional level, and still others are made between physician and patient. At each level, a set of moral dilemmas must somehow be resolved. In theory at least, there is some rational way to organize the decision-making process. This requires that the rationing decisions be made at appropriate levels by qualified parties using appropriate criteria.

The new health care proposals necessarily address the question of how health care is to be financed. How are the principles of fair and efficient taxation to be applied? Since health care creates private as well as social benefits, both the benefit and ability-to-pay principles will apply.

Should "money talk"? Assuming wealthy persons are to be allowed to purchase better health care than the poor, should there be limits on what can and cannot be purchased? How should scarce resources, such as organ transplants, be allocated?

Questions of intergenerational justice also arise in the health care debate. The Medicare program is financed primarily by payroll taxes. The benefits to the elderly are essentially a transfer from the working-age generations. Both the Medicare and the Social Security systems are financed in a similar way and must be organized to face the impending retirement of the baby-boomer generation. Is there some system of financing, featuring the buildup of trust funds, that will preserve the fairness of the necessary intergenerational transfers?

This brief survey demonstrates that, as public debate over health care coverage and costs proceeds, many related issues must also be resolved. We now turn to a closer look at issues related to coverage.

WHY GOVERNMENT INTERVENTION IS REQUIRED

Most health care markets depart from our ideal, perfect competition in a number of important ways. It follows that in those areas where health care is left to free markets a variety of market failures occur. It also follows that these unique characteristics should be appreciated when reform of public health care programs is undertaken.

Coverage: Who Is Covered and Why

In recent years the structure of the health care industry has undergone dramatic change. The reliance on employer-based insurance pools continues, but the pay-for-service system in which patients go to the physician of their choice is being replaced. According to where you work, you may or may not have options as to which HMO you join. Within the HMO you may or may not have a choice of physicians. At each stage of the health care delivery system there are "gatekeepers" to verify whether or not you need treatment and whether or not a specialist is required. The HMO networks have leverage not only over their members but over physicians, hospitals, medical equipment suppliers, and drug companies. Predictably, physicians and other health care suppliers are organizing so as to achieve countervailing bargaining power.

The Medicare and Medicaid programs, introduced in 1965 during President Johnson's Great Society initiatives, have grown rapidly. These programs have also been reorganized so that leverage can be brought to bear on doctors and hospitals. Rates for Medicare are set on a regional basis and by diagnosis. The resulting rate structures, based on "diagnostic related groups" are substantially below the market rates. Medicare and Medicaid are undergoing significant reform. Medicaid is being shifted to the states and will be restructured by each state within certain federal parameters.

Americans' concerns over health care coverage have many facets. When illnesses occur they can easily cost tens of thousands of dollars, and some can cost hundreds of thousands. For a family with no insurance this means the loss of all that they have worked for. As noted, over forty million U. S. citizens have no health coverage at all. Most of these uninsured people are low-income families who must run the risk of going without insurance because it is either unavailable or prohibitively expensive.

It is ironic that the United States has such a large percentage of its population with no coverage while at the same time we spend much more per person on health care than any other nation. Most European countries have national health programs that cover all of their citizens. These programs range from socialized medicine to national health insurance plans augmented with private insurance. Most of these government programs pay the great majority of expenses (typically over 70 percent). In Norway, for example, 98 percent of health bills are paid by the public system.

Paradoxically, although most economic analyses of rising health costs in the United States point to the third-party payment system (i.e., government or a private insurance company) as a major factor, most of the European countries with extensive third-party (i.e., government) financing devote a much lower percentage of their GDP to health care than does the United States. Norway, again, for example, devotes 8 percent, while the United States devotes over 15 percent.

In addition to the forty million Americans with no coverage there are other gaps. The existing array of insurance policies exhibit a diversity of limitations on coverage. There are substantial differences among policies in their coverage of catastrophic illness. Paradoxically most policies have *caps* on how much they will pay during the lifetime of a policyholder. This practice seems counterintuitive since the purpose of health insurance is to protect the insured against the possibility of large medical bills. Most patients have financial resources of their own that are sufficient for the less expensive treatment.

Medicaid covers virtually all of the costs when those who qualify become ill. The poor have no obligations; however, the doctors and hospitals are usually paid at rates below the normal fees. Medicare, by contrast, covers only 45 percent of the medical costs of the elderly and disabled. Here again the payment scheme seems counterintuitive. As a group the elderly are much more prone to prolonged, expensive illness that could ruin them financially. What is needed is a payment scheme that pays everything *after* a certain level is reached. Most of the elderly (80 percent) do in fact have supplementary policies. It is the elderly poor, those with the greatest risk, who are unwilling or unable to purchase supplementary policies.

Government Failure

Since World War II more than fifty initiatives for a national health insurance have been introduced and have failed. In the 1992 presidential campaign and during the first year of the Clinton administration, opinion polls revealed that, for the first time, a large majority of Americans favored a comprehensive national health care plan and radical overhaul to control costs and provide universal coverage. One poll during the 1992 presidential campaign revealed that a majority of those polled favored a national health service based on that of Canada. The plan that emerged during the campaign and Clinton's first year in office reflected the changing institutional structure in the health care industry, the rise of managed care arrangements such as HMOs. The Clinton plan was built around the idea of "managed competition," which featured regional organizations dealing with HMOs that would bid on coverage. However, when the Clinton initiatives were subjected to the politics of the Congressional legislative process and a concerted campaign of adverse publicity, they failed. During the bargaining process the integrity of the original plan was eroded. The repeated failure of Americans to enact universal health care insurance legislation underlines our differences with other Western democracies. Although Americans share both egalitarian and individualist values, the ascendancy of individualism precludes many social initiatives. We have much more faith in free markets and much more distrust of government than other democracies. The legislative process continues to reflect the original purposes of separation of powers, of checks and balances. The interests of small groups are protected and the government's ability to deal with social issues is curtailed.

Our nation's inability to address and act on health care issues does not mean that they go away, nor does it mean that health care markets remain static. The institutional setting is undergoing rapid change as more and more patients and health care providers are organized into managed care arrangements. As the idea of countervailing powers suggests, other players in the game—physicians, hospitals, employer consortiums, localities, and states—are also organizing so as to gain bargaining power. In summary, our national values, our health care institutions, and our perceptions of what is possible are all in a state of flux. It is within this context that we will now seek to apply moral reasoning to a few of the many health care issues.

Health Care: A Private Good or a Social Good?

Health care by nature has both private and public benefits. A good whose benefits are private can be priced and sold and will be provided efficiently by free markets. Obviously, health care can be sold; a physician can sell services to individual patients, as can nurses, hospitals, drug companies, and other health care providers. There would be a substantial allocation of resources to health care even without government programs.

But there are public as well as private benefits and costs. There are external benefits and costs that affect the family and friends of those who need health care. There are broad social and economic benefits from promoting a healthy citizenry and workforce.

These externalities and the several other market failures we have listed seem to justify several types of government intervention in the health care industry. In addition to these efficiency arguments there are important moral considerations.

Health Care as a Right

The argument that health care is a natural right is straightforward. If one has a right to life, the right to health care, as well as other necessities, is easily derived.

Arguments from Kantian ethics are equally straightforward. If we respect each person as an end and if we respect that person's right to follow her or his life goals, then health is a necessary condition. Certain mental and physical capabilities are required.

Rawls, we recall from chapter one, defines primary goods as "things that every man is presumed to want" and that "normally have a use whatever a person's rational plan of life."[1] There are social goods such as rights and liberties, powers and opportunities, income and wealth, and self-respect. Health, vigor, intelligence, and imagination all qualify as natural primary goods.

Without government intervention, the market would exclude many of the poor from receiving adequate health care. Even if health care markets were perfectly competitive, the moral standing of health care would require that it not be rationed by market forces.

As with many moral principles the idea that health and other necessities are rights has become a generally held social value. Over the centuries immigrants have arrived in America and many have taken low-income jobs. From these humble beginnings many of them and their children have become successful. For many the status of being poor is only temporary. These social myths or parables have some grounding in history; but more important, they have become expressions of our social morality. Our moral intuitions of fair starts and fair play tell us that good health is a necessary condition for the disadvantaged to have a chance to succeed. Without the means to purchase health care insurance many of the poor are at risk. Without proper health care they may fall victim to an illness that may result in death or permanent disability.

Query: If Health Care Is a Right, Who Owes What to Whom?

The utilitarian approach to this question is problematical. In applying the credo of the greatest good for the greatest number, the usual approach is to give no special value to the condition of a particular individual. Of course one must be alive to experience happiness, and society's happiness cannot be maximized unless most people are alive. Yet, if the loss of one life (or the slavery of one person) would create a greater net happiness for the rest of society, then that life should be sacrificed, according to this approach. On the other hand, Rule Utilitarianism could provide a more plausible approach, if, for example, a rule could be made that all should receive adequate health care. The argument would have to be made that a rule recognizing health care as a right would create a net long-run benefit to society as a whole.

The libertarian approach, although born of the values of individualism, is counterintuitive. Essentially the individual is responsible to no one. If I were to pass a small child who had fallen into a shallow pool, I would have no obligation to save his or her life and the child would have no right to expect me to act. Of course most libertarians assume that I would in fact save the child, but I am free to do as I wish. Moreover, in theory at least, everyone in society could unanimously agree to have government take the necessary actions to insure health care for all.

Under deontological approaches the duty to respect the life of another is given high priority. Deontological moral theorists would agree that resolution of some moral dilemmas may involve sacrificing one person's life for the lives of others or for other moral principles. But they would agree that the trade-offs are different in kind from the utilitarian argument; the life of each person has intrinsic value.

Now let us turn to another set of questions. Where does my own responsibility toward the health of others begin and end? Let us assume that I agree that I have a duty to save the child in the shallow pool. Perhaps I do not even have to get my feet wet!

But where does this all end? Am I now duty bound to answer every television appeal for charity, say, appeals by actresses asking for money to save a child in Biafra? Is this my duty or would it simply be a generous gesture? The question of who is owed what by whom covers the whole spectrum of social relationships: What do individuals owe each other? What are family members owed? What are members of society owed? One possible answer to the question of Whom do we owe? is to acknowledge some form of obligation to every other human being.

In an ideal Kantian world in which each has a duty to respect others and their goals, it follows that each person is also obligated to have self-respect and to follow one's own life plan. In practical terms each person must depend on larger organizations to fulfill such broad obligations. Returning once again to the constitutional convention analogy, we observe that many rights and duties have been enumerated in the Bill of Rights and in various other types of legislation. Moreover the enumeration of rights and duties, obligations and entitlements continues in current legislation to include the issues and programs of our study. The point is that, while we as individuals may acknowledge some obligations to every other person, we depend on a wide range of economic, political, and social institutions to carry them out. In each society there are different divisions of responsibility among individuals, families, and other social institutions. In most cases there are several lines of defense. In most societies, parents have primary responsibility for their children. However, if parents fail, secondary lines of defense such as the extended family and social workers come into play.

Query: Are There Limits to One's Health Care Rights?

How much health care is enough? When accidents and illnesses occur, how much effort and money should be spent? Is everyone owed some *satisficing* level of effort to restore or maintain one's normal functioning?

The idea of satisficing is more useful than the idea of maximizing for deciding what effort is owed. In the economics of the firm, satisficing refers to a method of setting priorities in which one goal must be reached first, and then attention can be turned to others. For example, the firm's managers may feel it necessary to first meet a certain, expected level of dividends to its shareholders. After that is met the remaining profits can be allocated using other criteria. With health care we may also wish to consider a satisficing level. Here our focus would be on maintaining or restoring a certain level of normal functioning for the individual. Thus, we do not ask whether or not we spend the same amount on each individual, and we do not set limits on what we may spend on each in-

> **Satisficing** is a method of accounting for two or more goals by satisfying one goal before turning to the others. Presumably the first goal can be achieved without exhausting all available resources. Once that is done, the attention and resources can be devoted to secondary goals.

dividual. What we ask is what it takes to maintain or restore an individual to a certain "acceptable" level of normal functioning. Obviously this idea creates its own set of problems and moral dilemmas. What exactly is normal functioning? What mental and physical capacities are included and how are they to be weighed? With some accidents and illnesses restoration of one or more important capabilities becomes impossible so we must redefine the satisficing level for that person.

Minicase: Should Health Care Insurance Cover Cosmetic Surgery?

Here the concept and definition of normal functioning becomes important. Since the term *cosmetic* is being used, we are not dealing with one's fundamental right to life. Instead we must ask what are the individual's legitimate expectations and aspirations. Consider first a purely cosmetic procedure such as a face-lift, in which the patient simply wishes to remove some wrinkles. Suppose that the patient's insurance is employer-based and covers this type of surgery. This coverage increases the cost of the insurance. The burden would be borne by fellow employees who would pay higher rates and receive lower wages (since in theory the employer's share is shifted to the employee as lower wages). Ultimately, taxpayers would bear some part of the burden since health insurance enjoys certain tax breaks.

Let us assume that most of those in the insurance pool believe that it is not fair for face-lifts to be covered. Say this elective, cosmetic surgery costs five thousand dollars. If not covered, it would be available only to those who wish to pay for it. Of course this type of cosmetic surgery may be very important to the self-image of some people. Should its availability be rationed by market forces? Should we deny a face-lift to persons simply because they have limited financial resources?

Consider next a case in which cosmetic surgery is not being done because of normal aging but is related to surgery for breast cancer. In fact there is an ongoing national debate as to whether or not reconstructive, cosmetic surgery should be covered when mastectomies are performed. Here, as in every case, the costs of such surgery must be considered. Let us assume that safe reconstructive surgery that restores the breast to its original contours is, in fact, available and available at an extra cost of six thousand dollars if performed at the same time as a mastectomy. Again we have the question of who should pay: fellow employees and fellow taxpayers or the individual? What part do psychological considerations such as one's sense of well-being and self-esteem play in our evaluation? Does it make a difference that in the face-lift case we are dealing with a normal aging process that perhaps we should all accept with some grace? By contrast, in the mastectomy case we are easing the burden of a surgical attempt to combat a cruel, arbitrary threat to a person's life.

It is not difficult to construct variations on this theme. We could describe situations in which some sort of cosmetic surgery is more or less crucial to a person's self-esteem or a person's chances of success in a given profession. We could vary the odds of whether or not the medical treatment will be successful. We could vary the cost of the procedure and thus the severity of the burden. We can also construct cases in which more basic functions are at stake: one's sense of seeing, hearing, feeling, smelling, or one's ability to walk, drive a car, or play golf. It is an understatement to say that the idea of "normal functioning" lacks precision. Nevertheless we will find it a necessary starting point for many health care related issues.

Query: What Is Society's Duty toward Individuals Who Behave Irresponsibly?

Consider first the question of buying adequate insurance. We start from an extreme libertarian position. Suppose a group of libertarians has somehow agreed to establish an economic system. All are free to find work, earn money, and purchase health care insurance if they wish. Some may decide to take their chances and invest their savings. Their hope is that by the time they experience a health problem they will have accumulated sufficient wealth to afford treatment. Libertarians would never limit an individual's freedom to make such a choice. Now suppose the strategy fails and an illness strikes. Other libertarians may well honor the individual's choice to bear the risk and suffer the consequences. Since the individual had no right to expect help in the first place, the question of whether or not the behavior has been irresponsible is moot.

By contrast, suppose we consider health care a right that is grounded in the duty of others to honor that right. What, if any, are the responsibilities of the individual? Is it the responsibility of society to give the individual an opportunity to buy insurance? Or is it society's responsibility to require that everyone buy insurance? When individuals are left free and decide not to buy insurance, what happens to society's responsibility?

Suppose further that some individuals are irresponsible with regard to their health. Should skiers, bungee jumpers, mountain climbers, and sky divers pay extra premiums? Should smokers, drug addicts, alcoholics, and gluttons pay extra premiums? Each of us may answer these questions differently. Answers to such questions may help give us insight into the nature and dimensions of the right to health care.

We now turn to a related question. What role would health care rights play if no efficiency problems existed?

IF HEALTH CARE MARKETS WERE EFFICIENT WOULD THEY ALSO BE JUST?

We have observed that market failures, such as those caused by asymmetric information, have led to employer-based health insurance and in some cases to incomplete markets. If the efficiency problems could be resolved, would that be enough? Or would there still be unresolved questions of fairness?

One problem, we recall, is that prospective policyholders know much more about their own health than does the insurance company. If the insurance company designs a policy for the general public, there is a danger that only those with the poorest risks will purchase policies. Insurance companies attempt to overcome their informational deficiencies by requiring physical examinations, medical histories, waiting periods, and exclusion of preexisting conditions. These practices are expensive. The insurance companies will only carry them to the point at which the added information costs are equal to the added revenue.

In practice it is not feasible for insurance companies to overcome the difficulties created by information asymmetries. But now suppose that the market failures could be overcome. Suppose, for example, that insurance companies found inexpensive methods for identifying the good-risk and bad-risk individuals and for offering policies that reflect those risks. The result would meet our efficiency criteria. Prices would reflect marginal costs and consumers would buy different policies according to the marginal benefits they expect. These market processes would lead to a more efficient allocation of resources.

We are left with the question of whether or not the efficiency and fairness criteria may be in conflict. The idea of *allocative efficiency* links consumer preferences to allocation at the lowest possible cost. When the opportunities of consumers to make choices are improved, their welfare will also be improved. Allocative efficiency will be improved as insurance companies are able to tailor their policies to the risks different buyers wish to assume. For example, policies could feature lower and higher deductible and copayment levels corresponding with lower and higher premiums. We might well agree that both efficiency and fairness would be improved if those who abuse their health were required to pay higher rates. But is it fair that some of the poor would be priced out of the insurance market because of health risks that are no fault of their own?

The debate over national health care insurance has raised other ethical and efficiency comparisons. We are members of many types of pools, but rarely if ever do we ask whether or not they are efficient and fair. Are there special characteristics that logically place some people in one risk pool and others in another? Are there special considerations that explain why some people should pay more than others? Who should be in what pool? In summary, we have observed that (1) health care markets are characterized by several types of market failure, (2) no pools would be necessary with perfect knowledge, and (3) even with perfect competition the market's allocation of health care would not be fair.

What rationale can there be for an employer-based care system? There seems to be no answer except that there are no other candidates. In one sense it is simply an historical accident that has been facilitated by government tax policy. Other nations have followed other paths to arrive at their present health care systems. An explanation of why we have arrived at our present system (in which coverage is not universal) would be complex and would require a thorough interdisciplinary approach. For a number of reasons, universal-health-coverage plans have failed to run the gauntlet of our legislative processes. There will continue to be tension between what is efficient and fair and what is politically feasible.

If we are hard pressed to justify employer-based insurance pools, are there more rational options? Would neighborhood, citywide, regional, statewide, or some other pooling be more efficient and fair? There may be efficiency considerations that call for a smaller or larger area to be administered. For example, local officials may be able to take better account of special local conditions. Alternatively, there may be economies of scale that favor larger numbers. These considerations, however, may not relate directly to the question of what should be the size of the pool. Who should be excluded and who included? Are there special relationships among ourselves and others that offer appropriate criteria?

We have used the idea of a constitutional convention to illustrate how rights and duties may be agreed upon within a society. Similarly, we have outlined the Rawlsian process of having founding fathers place themselves behind a veil of ignorance so as to arrive at principles and rules suitable for inventing social institutions. The perspective gained from such an exercise does not mean that we will always come to Rawlsian conclusions; we simply use it as part of our pluralistic approach. However, it seems that no matter what moral principles are brought to bear, we are led to ask whether the appropriate pool for health care should be society as a whole. The specific expectations and responsibilities built into the society's health care institutions should somehow reflect the social concern for each person's health and legitimate aspirations.

As argued earlier, the more egalitarian moral perspectives of the Kantian, Rawlsian, and other deontological approaches do not dictate a particular set of social institutions. If there is one *best* arrangement of institutions and rules, it has not been discovered. We continue to experiment, starting with the social arrangements at hand and asking if they can be improved so as to better reflect our moral principles. Our present health care system can certainly be improved. While the idea that all members should be in one pool seems to fit our moral intuitions, there may be other ways to accomplish the same goals. Since one of those goals is to insure that every person has access to a socially acceptable level of health care, a nationwide pool and program would seem appropriate. But, theoretically, other institutional arrangements may be effective.

In passing let us consider the question: Should the whole world be the pool? If we were to accept the principle that all persons have rights to life and freedom to pursue legitimate goals, then it would seem to follow that all other persons would have correlative duties. At the same time, since each person has her or his own life to live, it is unreasonable to conclude that each should spend all of her or his waking days concerned with the health and freedom of every other person in the world. Moreover, each person has a number of more immediate responsibilities to friends and families, as well as professional responsibilities and duties of citizenship. These relationships and the accompanying responsibilities have been formally or informally agreed upon and accepted. These responsibilities and duties are carried out within a set of institutions each with its own set of expectations. Except for various international agreements through the United Nations and other organizations, we have few explicit duties to the rest of the world. From a strictly libertarian contractarian approach it could be argued that our responsibilities to the rest of the world are limited only to those few to which we have voluntarily agreed. This approach has difficulties, the most obvious being that the opportunities we have for making actual contracts are limited and often flawed. There must be higher criteria for evaluating rights and duties than the specific contracts we make. Again, if we accept the principle that all men and women have a right to life and the pursuit of their own legitimate goals, then each of us has a responsibility to every other person. The remaining question is not whether we have a duty. We do. But how does our concern for the rest of the world fit in with the way we pursue our lives, our own goals, and our other, more direct, responsibilities? As individuals we address these concerns in different ways. Some become doctors and move to a poor country where they can be of great service. Most of us give occasionally to international relief funds but accept the idea that other, more direct, responsibilities have claims that are different in kind.

On a national level a strict libertarian could argue that our national government has no business giving foreign aid, that its responsibilities lie solely with its own citizens—that is the nature of the contract between citizens and government. But most citizens do not see their contract with society as so limited. If we were to use the Rawlsian analogy, the social contract that the nation's founders would make behind a veil of ignorance would be focused on the rights and obligations of the nation's citizens. This would not preclude society and its citizenry from having and acting on concerns for the rest of the world. Here again governments pursue international relations in many contexts and for many reasons. It is certainly appropriate for our government to be concerned about how other governments treat their own citizens. Are human rights being violated? We are interested in what other nations do not only because it affects our material national interests, but also because we have concern for others as persons. One aspect of our concern is for their health and the health care they receive. For practical purposes we would not expect health insurance pools to cross national boundaries. But in practical as well as moral dimensions we are affected by the quality of health care received by others.

COSTS AND RATIONING

Of the two major issues of the health care debate—Who is to be covered? and How are costs to be contained?—the question of costs is the more challenging. The answer to the coverage question is straightforward: *everyone* should be covered. But the answer to the question How are costs to be contained? is that health care must be *rationed*, and that answer is not very satisfying. We depend on market prices to ration most goods and services. But if we are unwilling to allow market prices alone to ration health care then we must find some more acceptable way to make rationing decisions.

Are there more rational ways to organize health care decision making? Are the important decisions made by the appropriate people? Are there incentives for the decision makers to use criteria that will enhance efficiency and fairness?

Part of the answer is to ascertain what are the appropriate institutional structures and where in them certain types of decisions should be made. Rationing and cost containment take place in every segment of the health care industry and in the government agencies that make and oversee health care policy. Within federal, state, and local governments different types of choices are made at different levels of the organizational structure. We can characterize the different levels as *macro, intermediate,* and *micro.* For example, the macro policy choices in the federal and state budget processes involve weighing major budget categories such as education, defense, and welfare in comparison with spending on health care. At this level, the idea of Pareto efficiency may be useful. At the macro level the appropriate efficiency standard is allocative efficiency. Spending on public programs should reflect the preferences of voters and should be carried out at the lowest cost possible. Each category program should be carried to the point where marginal benefits are equal to marginal costs. The budget as a whole is balanced against taxes and the opportunity costs of what citizens would otherwise purchase in the private sector. At the intermediate level of the budget process, departments and agencies make more specific choices among various health care programs. Goals are specified and related to costs. The departments and agencies of federal, state, and local governments administer government health care programs. Within the institutional structure of federal, state, and local governments administrators have varying degrees of flexibility in carrying out the program's goals. There are hierarchies of decision making in the other segments of the health care industry as well: insurance companies, HMOs, hospitals, and the medical profession.

At the micro level, rationing decisions must be made by hospitals, doctors, and patients. These decisions deal more directly with persons, rather than with budget categories and balance sheets. At this level, the broader definitions of efficiency have little applicability; the focus is what can be done for the patient with the resources at hand. It may be appropriate at times to employ Pareto efficiency reasoning. Can resources be reallocated in ways that help patients without making others worse off. The approach to social ethics presented in chapter one proposed that moral principles take on different relevance and weights in different situations. This implies that the moral *nature* of the decisions is different in some important way. As we survey the various types of health care cost containment and rationing, we will keep these propositions in mind.

In chapter two we asked whether or not it was possible for decision making within the legislative and administrative processes of government to accurately reflect social preferences. Arrow's impossibility theorem suggested that no voting system could insure a consistent result. In reality we expect something less than a perfect ordering of social preferences. Our democratic system relies on elected representatives to interpret society's preferences. Ideally, they also use their own judgement to promote allocative efficiency and fairness. But we are aware that various *government failures* frustrate this process: the system of checks and balances can at times make it difficult or impossible to adequately address social issues; the political and legislative processes offer opportunities for special interests to exercise undue influence; and the incentives faced by bureaucrats within administrative agencies may undermine efficiency and fairness.

At the macro policy level, government has some responsibility to set parameters for the evolution of the health care industry. It is important that the criteria for these policies not be limited to efficiency considerations. Ideally, at each level of decision making, the right people should be making the right decisions for the right reasons.

In the era when the costs of new technology and treatment were paid for by third parties (Medicare, Medicaid, and private insurance), costs and quality rose dramatically. Necessarily this process has been slowed. The Medicare and Medicaid programs have begun to place strict limits on how much is to be paid for particular diagnoses. Many of these limits are unrealistically low. This in turn has led to cross subsidization of the Medicare and Medicaid programs by the private insurance companies and their policyholders. In response, private insurance companies have sought to control treatment costs by such methods as setting price limits and requiring diagnoses to be verified by second opinions. Health maintenance organizations have achieved substantial monopsony power. They are able to enforce strict guidelines for the prices of treatment. In some cases physicians are paid by the number of patients assigned to them rather than the costs of their treatments. The developers of expensive new techniques no longer can be assured that they will be approved for payment.

In those cases where managed care providers have been able to employ physicians on a capitation basis, the incentives shift dramatically. With some exceptions, physicians are paid according to the number of patients assigned to them regardless of the level of care given. The physician has incentive to insure the long-term health of the patient by emphasizing preventive medicine. However, the physician also has incentive to keep down the costs associated with chronically ill patients. The effects of those new incentive patterns are now being assessed. In most managed care arrangements, the care given is adequate, but in some cases, costs are being contained by overly strict rationing of expensive procedures.

There are proposals to shift Medicare and Medicaid to managed care arrangements. The government would contract with managed care organizations on a capitation basis. Some of the managed care organizations would then, in turn, contract with physicians and other health care providers on a capitation basis. Thus, incentives would be changed radically, with costs being curtailed but possibly at the expense of needed care.

These trends in the evolution of health care institutions are gaining momentum. These new institutional arrangements mean that a new organization of decision making is also evolving. It is not at all clear that the right people will be making the right decisions using the right criteria.

Query: How Should We Pay for Health Care?

In the United States most health insurance is employer-based, with the employer paying part and the employee paying part. Economic analysis suggests that a large part of health care insurance paid for by the employer is shifted to the employee in the form of lower wages; thus the employee pays most or all of both parts. Companies with no health plans pay higher wages for workers with comparable skills.

Economists describe the government's contribution as a *tax expenditure.* Since the part of the employee's benefits and income that goes to pay for the health care policy is not taxed, government revenues are less than they would have been. In one sense this represents an expenditure going toward health care, a tax expenditure funded from general taxes (primarily the personal income tax). If, on the other hand, we compare the present system, in which most of the cost is borne by employees, to a system financed, say, by the personal income tax, we find the present system is much more regressive. A regressive payment system is not necessarily unfair. As we may observe, the market's rationing system of charging the same price to all is similarly regressive. If we focus on the private-good characteristics of health care, the problem of regressivity is less objectionable.

The tax expenditure part of health care insurance costs obviously comes from general tax revenues, since employees escape paying income tax on their insurance premiums. There is a certain logic to having health care paid for at least in part by general taxes since some of the benefits are public in nature.

Medicare's two parts each have their own trust funds. Part A covers the care provided at hospitals and post-acute care at skilled nursing facilities or home health agencies. Part B covers physician services. The Hospital Insurance Trust Fund (HI) is financed from payroll taxes at the rate of 2.9 percent (the employer ostensibly pays half of the tax). Part B, the Supplemental Medical Insurance Trust Fund (SMI), is voluntary and is paid for by premiums and heavily subsidized by general taxes (the latter pays 75 percent).

Current projections anticipate short-run deficits, starting in the year 2001, that require our immediate attention. A much more challenging problem looms after 2010 as the baby-boomers retire. By the year 2030, the elderly population and the total cost of Medicare will more than double.

There can be little debate over the importance of medical insurance to the elderly. It provides insulation from the devastating financial burdens that accompany poor health. These burdens would usually be shared by children and grandchildren of the elderly. Although we generally assume that Medicare covers virtually all of the elderly's acute health care expenses, it actually covers only 45 percent. The elderly presently spend 21 percent of their income on additional health care insurance, copayments, deductibles, and various types of treatment not covered by Medicare.

Recent cost reduction efforts have focused on cutting payments to hospitals and physicians. These efforts have been quite successful, primarily because providers have been able to shift part of the burden to other payers. This strategy will remain important in efforts to resolve the short-term shortfalls. President Clinton supported shifting home health care services from the Part A hospital trust fund to Part B. As noted, this involves a shift in who pays. Some of the burden is shifted from payroll taxes to premiums and general tax revenues.

The premiums for Part B in 1997 were $43.80 and covered only 25 percent of the cost. How much they will have to be increased depends in part on the share to be paid by general revenues (primarily the personal income tax). Moving home health care to Part B would cut in half the expected shortfall in Part A for the year 2000.

Other short-run remedies may include further increases in Part B premiums for the wealthier beneficiaries and further incentives for participants to move into managed care plans. There is some question as to how much money greater movement toward managed care will save. The current trend has been for the HMOs to enlist healthier people whose costs are generally lower.

The long-term challenges for Medicare are the most serious. As with Social Security, the demography of the baby-boomers requires that huge trust funds be built up if intergenerational equity is to be restored and maintained. While premiums paid by the elderly will continue to be a significant part of the solution, their potential is limited. One difficulty is that most of the elderly have relatively low incomes. As of 1997, about 80 percent of the elderly had incomes less than $25,000. The tactic of increasing premiums for higher income beneficiaries is also limited. There are simply not enough couples earning over, say, $100,000 a year to make a substantial difference in the funding dilemma. Moreover the strategy of restraining provider payments will eventually run its course, especially since it is being used across-the-board to reduce health care costs, not simply for Medicare and Medicaid. This means the burden can no longer be shifted to other payers. A major factor in rising costs has not been payments to doctors but advances in technology such as diagnostic procedures.

It may be possible to raise the eligibility to receive Medicare from age 65 to 67 or higher. This would agree with scheduled and proposed increases in Social Security retirement ages. These proposals require a change in the conventions of the workplace; they assume that people will be willing and able to put off retirement.

The most feasible political solution to long-term funding problems for our social programs requires the appointment of a respected bipartisan commission. Ideally, many of the necessary tradeoffs can be accomplished before the final plan is subjected to the vagaries of the legislative process. The tradeoffs involve many of the principles of efficiency and fairness we have considered in several contexts. Solutions to Medicare funding require that ground rules be set for the treatment of the elderly by managed care organizations. The commission must also make proposals as to how financing should be reorganized: how the types of care now allotted to Parts A and B should be reassigned and whether long-term health care should be included. This in turn leads to the question of the roles to be played by payroll taxes, beneficiary premiums, and general revenues. The commission must also address the question of what treatments should be completely covered, partially covered, or not covered at all.

Assuming that long-term health care funding is transferred from Medicaid to Medicare, how should the new insurance be organized and funded? What parts should be played by payroll taxes and income taxes in building up the necessary trust fund? As noted, the income distribution among the elderly sets limits on the role premiums can play. Income distribution among the elderly is very unequal. The average is $11,000 and the lowest 20 percent earn an average of only $6,272.[2] Again, there are not enough couples at the high income levels to allow a progressive premium schedule to have great effect. Generally, the elderly poor are members of families with low-income children and grandchildren. Thus, increases in premiums and cuts in benefits weigh heavily on several generations.

Any rational long-term solution must feature higher payroll and income taxes so that sufficient trust funds can be built up during the working years of the baby boomer generation. Both Social Security and Medicare face two demographic challenges that necessitate the buildup of the trust funds, the baby boomer phenomenon and increased longevity. If present day taxpayers plan to live more years in retirement, intergenerational justice requires that they invest more during their working years. Although the financial logistics of meeting these challenges are not difficult to comprehend, the advocacy of tax increases in recent years has amounted to political suicide. There remains the question of whether a responsible commission can be appointed that will be able to make hard choices and, in turn, make proposals that will gain sufficient public support.

Medicaid, the health care program for the very poor, is paid for by general taxes. Medical care for the poor is clearly a broad social goal and is redistributive in nature. Its financial burden should be shared by all according to ability-to-pay and equal-sacrifice principles. While no tax apportions burdens equally among income levels, the personal income tax comes closest; therefore, its use to pay for Medicaid is appropriate.

In summary, the various revenue sources used for employer-based insurance, Medicare, and Medicaid are not demonstrably unfair. The glaring deficiency is a sin of omission; there are some forty million Americans who effectively have no coverage.

Some Questions Concerning Medicaid Reform

Reforming the Medicaid system by shifting responsibility to the states will certainly allow for innovation and experimentation. State governments are assumed to be more in touch with the particular needs of their constituencies. State bureaucracies are assumed to be less inept and wasteful than their federal counterparts.

The process of reorganizing Medicaid may offer opportunities to increase health care coverage to some or all of those who now have none. Medicaid reform will be part of each state's comprehensive welfare reform designed to encourage more responsible behavior on the part of welfare recipients. The plans must include expanded day-care provisions for the children of mothers required to work.

The new welfare initiatives of the states have moral as well as economic dimensions. The perspectives developed in chapters one and two can be applied in their analysis and evaluation. Will the results of new initiatives be efficient? Will they be fair? Do the new programs address our social goals? Is sufficient account being taken of the potential market failures?

Although shifting Medicaid to the states promises several advantages, there are at least two difficulties that have not been addressed. The first concern is that welfare and Medicaid is a *social risk*. The federal government is much better situated than the states to finance the Medicaid system.

If the nation experienced a number of years of recession, the states would not have the financial capability to finance extended benefits (to include Medicaid). It is only the federal government that can run a deficit for a long period of time. Similarly, the social risk of long-term inflation cannot be met by states.

Second, the promised cost containment of Medicaid is unlikely to occur. The demographic time bomb of the baby boomers will go off in 2010. Although the Medicare program is designed to provide health care for the elderly poor, in recent years Medicaid is assuming a large and expensive role in providing long-term health care.

Ideally, the federal government would expand the Medicare program to include insurance for long-term nursing home care. Currently the market is incomplete, due to the problem of adverse selection. Medicaid comes into play as the elderly who need long-term health care spend down their wealth in order to become eligible. Although unintended, this part of Medicaid is large and increasing rapidly. We will consider the moral and economic ramifications of this phenomenon later.

What is required is a social insurance program that covers nursing home care. The demography of the baby boomers requires that a trust fund be built up now so that it can be brought into play when they become elderly.

Neither the new initiatives of the states nor the federal government appear to be giving attention to these problems.

Query: How Should We Pay for Long-Term Health Care?

Many elderly persons require some form of long-term care. The need may range from nursing and custodial home visits to residence in a nursing home with various levels of care.

One risk that healthy individuals face is that at some point they may reach old age and need long-term care. The risks associated with long-term care are in theory insurable, but most private firms fear the problem of adverse selection if they were to offer such policies. This would be the case if most of the actual purchasers of a given policy would be those with the worst risks. The market for long-term care insurance, in fact, is best described as an "incomplete market." There are some policies available, but they are expensive and limited in coverage.

There have been a number of legislative proposals to extend Medicare coverage to long-term care. These, like most other health care initiatives, have failed. Thus, when elderly persons require long-term health care, the responsibility falls on their own resources or those of their family. In some situations the individual's own resources may be sufficient; in others, the individual must rely on children or grandchildren, or whomever may be able or willing to provide care. Some families are in better positions than others to provide long-term care.

As we consider this gap in health care coverage it seems out of sync with our social values and intentions as to the division of social and familial responsibilities. Most health care for the elderly is provided through Medicare. Spouses, children, and grandchildren can usually be relied upon to fill any gaps the system does not cover. But when long-term care is needed there is no satisfactory system, and the demands placed on family seem unreasonable. Moreover, many of the elderly have no family or have families with limited means.

In practice there is a safety net. This occurs because Medicaid, which provides health care for the poor, will come into play when the elderly person on long-term care finally runs out of resources. In fact the process, as noted, is known as "spending down" and has become standard. Each state has developed rules for spending down an elderly person's wealth and income. The formula states how much can be retained, how much can be given to spouse or children, and how much must go toward paying for long-term care. When the elderly person's wealth is finally exhausted, Medicaid takes over. Remarkably, neither the spouse nor the children are held legally responsible.

Query: What Is Society's Responsibility in Health Care Provision?

Is the spend-down process a morally defensible process for meeting society's responsibility to provide health care? We need to focus on the question of whether or not this responsibility can be met by providing a safety net or whether it requires an insurance program. Certainly society is meeting part of its responsibility; it is providing that no one will be denied long-term medical care. How would our evaluation be affected if the adverse selection problems were overcome so that an acceptable array of policies became available? Some individuals who were given the opportunity to buy their own insurance would still be unable or unwilling to buy. Would the spending down safety net then be an acceptable way of meeting society's responsibility?

Consider also several attributes of the Medicare program.

1. The elderly who have contributed to the program believe they are entitled to receive benefits.

2. The free-rider problem, in which working-age persons are tempted to refrain from buying insurance, is overcome by making contributions compulsory.

3. The market failure caused by the adverse selection phenomenon is overcome by including everyone in the pool.

4. Intergenerational equity is preserved to the extent that the trust fund is kept sound. The spend-down process shares none of these attributes.

Query: What Is the Family's Responsibility in Health Care Provision?

Many families face questions of their responsibilities when one member chooses or finds it necessary to use the spend-down procedure. The spouse, children, or other family members do in fact have responsibility; but how is that responsibility to be exercised? Society, that is government, is partially meeting its responsibility by means of the spend-down process. Moreover the family has no legal obligation to pay for long-term health care.

If, as we have argued, family members do have some ultimate responsibility, how is that responsibility to be expressed? Long-term care is very expensive. We can easily visualize a process in which the wealth of the elderly person is spent down, as well as that of the entire family, including children and grandchildren. Many families have been faced with this dilemma. A very large percentage of the elderly in long-term care facilities have chosen the spend-down method to qualify for Medicaid.

Summary

The answer to the question of long-term health care is that there should be insurance. For most of our citizens, the financial demands of long-term health care would cause great hardship to themselves or their families. It is neither logical nor feasible for all persons who are at risk to be required to build up the necessary savings.

But what kind of insurance? What should be covered? And how should it be financed? The most straightforward solution would be to make it part of the Medicare program. The payroll tax would be raised to include both types of health care. Working-age persons, therefore, would be given the opportunity; that is, they would be required to purchase insurance against the time they might have need of long-term health care.

There are other possible approaches that would engage private insurance companies. There may be some way to overcome the adverse selection problem by widening the pools of potential policyholders. Alternatively, the government could give tax incentives to working-age persons to encourage them to purchase long-term health care insurance. Or it could simply require that all persons purchase some insurance. If somehow the great majority could be induced to purchase their own policies, the Medicaid spend-down process could still be left in place as a safety net for the poor.

Long-term health care does not always require going to a nursing home. Many elderly persons would rather receive long-term care at home if their needs could be met by home visits of health care providers. When insurance policies are designed, the benefit structure should not create incentives that put undue pressure on the elderly to leave their own homes.

To the question What are the responsibilities of spouse and family? the answer seems to be that, while there are fundamental familial duties, the financial burdens of long-term health care expense can and should be avoided. When an elderly person is in need of long-term health care, the person's family and friends will still have ample opportunity to demonstrate their love, respect, and caring.

There is an underlying issue that is often overlooked in discussions of health care for the elderly: How important are self-respect and dignity in social relationships? Even though family ties may be strong and family members may be interdependent in many positive ways, parents will be naturally reluctant to become a burden to their children or to anyone else. One of the attributes of the Social Security system and Medicare is that they have made possible a much greater degree of financial independence for both children and their retired parents. Without government initiatives of some sort, the threat of facing either a substantial financial drain or resorting to the spend-down solution is a very real risk for most families. Again the question is not whether children have responsibility for their elderly parents; the question is whether insurance should be available to mitigate the burdens of long-term health care expenses. In that sense, Social Security and Medicare are insurance to ease the burdens of becoming old and infirm.

Many macro budget decisions involve these and other questions of costs and rationing. Let us consider the rationing criteria in more detail.

THE ISSUE OF RATIONING: WHAT CRITERIA?

Assume you have influence over the nation's health care budget. A review of the demographic statistics reveals that out of one million deaths per year most (600,000) come from the age brackets above seventy years. Still, 400,000 come from younger people, and more alarmingly, accidents and suicides account for a large percentage of deaths among the very young. If we were to define the health care benefits to be maximized in terms of *life years saved*, it may well be that we should shift the budget toward accident and suicide prevention and away from the care of "old people's diseases" such as heart disease, lung disease, cancer, and kidney failure.

While the criterion "maximize life years" is open to criticism, it makes a good starting point. We have already professed a high regard for life; and the criterion has the attribute of being impersonal, that is, treating the life years of everyone the same. Similarly, the conclusion that we should put more money into saving the lives of the young is consistent with the set of principles we have developed based on the ideal that each individual should have the opportunity to realize life goals of his or her own choosing. The "fair innings" argument would require that one live long enough and have the resources to accomplish one's goals.

Although our present concern is the maximize-life-years criterion, at some point we must consider how far we may wish to take the "maximize opportunity to achieve individual goals," or fair innings, criteria. For me, the author, and perhaps for each of you, these criteria will turn out to be very important. That does not mean that other values will not also be important. Just what are the goals of others? But the difficult issue remains. If we accept the fact that the elderly can achieve fewer goals than the young, is that a legitimate consideration for social policy? Just because the elderly may have accomplished some of their own goals, does that mean their lives are of little value? Of course not. We would hope that they may continue to flourish. We would encourage them to continue to set and achieve further goals, to enjoy their lives, and to enrich the lives of others. We may also appreciate the fact that many of the elderly have "earned" their right to a comfortable retirement; many have contributed much to family, to friends, and to society in general.

Since resources are always scarce, there may be some conflict between the social goals of providing opportunity for the young and care for the elderly. The point to be made is that a number of moral principles relate to such trade-offs. An obvious weakness of the strict maximize-life-years criterion is that it ignores quality-of-life considerations. The extension of life for someone in a coma or in great pain may have negative value.

The QALY as a Policy Criterion

One criterion that can be used to bring quality of life into policy considerations is the QALY. As defined by Alan Williams and others at the University of York the QALY is a *quality of life adjusted year*. The essence of the measurement is that it represents a year in which the person is fully healthy, fully functional, with only a few, if any, colds or minor health "annoyances." If we define the value of a year of health as 1, then years of bad health are less than 1 and being dead is 0. For most individuals there is some level of pain that has a negative QALY value, being worse than dead. Of course most of us have to settle for years in which we are not perfectly healthy. And most would settle for life with various disabilities before deciding it was not worth living.

The general idea is to get the most for dollars spent on health, that is, to get the most QALYs possible. Looked at from the cost side we want to reduce the cost per QALY.

The QALY approach has been used in a number of evaluative studies of health care systems, including, of course, Britain's National Health Service. Let us consider a hypothetical case to see how it can be employed. The country in question spends a large part of its health care budget on expensive treatment for the elderly with diseases such as emphysema and kidney failure. These individuals will typically have more than one health problem, and some have permanent disabilities. On the other hand the country spends very little on research toward eliminating birth defects and related disabilities. Similarly the funds available for correcting eye disorders among the young are quite low, especially among low-income groups. The results of our hypothetical study place the cost of a QALY for treatment of emphysema at $60,000, whereas a QALY for treatment of a typical eye disorder is $6,000. Of course few of the elderly in question actually experience a full QALY in a given year, so that the cost calculation involves dividing by some fraction of one. Moreover, cost-benefit analysis of the present value of future QALYs naturally favors the treatment of the young, whose long-term potential for enjoying QALYs is greater.

The policy recommendations of our hypothetical study would specify amounts to be shifted from one category to another. Funds would be shifted so as to maximize total QALYs. In cost terms, funds would be shifted until the marginal costs per QALY were equal. Obviously the life prospects of some individuals will be changed by redistribution of funds. Some of the elderly with diseases such as emphysema and kidney failure will receive little or no treatment. They will die sooner than they otherwise would have.

Macro policy decisions necessarily trade some lives for others or some lives for a greater quality of life. There are no easy answers. We must find some way to compare the quality of life that various people experience. From the utilitarian perspectives we would extend the lives of those who contribute most to the general welfare. We would also extend the lives of those who get the most happiness out of life. These choices seem terribly undemocratic. Our deontological, rights-based principles place value on each individual for her or his own sake. We are reluctant to discriminate against one person who chooses the simple way of life or another who has various disadvantages and few talents. The QALY claims only to be a rough measure of the "quality of life"; it does not discriminate on other bases. But is that an advantage or a disadvantage? Just how do we want to discriminate?

A quantity-of-life principle would improve the present allocation of resources, and the QALY approach would be a further improvement. But the QALY has its own weak points. The QALY values the life years of those with disabilities at less than those with no disabilities. Certainly this is a way we do *not* want to discriminate if it means that we further diminish the quality of life of those, say, who have been born with disabilities. We must somehow bring such considerations as need and desert into the equation. Neither the utilitarian nor the QALY approach does this well. The QALY approach favors the young, as do the fair-innings and opportunity-to-realize-one's-own-life-goals principles. But it does not specifically address these values, nor does it address questions related to need, to potential, or to the needs of others. The idea that women and children should be first out of the burning building or first into the lifeboats is perhaps an outdated form of chivalry; but one intuition that still holds is that those who are weaker, especially children, deserve to be given priority when in need. Similarly, we have from time to time exempted some men from military service because of familial responsibilities. When calculating the value of a person's life, it seems appropriate to consider what affect his or her life has on the lives of others. Again, how far do we go in that direction? How much greater is the value of the life of an entertainer than of the average person? And do we subtract value if the personal life of the entertainer is less than praiseworthy? As we have observed, the QALY has the advantage of being very democratic. Its focus is on the health of the individual; no account is taken of the individual's political or economic power or even her or his contribution to society.

Who then should we discriminate for and against in health care policy? We will leave the macro question for now with a proposition that deserves further thought.

Proposition: Both from the quantity- and quality-of-life perspectives, health care policy should shift resources toward the young.

This implies that more resources should be shifted from other goods to health care. Possibly this redistribution should be at the expense of the elderly.

In further discussion of this proposition we should ask what claims the elderly may have. Obviously the elderly have a right to life. We would agree that prolonging the life of an elderly person is worth more than some sorts of cosmetic surgery. We would observe that during their lives many elderly persons have contributed and continue to contribute to the lives of others. How do such considerations enter into macro policy decisions: the level of spending on health care and the division among prevention, current treatment, and basic research?

WHO DECIDES WHAT?

The question of who should decide what has been implicit in a number of the issues we have discussed. When we consider the institutional structure of the economy, the government, and society in general, we ask if there are ways to organize decision making in economic, political, and social activities that will enhance efficiency and fairness. We have considered a number of health care issues that arise in different institutional contexts. Before summarizing, let us once again consider the decisions made at the most basic level, the patient and the physician.

The "Spare-No-Expense" Dilemma

In contrast to the relatively impersonal rationing that takes place when legislators consider health care among other budget categories, decisions among doctors and patients become very personal. At the personal level, the usual attitude is to use whatever resources are available. Patients or family members typically respond to the choices, say as outlined by their physician, by saying: "spare no expense." If the patient's life is in danger the physician and hospital are expected to do all that is possible. If a promising treatment is not covered by insurance, then some other way of financing it will be found. The question is whether or not we as a society want to preserve the traditional advocate role of the physician or have him or her play some prominent role in the rationing process. It may be possible to preserve the physician's role as advocate if the more difficult rationing decisions can be relegated to other levels in the process. For example, the introduction of new technology depends on whether or not it will be covered by Medicare, Medicaid, and private insurance. Similarly, boards at regional and state levels must decide whether or not various treatments will be approved for certain diagnoses. It may not always be feasible to preserve the advocacy role for physicians. Even at this most basic level, there may be scarce resources that must be rationed.

As the health care industry evolves toward more control over costs by HMOs and private insurance companies, the question of how decision making is best organized cannot be avoided. The general consensus is that decision making must be rearranged so that the supposed tendency of physicians to order unnecessary, wasteful treatment is constrained. In many situations the physician will become an employee of the HMO with incentive to keep costs down. In other situations the physician's authority to make decisions will be subject to approval by employees of an insurance company. The goal of these new decision-making arrangements is efficiency. As these trends continue and intensify, there is widespread concern that considerations of fairness may be given less weight.

When Life Is Not Worth Living

There are situations in which no medical treatment, no matter how costly, can make life worth living. If expressed in terms of the QALY concept, the quality of life would have a negative value. The relevant question changes from one of rationing to one of the morality of ending a person's life. Who should decide and on what basis?

This moral dilemma, like several others we have considered, involves two dimensions. The first requires a realistic assessment of what is possible. What treatments are available and what are the probabilities attached to each? The second involves the balancing of the relevant moral principles.

Let us first consider the case in which the illness is certain to be terminal and the person is in considerable pain. The application of utilitarian cost-benefit principles would seem to be straightforward. What justification could there be for keeping the person alive? This is not to say that we cannot think of other situations in which the utilitarian approach would be problematical; for example, in which the quality of life is low and the treatment very expensive. In such a case we may be reluctant to rely solely on cost-benefit calculations; but in the case at hand, it would seem that a utilitarian judgment to end the life would be unassailable. Let us go further and specify that the person now expresses the wish that life be terminated. This brings several deontological considerations into play. We should have respect for the person and her or his right to determine her or his own course of life. Can there still be moral principles brought to bear on behalf of sustaining this person's life?

In fact, there are moral, legal, and religious sanctions against ending such a person's life. Again we will not attempt to explore all of the possible situations and relevant moral principles. We do observe, however, that the proper role for society may be ambiguous. The argument can be made that in social policy it should be made clear that the life of every person has value. It would be unfortunate if a public policy allowing for the termination of life were ever interpreted as encouraging the termination of life.

Rationing among Patients

Medical ethicists have given much thought to which moral criteria should be used in rationing scarce resources among patients. We will only introduce the subject. At most large hospitals, physicians or committees of physicians have been designated to make some of the more difficult rationing decisions such as which patients will receive organ transplants. The concerns we outlined previously are directly addressed. Thought is given to the makeup of the committee and the ethical criteria to be used. The criteria used by such committees include the following: the quantity of life (how long life will be prolonged), the quality of life (say, whether normal functioning will be achieved), the patient's potential (for surviving the treatment, etc.), and the value of the patient to others and to the community as a whole.

Among physicians and medical ethicists the motorcycle is affectionately termed the "donorcycle." Suppose a young man has just died in a motorcycle accident and has left his organs to be used in transplants. We assume that the committee has given some consideration to all of the principles and conditions that we have discussed. Teleological principles such as the utilitarian greatest-good-for-the-greatest-number principle are inherent in the quantity-of-life, the quality-of-life, the potential-for-success, and certainly the potential-contribution-to-society criteria. Likewise deontological principles such as treating each person as an end are also inherent in all of the criteria, including the deservedness criterion.

Now suppose first that we have two candidates who are rated the same. They are the same age, have the same potential for a successful transplant, and so on. How do we decide? One method that ethicists claim is fair is to leave the decision to chance—to flip a coin, or if there is a larger number, to have a lottery. In the United States during the Vietnam War a lottery was used in connection with the draft. Is it appropriate to use a lottery to decide among candidates for organ transplants? Should a lottery be used when all of the other criteria are equal, or should it be used even when candidates are not equal? Suppose for example that a person is fairly healthy but is slightly diabetic. On each iteration of the committee's decisions this candidate loses out and will always lose out. Should this disability continue to rule him or her out? Put another way, should we further punish this person for his or her disability? Again, we must discriminate, but on what grounds?

Suppose instead that there are three candidates for transplants: one needs a heart, one needs a lung, and one needs a lung and a heart. Since there is only one donor, we can give transplants to two persons or to one. Suppose that all three will probably live until other donors are found. Nevertheless on each round of decision making, their odds are reduced. Certainly on the bases of quantity-of-life, quality-of-life, and other criteria, we would expect the committee to decide in favor of two lives rather than one. But let us again put the decision in iterative form: there will be other donors and other candidates in the future. We ask, do we want to continually rule out the person who needs a heart and a lung? Our respect for the person, the deontological approach, especially the Kantian principle of treating each person as an end, would seem to argue for giving each person a chance, even a small chance. The case is similar to that of the diabetic candidate. Perhaps our respect for each individual person as an end in herself or himself would lead us to want to put even the diabetic and the heart and lung transplant into the lottery.

One possibility is to use the other criteria (quantity, quality, recovery potential, etc.) to rank each candidate and then to run the lottery giving greater odds to the higher ranks; the best candidate gets ten chances, the next nine, and so on. The diabetics and the heart-lung candidates would have the odds stacked against them, but they would at least have a chance. Through successive iterations they would still be considered and thus their overall odds would improve if they lived that long. This method is not presently used. Would it be more fair?

A point should be reiterated concerning the economics of medical ethics at the micro level. At the personal level, it is more difficult to quantify the costs and benefits of the decisions that must be made. In situations in which resources are not scarce, the decision makers focus on the most promising treatment regardless of cost. When resources are scarce and one life must be traded for another, decisions are more a question of fairness than cost effectiveness. We can expect the use of cost effectiveness to be appropriate at the macro level, but even there analyses must be framed in moral terms. These examples of decision making at the level directly concerned with physicians and their patients make a strong point. We are unwilling to allow the market to ration health care resources. Yet within other levels of the emerging institutional structure, the introduction of market incentives is being encouraged.

Let us return to the larger social issue: Who will ration health care and on what bases? There are some health care decisions that are highly personal and should be left to the patient. Others require the physician, the family, or, in the case of scarce resources, an appropriate committee. The higher-level decisions, such as how health care fares in federal and state budgets, are made by our representatives through democratic processes. At each level a number of social issues arise that demand careful analysis and application of moral principles. There are many intermediate levels of decision making in which rational, cost-effective criteria must be better integrated. As the institutions of health care delivery continue to evolve and to be shaped by public policy, we will be challenged to find the best way to organize our thinking. Who should be the decision makers? What criteria, incentives, and goals are to be employed? Ultimately, how can we influence the shape of these institutions so that the decisions that emerge will incorporate and balance principles of ethics as well as efficiency?

COVERAGE AND COSTS: SOME FINAL WORDS

Two broad social concerns, coverage and costs, run through our discussion of health care policy. As the health care industry evolves, we are interested in how costs will be contained. *Who* will decide how scarce health care resources will be rationed? What will be the criteria they use? What treatments will be available and who will receive them?

Although we have failed to formulate a comprehensive health care policy, rationing processes are evolving rapidly. There are efforts to restructure Medicare and Medicaid and to curtail costs. In the private health care markets, managed care organizations are playing larger and larger roles as health care providers for the employer-based insurance plans. The traditional system in which fee-for-service charges are paid for by a third party (the insurance company) is being replaced by one in which employers contract with managed care organizations to cover all employees on a per capita basis. Incentives are changing in favor of cost containment. At the same time, decision making power is being rearranged; there are now gatekeepers who determine whether patients need treatment and whether a specialist needs to be called. Managed care organizations will gain more and more leverage over physicians, hospitals, and manufacturers of drugs and other health care products.

Will the choices that emerge from these new institutional structures be efficient and fair? As patient–physician advocacy relationships change, will there be other means for protecting the interests of individual patients? More generally, how will the duties and responsibilities of patients, families, and physicians be redefined? There is a real danger that, as new health care reforms are developed, considerations of fairness will be subjugated to the efforts to reduce costs.

Our discussion of coverage explored a number of related issues: the basic question of whether or not health care is considered a right; questions of the responsibilities of individuals, families, and society; questions of what should be considered an adequate level of health care; and questions of how it should be financed.

If we accept universal coverage as a social goal, we are still left with the question of how that can be accomplished. The answer depends in part on the nature of health care insurance and the associated market failures. We are aware of the reasons private insurance companies have failed to provide adequate insurance, but it is unlikely that, if market failures could be overcome, our social goals would be met.

The present structure of the industry features employer-based insurance pools augmented with the Medicare program for the elderly and the Medicaid program for the poor. Our efforts to adopt a national health care insurance plan have failed for the foreseeable future. Similarly, we have no comprehensive policy for containing health care costs.

The absence of a rational and comprehensive health care policy does not mean that the issues go away; it means they are exacerbated. Indeed, new issues will arise as the structure of the industry continues to evolve. There will be proposals to deal with the problems of those who have no coverage. There will be proposals to insure that managed care organizations will not deny needed health care in their efforts to economize. There are proposals to reform Medicare and Medicaid to curtail costs by greater reliance on managed care arrangements. There are reforms in Medicaid to curtail costs by shifting functions to states.

As new proposals are advanced, the perspectives we have presented will facilitate our evaluation of them. Do they address the moral and economic dimensions of the issues? Will the proposals overcome the efficiency problems or make them worse? Will the proposals accomplish our social goals or will they promote special interests? Will the distribution of tax burdens be fair?

Finally, there are questions of intergenerational justice that should be addressed. The concept of generational accounting allows us to calculate the lifetime distribution of benefits and burdens among various age cohorts.

The use of Medicaid to provide long-term nursing home care for the elderly poor is inefficient. As the baby boomers retire, this burden to then current tax-payers will become intolerable. We must address this issue now. Should our approach include a national (and compulsory) insurance policy to provide for long-term health care for the elderly? And can we assume that such a program would necessarily include the buildup of a trust fund in anticipation of the baby boomers reaching old age? Public discussion must address the issue of maintaining trust funds for Medicare and Medicaid so as to preserve intergenerational fairness.

As usual, our consideration of social issues asks more questions than it answers. Our goal, we recall, is not so much to find *the answer*, instead we seek to find ways to better organize our analyses and evaluations.

SUGGESTIONS FOR FURTHER READING

Is Health Care a Right?

Kenneth N. Buchi and Bruce M. Landesman "Health Care in a National Health Program: A Fundamental Right," in *Changing to National Health Care* eds. Robert P. Huefner and Margaret P. Battin (Salt Lake City: University of Utah Press, 1992), pp. 191–208.

James Childress, "A Right to Health Care," *Journal of Medicine and Philosophy* 4 (1979).

Norman Daniels, *Just Health Care* (Cambridge: Cambridge University Press, 1985).

The Issue of National Health Insurance

Henry J. Aaron, ed., *The Problem That Won't Go Away* (Washington, D.C.: The Brookings Institution, 1996). A collection of observations on why the Clinton Plan failed and what the future holds. The entire political spectrum is represented.

Huefner and Battin, eds., *National Health Care*. A collection of articles on the various issues of national health insurance.

On Cutting Costs

Henry Aaron and William B. Schwartz, *The Painful Prescription: Rationing Hospital Care* (Washington, D.C.: The Brookings Institution, 1984). An assessment of the various concerns arising from the rationing of health care.

Larry R. Churchill, *Rationing Health Care in America* (Notre Dame: University of Notre Dame Press, 1987). Churchill examines various moral issues of health care rationing.

David M. Cutler, "Cutting Costs and Improving Health," in Aaron, *The Problem That Won't Go Away*.

———, "The Cost and Financing of Health Care," *American Economic Review*, 85 (1995), pp. 32–37.

ENDNOTES

1. Rawls, *Theory of Justice*, p. 62.
2. Marilyn Moon, *Medicare Now and in the Future* (Washington, D.C.: Urban Institute, 1996).

6

Social Security, Old Age, and Retirement

The phenomenon is of recent vintage. Only in the last few decades have we had a significant part of society who are elderly and retired. Since this social phenomenon is so new, many of its moral implications have not been fully addressed. What are the responsibilities of the individual, the family, the government, and other social entities in providing for retirement? As with other social issues, it is possible to have various overlapping spheres of responsibility among individuals and families, as well as federal, state, and local agencies.

In our system, the individual bears primary responsibility; yet our Social Security program is compulsory, financed by a payroll deduction. But upon this base individuals are free to construct their own more elaborate retirement plans. Most individuals also participate in a program organized by their employers. These programs differ in what flexibility they offer the employee: what choices with respect to how they are invested, what choices in the level of contribution, what choices with respect to the type of annuity (or equity at retirement), and the degree of flexibility when changing jobs. Government has given these employment-based programs and additional individual retirement possibilities substantial encouragement through tax incentives.

The ability of the elderly to live comfortably and to realize their goals in retirement depends on a wide range of factors. Income from Social Security, employer and individual retirement programs, home ownership, and Medicare are contributing factors. We now consider the part played by Social Security.

The Social Security Retirement Program: Two Purposes

Our Social Security system (OASDI) has a number of purposes in addition to its retirement program. These include providing for the families of those who die before reaching retirement age and providing benefits for those with disabilities. The retirement program, our focus here, has two related but distinct purposes: (1) to insure that the elderly poor have an income that meets a socially accepted level, and (2) to provide a base upon which all citizens can build their own individual retirement programs.

For many years, 1936–1983, the program worked very well as a pay-as-you-go scheme, with working generations providing benefits to those who had retired. The unprecedented population growth of the late 1940s and 1950s (the baby boom) will make great demands on the system starting in the year 2010. Moreover, several severe recessions in the 1970s and early 1980s put great strain on the Social Security budget. In the late 1970s and early 1980s new arrangements were set up. Working-age generations still provide benefits for the elderly, but they also must build up a trust fund for the extra demands that will be put on the system when the baby boomers begin to retire in the year 2010. The mechanics of this trust fund are straightforward, but, unfortunately, political rhetoric often seeks to confuse the issue. It is important that the general public have a clear understanding of what is required for intergenerational fairness.

Analysis and evaluation require that we first understand what Social Security is and what it is not. An analysis of the retirement provisions of Social Security based solely on, say, the retirement programs offered employees by their employers would be misleading. On the one hand the benefits for those who retire under Social Security have far exceeded the rates of private-sector retirement plans. On the other hand contributions to Social Security do not build equity that can be passed on to children and grandchildren. For individuals who die at sixty-five with no surviving spouse, Social Security will have been a poor investment. It guarantees a retirement base for old age: if one is destitute, the benefits provide a minimum level of income; if one is better off, the benefits provide a foundation for building a more comfortable retirement program. In fact it is essentially a special kind of insurance for retirement: insurance that provides benefits if, and only if, one reaches old age.

Social Security and Familial Responsibilities

It is useful to evaluate the Social Security program as a contract among generations to provide insurance for retirement. This contract works within the context of a myriad of other responsibilities, claims, duties, and obligations that we have as members of families, communities, and society. Within a given family there are various explicit and implicit responsibilities shared among children and parents. Through time the makeup of these responsibilities is affected by changes in social and economic institutions.

When the Social Security system was first introduced, the more immediate responsibilities of children toward their elderly parents were immediately altered. Of course the underlying familial duties still existed, but at the societal level, a new intergenerational contract was written. The elderly were immediately made more independent, and their children's responsibility to support them was eased. At the same time, the working-age cohorts became obliged to pay benefits to the elderly. Thus, in many families the immediate responsibility for children to support their elderly parents was replaced by an obligation to pay taxes. The working-age cohorts, in turn, began participating in a program that insured that they would have a retirement base. They themselves were also insured against ever becoming destitute in their old age. Future generations would provide them with benefits when their time came to retire. For most of the years of the program's existence, the pay-as-you-go system allowed the "contracts" to be fulfilled with relative ease; and, in fact, generous bonuses were given to retiring generations. In the last decade, however, it was recognized that demographic changes in birth rates and longevity and changing work and retirement patterns made a pay-as-you-go system no longer viable. A new system would have to be devised in order for a fair distribution of costs and benefits to be maintained through time.

The changes that were made in 1983 will make an excellent case study combining ethical and economic considerations. It features a trust fund that will augment tax revenues when the baby boomers begin to retire in the year 2010. It uses the idea of *close actuarial balance*, a method of relating the trust fund to expected benefits and contributions through time. First let us analyze the mechanics of the program using the perspectives from economic theory. Interesting questions arise as to how the interests and behavior of individuals, families, and businesses are affected through time.

The Peculiar Economic Characteristics of Social Goods

The relationships among individuals, families, and generations with respect to risks and insurance were changed with Social Security. Those relationships will continue to change. Many individuals do not clearly understand how the present Social Security and national health programs relate to their own risks and retirement possibilities or to their changing responsibilities to family and community. In the preceding chapters we have considered several of the social, or public-good, characteristics of programs that address such social issues as unemployment, income distribution, and health care. A public good or bad, we recall, has the characteristics that its benefits or costs are not assignable or divisible, nor are they exhausted by individual consumption. The classic case of a pure public good, national defense, exhibits these two characteristics. First "defense benefits" are shared by all, and no one person's "consumption" of "defense" dilutes the consumption of another. In addition, it is impossible to exclude any citizen; "defense units" may not be packaged and sold to individuals. If exclusion were possible, competitive markets would organize its production quite efficiently. Consequently, the public sector must be brought into its financing and production.

Social Security is not a pure public good, since individuals *could* be excluded from receiving the program's retirement benefits. Nevertheless, there is a public character to the provision of Social Security, as with other income transfer programs. This is true because most citizens think that some basic needs should be available to all, even though some may not currently have the ability to pay. Most citizens would suffer psychic discomfort if they were aware that others were unable to obtain such essential goods as food, clothing, shelter, education, health care, or more generally, life and economic opportunity. Thus, these goods take on the character of public goods. The psychic comfort or discomfort is public in the sense that it is not divisible or assignable. Of course there are several other lines of moral argument that can be used to justify a person's claims to goods essential for life, but that is not our point here. The point is that, if most citizens feel empathy for others who are old, infirm, and destitute, their welfare takes on the characteristics of a public good. As with all goods that create social benefits, a free-rider problem arises. Accordingly, the public sector must use its taxing power to insure adequate financing. While I, as an individual, support income redistribution to insure the elderly against destitution, I would prefer that others pay for it.

A second free-rider problem has to do with how individual benefits are calculated. In our present system, there is a link between individual contributions and benefits, but it is not sufficiently direct to discourage some free riding. One may try to contribute less during one's working years, if such behavior means only a small reduction in expected benefits. This free rider problem provides further justification for a government program with compulsory contributions.

There are additional economic characteristics of these issues that must be considered when we evaluate the particular approaches we have taken. Moreover, there are important changes taking place that will require new initiatives.

Informational Costs and Product Differentiation

There is a tendency in the marketing of insurance and real estate for competition to lead to excessive duplication. In insurance markets, there are often too many salespersons and a confusing array of policy options. Typically, the variety makes choices more difficult rather than more efficient. The net result is that information costs are high and too many resources are devoted to the marketing process. Each agency is unable to realize the economies of scale that would be available in a larger operation.

By contrast the Social Security program is by far the most efficient insurance program ever devised. There are substantial economies of scale, low administrative costs, and practically no marketing costs. In spite of these advantages the system faces serious challenges, some real and some the creation of political rhetoric.

In comparing Social Security insurance to the variety of retirement plans offered by private companies, we must ask if the efficiency gained is worth the loss in freedom of choice. We observe that excessive differentiation may often carry a nuisance factor such as being inundated by advertising, telephone salespersons, and so on. More important, since the Social Security program features a minimal level of benefits, it will not satiate the demand for retirement plans. For the great majority of citizens who see their Social Security plan as simply a base upon which to build, there is no loss in freedom of choice. They can obtain whatever variety they wish with the supplemental plans they choose. Some private markets for insurance and retirement plans exhibit some of the inefficiencies we have enumerated, but for most employees a retirement program is offered through their employer. While in many cases the individual has several options as to the level of participation, the nature of the investment portfolio, and the type of annuity, these do not create excessive informational costs. Most individuals are free to augment their Social Security and employer-based retirement programs by building equity in their home or in other types of investment.

Employer-Based Retirement Programs

As our demography has changed over the years, with people living longer and into the "golden years" of retirement, insurance companies have been slow to respond. Almost no retirement policies were available in the years preceding the Great Depression of the 1930s. When the depression occurred it wiped out the savings of many older citizens. Simultaneously it wiped out their jobs and the prospects of finding other employment. Individuals had previously relied on building up their own wealth so as to be secure if they reached old age. The market was *incomplete* in that, although there seemed to be a demand for retirement plans, no firms in the private sector seemed willing to embark on such a project. The implementation of the Social Security program was in part an emergency measure to provide for this new class of elderly poor. Social Security is designed to provide only a "social minimum" of support. As noted, there has been ample room for supplementary pension plans to emerge in the private sector. Due in part to tax incentives, pension plan coverage by employers has grown rapidly, especially in the decades from the 1950s until the 1980s. Since 1980, jobs in the large manufacturing industries have declined while the poorly paid and poorly covered jobs in the service industry have increased. Correspondingly, the percentage of workers enrolled in employer-based retirement programs has declined.

The public sector provides tax incentives to employers to set up retirement plans for their employees. Usually the employer makes part or all of the employee's contribution to the retirement fund. In any case the tax advantage makes this form of remuneration attractive, since personal income taxes are avoided. Because many of these plans are not transferable, they give an advantage to the employer in that they enhance employee retention.

The government has the responsibility of supporting private pension plans by regulating the industry and providing insurance so that each plan will be able to meet its obligations. A great diversity among employer-based pension plans has evolved, and government guidelines and regulations have not always been successful. During the 1980s, the parts played by pension funds in takeovers and bankruptcies raised difficult questions that have not been satisfactorily resolved.

Social Risks

The private-good nature of Social Security is that it provides an individual with insurance against being destitute in old age. It also provides psychic insurance for those who care about their neighbors. I am assured that few of my fellow citizens will ever become destitute in their old age. Private insurance companies are adept at pooling risks within a given group when the occurrence of the event to be insured against can be predicted with some accuracy. Generally, although life spans continue to increase, the demography of the various age cohorts is predictable. Yet, there are a number of reasons why private insurance companies cannot fulfill the insurance roles now played by Social Security.

One reason can be seen in the concept of *social risks*. Social risks involve events that are so widespread and random that they cannot be insured against by private companies. While the actuarial account of life spans allows private insurance companies to offer life insurance in normal times, we cannot expect their policies to cover deaths due to war. Similarly, we cannot expect private companies to offer policies that protect against widespread unemployment and forced retirement during a depression. Inflation is also a social risk, a risk of such widespread impact that we cannot expect the insurance industry to insure against it. Although an actuarially sound and properly invested retirement program may increase in value as other prices increase, it does not always keep pace with inflation. As we observed in the 1970s, it is possible to have inflation and recession simultaneously. In these and other periods of inflation there is no assurance that the values of insurance company portfolios will keep pace. Thus private-sector life insurance or retirement plans are not so confident of their investment portfolios that they are willing to index the returns they promise against inflation.

Government has the ability to compensate for social risks. Its powers to tax and create debt give it a greater ability to spread risks over time and geographical locations. While a hurricane, drought, or flood could wipe out a regionally based insurance company, the government can spread such risks over larger populations. Even during a period of war the government can redirect resources from present private-sector consumption and investment to the war effort and then spread the burden among future generations of taxpayers. Challenging questions of intergenerational justice arise as to how various monetary and fiscal policies affect private and public debt and private and public investment, and in turn the distribution of income and claims within and among various age cohorts. Similar questions arise with the Social Security program.

Risk Pooling: What Is the Appropriate Pool?

Different individuals have different expectations with regard to health, income earnings, and life spans. As we observed with the issue of health care, some interesting ethical questions arise when we ask who should be in the pool. One obvious difference between a retirement pool and a health care pool is that, in the first, you want to be grouped with those who die young, and, in the latter, you want to be with those who are very healthy.

When we have considered the question of who should be in the pool in other contexts, such as health care, most of the relevant moral principles seem to have favored larger, more inclusive, pools. Let us assume that a given community includes two major types of employment: coal mining and university teaching. Generally the coal miners have more health problems and shorter life spans than the university teachers. Consider the potential markets for health and retirement insurance. What sort of pooling could we expect to evolve? First we must recognize that private firms face several difficulties in formulating any plans they may offer. Second, we must consider whether or not there are efficient and fair ways to "pool" individuals. What is the nature of the community? Who belongs to the community and what sorts of obligations are inferred? Does everyone have an obligation to belong to one of the pools and thus share the costs of insuring against the pooled risks? We could expect the coal miners to prefer being pooled with the university teachers for purposes of health insurance but would not expect them to be enthusiastic about such pooling for a retirement plan, especially one that pays lifetime annuities to retirees. We would expect an individual to attempt to join those pools made up of others with more attractive risks and benefit profiles. The adverse selection problem, therefore, affects annuity-based retirement programs in the same way it affects health care insurance.

Query: What Moral Principles Are Relevant to Retirement Annuity Plans?

As individuals we belong to families and communities; we may be an employee in a private or public organization; we are all citizens within local, state, and national government boundaries. Within these complex layers of family, friends, and wider circles of attachments, what rights and obligations are affected when risks are shared? Moreover, what configuration of institutions is most appropriate for the pooling of these risks? Again, these questions are not simply questions of efficiency. Even if the various market failures could be corrected so that resource allocation would approximate that of the laissez-faire, perfect competition norm, not all of the important issues would be resolved. As we have argued, the nature of the various risks that individuals share includes social as well as individual concerns.

For a given group to be viable those receiving the lowest benefits must have sufficient reason to remain in the group. But no matter how the adverse selection problem is overcome, questions of fairness still arise. In life insurance pools those with poor life expectancies get a bargain if they are pooled with those with longer life expectancies. The latter can be thought of as subsidizing the former. Within a retirement annuity plan, those with longer life expectancies get a bargain if pooled with those with shorter life expectancies. Generally, when women are pooled with men in a retirement annuity plan, women, who usually live longer, are being subsidized by the men. Women are being given a subsidy in that they have a longer life expectancy. Of course, other considerations, such as job discrimination and historically lower pay for women, should be taken into account when questions of fairness are addressed. If it were possible to offer separate retirement annuity plans to women and men, would it be fair? Are there different moral principles that argue for and against separate pools? Our point is that such questions, although difficult, are germane to all retirement plans, including Social Security. The government has the means to overcome adverse selection in that it can use coercion to stop those who would withdraw from a given pool. The Social Security program requires almost all working individuals and their employers to pay premiums. One important question is whether or not the reasons we are presenting here are sufficient to justify the use of coercion.

The primary reason that retirement plans, as well as life and health insurance, have been organized on employer lines is that an employee is unlikely to change jobs in order to get a slightly better rate. As noted, the government's tax incentives have encouraged the evolution of this arrangement. Employer-based retirement plans clearly cannot satisfy social goals with respect to insurance against poverty among elderly persons. Moreover, as we observed in chapter five, employer-based health insurance has failed to satisfy social goals regarding the right to health care. In both cases the market failure caused by adverse selection is overcome, but employer-based pooling fails several of the fairness criteria. Of course, the extreme example of unfairness in health care insurance coverage is the case of over forty million Americans who have no coverage at all. The Social Security pool is much more inclusive.

Moral Hazard and Social Security

The term *moral hazard* is somewhat of a misnomer when applied to individual behavior and Social Security; but it is an influence that can create difficulties, if not failures, in private insurance markets. Moral hazard is the lessening of incentives individuals may have to avoid the insured-against events. If one's jewelry is insured one may wear it more often. If one's car is insured one may be less reluctant to park where it might be dented.

Individuals face the risk of becoming old, infirm, and thus unable to support themselves. They can insure against this by creating an adequate stock of wealth or by taking out insurance that will guarantee an annuity. One problem with the stock-of-wealth approach is that few individuals know how long they will live and what will be their state of health. Most individuals choose to make annuity insurance part of their retirement plan.

A particular type of moral hazard problem arises for some individuals when they approach retirement age and see that the income they will receive after retirement (their *replacement rate*) is in a range they consider quite adequate. Insurance for retirement can become a moral hazard if it creates incentive to actually retire. It is not clear whether or not this type of moral hazard problem is important for Social Security. On the one hand Social Security is simply a substitute for private retirement annuity plans an individual may purchase. If Social Security were not available most individuals would increase their investment in private retirement plans. On the other hand, we have observed that Social Security differs in important ways from private retirement plans. And these differences suggest that the moral hazard problem may not actually be detrimental to the purposes of the program. First, Social Security is compulsory; we assume that a significant number of persons would choose not to purchase old age annuity insurance unless required to do so. Second, there are great economies of scale in the Social Security program, so that, as a form of old age insurance, it is much more efficient than its private-sector counterparts. Third, there is some income redistribution involved, in that the low-income elderly have a proportionately better payoff than do the wealthier elderly. The payoffs for all groups have been generous relative to contributions. For all of these reasons most individuals contemplating retirement have better prospects than they would have had if the Social Security program did not exist. Certainly those elderly persons who would have been forced to work simply to survive, many of whom would have attempted to work even though they were in ill health, are able to retire instead. Others in better circumstances face improved retirement possibilities as well as greater incentive to retire.

Until recently, Social Security benefits were substantially decreased for those who earned income over certain levels. This disincentive is being reduced as the income test is being raised from $13,000 to $30,000 over a number of years.

As Social Security is reformed so as to reestablish its rationality and solvency, benefits will be reduced and more of them will be subject to taxation. Questions of fairness will be raised: Why should Social Security subsidize older and high-income workers, especially if that means higher tax burdens for younger workers?

It may be argued that all Social Security benefits, like other income, should be taxed. If we accept the principle that progressive income taxes are more fair, then this form of income should also be subjected to progressivity. It would be possible to raise benefits and tax coverage and be revenue neutral. The point of most public debate over benefits, however, is that the net benefits to the middle- and upper-income retirees should be reduced so as to improve the program's viability. But how far should we go in this direction? To the extent that Social Security attempts to provide a social minimum for the elderly poor, little reduction in their benefits is possible. The limits for benefit reductions and tax increases are questions of efficiency and fairness. If we see the retirement-base insurance as a private good, then the net benefits to all participants should be kept at a level where they are considered efficient and fair. This would seem to require that the benefits should at least be comparable to other investment opportunities. Considering the special characteristics of this type of insurance, which is that the retirement payoff goes only to those who survive and that there are substantial economies of scale, it should be possible to keep benefits high enough to maintain wide public support. As we shall argue, the rationality and intergenerational fairness of the program depend on how the trust funds are managed.

In one sense the moral hazard problem is no problem at all. Surely the purpose of social security is to enable elderly individuals to retire. Likewise the purpose of health care insurance is to enable individuals to obtain medical treatment. Even so, there are some work disincentives built into the Social Security system that should be removed. Certainly we do not want to discourage the elderly from continuing productive work if they enjoy it. More generally, as our population tends toward an older and healthier distribution, we need to consider redesigning all of our various institutional arrangements concerning retirement annuities, tax incentives and disincentives, and availability of full-time and part-time employment possibilities for the elderly.

Market Failure, Merit Goods, and Social Security

A basic tenet of our social ethics is that every person has a right to life and thus a right to certain things essential to maintaining life. These natural primary goods include food, shelter, clothing, and health care. Retirement insurance may be included if we reason that it insures at least a subsistence level of income for those who happen to live to old age.

By definition, a free market cannot require individuals to contribute to a retirement plan. But government, through its Social Security program, does in fact require that individuals contribute. One rationale for such paternalism is the argument that members of society feel an obligation toward each other. This obligation requires that those goods essential to life be available to all. It seems to follow, according to this argument, that all members of society have some obligation to insure themselves against becoming destitute in old age. An extreme libertarian approach would be to "respect" an individual's liberty to make his or her own choices; and this respect would outweigh any sympathy one felt for an individual who had chosen unwisely. As Milton Friedman has argued:

> Those of us who believe in freedom must believe also in the freedom of individuals to make their own mistakes. If a man knowingly prefers to live for today, to use his resources for current enjoyment, deliberately choosing a penurious old age, by what right do we prevent him from doing so.[1]

If one falls short of such ideological purity, or alternatively, if one believes that we have an obligation to the elderly, an obligation that outweighs our respect for their previous choices, then Friedman's argument fails. His argument also fails to take account of the fact that many poor individuals have current needs that seem to require all of the income they can muster. One does not have to be overly paternalistic to realize that, to a young person, old-age retirement insurance involves risks that are not always obvious and certainly not always pressing. Without compulsory insurance many poor people would choose not to insure against the possibilities that they could (1) lose their health, (2) lose the ability to support themselves, and (3) happen to live long enough for that to become a problem. Since later generations would bear the burden of such "irresponsible" behavior, we feel justified in requiring participation.

ETHICS, INVESTMENT, AND CLAIMS AMONG GENERATIONS: SOME RAWLSIAN PERSPECTIVES

Rawls's Social Minimum and the Problem of Justice among Generations

Rawls is quite clear that a "social minimum" relates to the problem of justice among generations. The social minimum is defined in terms of his difference principle:

Once the difference principle is accepted, however, it follows that the minimum is to be set at that point which, taking wages into account, maximizes the expectations of the least-advantaged group. By adjusting the amount of transfers (for example, the size of supplementary income payments), it is possible to increase or decrease the prospects of the more disadvantaged, their index of primary goods (as measured by wages plus transfers), so as to achieve the desired result.[2]

We should note that Rawls is suggesting a very specific and a very pervasive redistribution scheme. Interpretations vary as to just what policies would be required to implement the difference principle. Rawls himself is at times unclear as to whether or not radical redistribution is required. In this quotation, at least, the difference principle is to be achieved by a direct implementation of transfers by government. What is striking is that Rawls's application of the difference principle here is so radical relative to the more traditional tax and transfer principles. Except for questions of incentives, there seems to be no restriction on the use of taxes and transfers to raise the incomes of the least-well-off. What is being ignored is a principle of distributive justice usually given considerable weight in a free market economy: "to each according to his or her contribution."

What are some of the implications of this interpretation of Rawls's approach and the radical redistribution it seems to require? With respect to the question of intergenerational relationships, one incentive we must worry about is whether or not an appropriate amount of saving will take place in each generation. When we apply the difference principle we cannot simply apply the highest possible social minimum to the income distribution of the present generation. We cannot simply scale down the wealth of those better off "until eventually everyone has nearly the same income." We must also consider the "long-term prospects of the least-favored extending over future generations."

Rawls begins by visualizing cultures starting at levels of wealth in which a well-ordered society is not possible. There is a "burden of capital accumulation and of raising the standard of civilization and culture" to be shared among generations. This is certainly a difficult question in the context of a "state of nature" model. It also seems an appropriate concern for many third-world countries. But, considered in terms of a contract among citizens of one of the Western democracies, the question of capital accumulation is entirely different. Indeed, the accumulation required of this Rawlsian stage has long ago been achieved by all Western industrial nations. We will return to this proposition shortly.

We first note that Rawls admits to having no satisfactory approach to deciding what should be the savings goals for different generations in developing nations: "How the burden of capital accumulation and of raising the standard of civilization and culture is to be shared between generations seems to admit of no definite answer."[3] Thus Rawls essentially fails in his attempt to apply his principles to the question of a "just savings principle" for developing nations. He resorts to the "veil of ignorance" and suggests that in the "original position" the participants, theoretically not knowing to what generation they would belong, could come up with a specific set of savings rates showing what would be required of each generation. "Presumably this rate changes depending upon the state of society. When people are poor and saving is difficult, a lower rate of saving should be required; whereas in a wealthier society greater savings may reasonably be expected since the real burden is less."[4] Rawls's description of the way those in the original position decide upon each generation's "just" savings rate is quite awkward: "They try to piece together a just savings schedule by balancing how much at each stage they would be willing to save for their immediate descendants against what they feel entitled to claim of their immediate predecessors. Thus imagining themselves to be fathers, say, they are to ascertain how much they should set aside for their sons by noting what they would believe themselves entitled to claim of their fathers."[5]

What are we to make of the analogy of the feelings of fathers and sons? Surely the capital accumulation in the United States and most Western democracies has progressed beyond what one generation "owes" another. Intuitively we feel that fathers (parents) would be generous to their sons (children). And in most families children would expect their parents to be equally generous toward them. What is confusing here is that Rawls speaks of what the father is "willing" to save and what the son feels is his "entitlement." This would seem to leave a wide range within which the savings rate is to be decided. Our more general criticism, which we will consider later, is that use of the difference principle leaves little room for parents to be generous to their children. The radical redistribution required under the difference principle means that most extra income above the social minimum will be taxed and transferred to the least-well-off. (As noted, the only exception will be when higher incomes provide incentives that work to the advantage of the least-well-off.) It seems inappropriate to resort to the feelings of parents for their children if, as Rawls claims elsewhere, we should be in the process of applying the difference principle. His final scheme has little to do with the difference principle either at individual or at societal levels of conscience.

It seems clear that the present stock of capital of most developed nations qualifies as a Rawlsian final stage:

> The last stage of which saving is called for is not one of great abundance. This consideration deserves perhaps some emphasis. Further wealth might not be superfluous for some purposes; and indeed average income may not, in absolute terms, be very high. Justice does not require that early generations save so that later ones are simply more wealthy. Saving is demanded as a condition of bringing about the full realization of just institutions and the fair value of liberty. . . . It is a mistake to believe that a just and good society must wait upon a high material standard of life. What men want is meaningful work in free association with others, these associations regulating their relations to one another within a framework of just basic institutions. To achieve this state of things great wealth is not necessary. In fact beyond this point it is more likely to be a positive hindrance, a meaningless distraction at best if not a temptation to indulgence and emptiness.[6]

Although parts of his argument are awkward, the questions Rawls presents are similar to our own. Therefore, we can make use of some of the insights gained in our assessment of his theory. We should note, however, that, in applying his theoretical models to current social issues such as Social Security, we must pay attention to some of the more abstract and thus unrealistic assumptions of his models. We are left with the question of how to assess the potential of capital accumulation when the society in question is unlikely to implement the difference principle or to fully establish the institutions required for justice. Is the appropriate savings rate the same in an actual society as it would be in an ideal model? Rawls assumes that there will be zero population growth and no changes in technology. By assuming that technology does not change, he ignores the most important component of economic growth. It turns out that technological change is much more important than capital accumulation. Moreover, technological change is unpredictable, making it difficult to formulate a just savings rate as envisioned by Rawls. Over much of our history the introduction of new technology has so increased productivity that the difference principle would have required dissaving rather than saving.

Query: What Do We Owe Succeeding Generations?

Rawls's attempt to apply his theory to the question of intergenerational duties seems to create more problems than it solves. The radical redistribution required by a strict application of the difference principle is already problematical, but it seems even more so when applied to intergenerational obligations.

Let us consider the applicability of the other moral perspectives outlined in chapter one. The utilitarian principle, "the greatest good for the greatest number," necessarily focuses attention on how increased savings directed toward capital formation and research pay greater dividends to future generations. The utilitarian version of a "just savings principle" would reward present generations in a manner just the opposite from Rawls's difference principle. Although the present generation would be the least well off, it and each succeeding generation would continually be sacrificed for the greater good of an ever-increasing population.

By contrast, deontological arguments can more readily be made in support of the claims of present generations. According to Kant an act has moral worth only if it is done from a sense of duty to principle. The principle in turn must pass the test of the categorical imperative; Could we will that the rule become universal law? When we, as a generation, decide on what is fair for us to do, could we will that other generations follow the same principle? Or, similarly, could we will that preceding generations would have followed the same principle?

Very generally each generation has the responsibility to build and to maintain political and economic institutions that make for a fair game in which each person has opportunity to follow her or his own chosen life goals. To the extent that the game is fair, each person has a claim to rewards fairly earned.

As with other social issues, the conflict between utilitarian and deontological principles once again presents a moral dilemma. Should we ask if the results represent the greatest possible social welfare? Or should we ask if the processes and actions have moral worth? Is there an appropriate way to balance these principles?

One possible compromise among these principles may be to resort to the related ideas of satisficing and an acceptable social minimum. One generation should be able to meet its obligations to the next by passing on a situation that features an acceptable level of well-being and opportunity. Moreover, some room should be left for individuals and groups within each generation to devote their efforts and resources to their own goals. This satisficing level would require a distribution of income within each generation so that the basic needs of all individuals are met and an acceptable range of economic, political, and social opportunities are available to all. These intragenerational and intergenerational requirements are demanding but not as demanding as a strict application of the Rawlsian difference principle.

Let us agree that we do not know exactly what we *owe* succeeding generations. They are owed something. The acceptable social minimum is similar to the welfare concept, "minimum standard of living," but the former includes not only income but all of the Rawlsian primary goods. It also includes an acceptable range of economic opportunity. Thus, although we do not attempt to specify exactly what is required for an "acceptable social minimum," the idea is a useful standard.

All of this tells us nothing about what is allowable as an upper limit to what an individual or an entire generation can receive from its predecessors, nor does it say what the average or total should be. If we are comfortable with the idea that fortunes can be legitimately won (or lost) through luck or hard work, we must also accept inequality in incomes and wealth. If we also allow parents and others to give to individuals in succeeding generations, then we can expect further disparity. In earlier chapters we addressed the questions of placing limits on inheritance and of formulating other parameters as rules of the game, and we will occasionally return to that theme. If there is a general theme that runs through most discussions of what is owed to individuals or to generations, it is the Kantian injunction that each person deserves respect. This respect extends to the person's aspirations. In meeting our obligations, there is still room for generosity toward ourselves and others. Our duties to succeeding generations are not pervasive.

The public debate over the fate of Social Security is taking place within the larger context of demographic changes and questions of intergenerational justice. Moral arguments that relate to the Social Security program are essentially the same moral arguments that are relevant to the broader question of what one generation owes another. If we were to take a utilitarian perspective, we would question whether or not so much of our nation's resources should be devoted to the elderly. If we focus only on the "redistribution goal" of the program, there seems to be no justification for the benefits received by the elderly who are better off.

On the other hand, the deontological perspective of the fair game supports the claims of the elderly. They have contributed over the years and have been promised a substantial base upon which their other retirement investments have been built. Given the demography of the retirement of the baby-boomer generation in the year 2010 and beyond, the fair-game claim will be legitimate only if the program's trust fund is increased proportionately. Each generation has the responsibility during its working years to keep the system financially sound so that the inherent promises can be honored. The integrity of the system should never be allowed to deteriorate as it has in the 1980s and 1990s.

As with the broader generational debate, evaluation of the Social Security program presents a moral dilemma between principles focusing on how the pie should be divided or how the pie was made. The conflict can also be expressed in terms of principles of distributive justice: "to each according to need" or "to each according to contribution."

The present Social Security program is, in fact, a compromise or balance of these principles. Each of the two social goals relates to one of the principles: to provide for the basic needs of the elderly poor and to reward the other participants with a retirement base that partially reflects their contribution.

SOCIAL SECURITY AS A CONTRACT AMONG GENERATIONS

The present Social Security contract links the individual to society and one generation to another. Since the retirement program necessarily involves the public sector, we must now consider how the contracts among members of multigenerational families, and among generations in the broader sense, are affected. We need to be more specific about what is meant by various definitions of "generation."

What Is a Generation?

We have been using the term *generation* in several contexts, each of which has a unique and important meaning. When referring to one family made up of several generations, the meaning is clear: grandparents, parents, and children make up distinct generations. Of course, one model will not suffice, since there are many types of family units including single persons, couples without children, and single-parent families. It follows that the implicit and explicit contracts among family members will differ according to the nature of the family relationships.

Our second broad meaning of the term refers to age cohorts that share experiences and events such as economic depression, war, inflation, and technological change. These shared experiences and events tend to distinguish them and perhaps alienate them from other age cohorts. The same events affect individuals differently according to their age. The Great Depression affected children, young singles, married couples, older parents, and the elderly in different ways according to the needs, wants, and responsibilities of each. Similarly, World War II and the wars in Korea and Vietnam had different effects on different age cohorts. We will not attempt to survey and evaluate all of the theories of social scientists that seek to explain how particular generations share and respond to social institutions and events. Instead, we will pick a few perspectives that seem to offer insight into the questions we are asking.

There are two points of departure important to our understanding of the idea of a generation. First we must realize that strictly temporal and biological factors are important; but second, we must also realize that social, economic, and political events are crucial to the turning points that mark new generations and their perceptions of social issues. There is a danger of either placing too much emphasis on measurable temporal and biological data (such as birth, death, life span, age distribution) or placing too much emphasis on the political and economic events that tend to differentiate and shape generations. David Hume speculated that, if human generations were structured like the caterpillar-butterfly metamorphosis, a whole new set of institutions could be invented each new generation. It is the biological continuity and overlapping of generations that necessitates accommodation among generations and affects continuity or change in social institutions.

One important way to define the phenomenon of a generation is in terms of an intellectual movement, a new frame of reference for intellectual discourse. A generation contributes to intellectual and social movements according to its own experiences and how it interacts with other generations.

We observe that periods of social and economic change affect the choices open to individuals within various age groups, New sets of challenges and opportunities are being placed before each age cohort. In the first place, the traditional ways of applying ethical norms, say, the accepted fair rules of the game criteria, become difficult simply because the game itself is changing. Old norms of parental responsibilities toward sons and daughters preparing for and entering the job market or homemaking necessarily change, just as those institutions and the roles of men and women change.

If we define generations as age cohorts, we observe that the responsibilities of younger, working age cohorts change as life spans and retirement years increase. Since the "game" itself is changing, social norms are also changing. This includes generally held ideas as to what are the responsibilities of children toward their elderly parents and what are the responsibilities of one generation of taxpayers toward Social Security beneficiaries.

Individual Choices within Multigenerational Families

The roles individuals are expected to play and the choices open to them within familial, economic, and societal settings are circumscribed in many ways. When an important social or economic event occurs that evokes a turning point in attitudes, it is experienced in different ways by the individuals within families with different age groupings. Consider, for example, how the 1929 stock market crash may have affected a three-generational family that had children in college, parents in their mid-forties, and grandparents who were elderly and retired. Each age group would be affected in different ways. Alternatively, consider the effects on another three-generational family; one with very young children, parents in their late twenties, and grandparents who were still working and held positions of great responsibility. The challenges to each age group would have been quite different from the other three-generational family. In addition to the different responses within families to an important social event, there is a larger social context in which each family is affected by the responses of other families with different age dispersions.

The dynamics within a multigenerational family and among overlapping offset generations give us insight into the possible responses to events that affect the age cohorts in different ways. The combined effects of the Great Depression and World War II shaped a unique worldview for those who turned eighteen in the late 1930s and early 1940s. The experiences of having taken part in successful individual and social responses to those challenges made for attitudes and aspirations quite different from those of preceding generations. A veteran's return after World War II meant that college education could be begun or completed, with marriage, children, and a new career to quickly follow. For those in an offset generation who were, say, twelve years older, the Great Depression and World War II severely interfered with careers and family responsibilities that had already been undertaken. Veterans who were in their mid-thirties when they returned from World War II faced a different set of responsibilities and opportunities. For some, the interruptions in their careers would allow new opportunities to be considered; for most, however, the lost ground would never be regained.

If we are to analyze the implicit contracts within families we must recognize that the expected familial roles are changing, especially the intergenerational responsibilities. Not only are intergenerational "demands" changing with demographic change, but ideas as to appropriate roles and responsibilities are changing; thus, traditional responses cannot be expected.

Retirement conventions and policies have changed within the economy but have not kept pace with important demographic and sociological developments. Legal and economic institutions have failed to provide productive opportunities for older generations and, in fact, provide disincentives. Longer life means more generations within a family and new sets of responsibilities and dependency relationships. Divorce and remarriage, combined with increased longevity, make for complex relationships among dispersed kin and step-kin.

For obvious reasons, we like to think in terms of decades such as the 20s, 30, 40s, 50s, 60s, 70s, 80s, 90s, the turn of the century, and so on. Unfortunately, decades are not good demarcations for the events we usually acknowledge as important for shaping particular generations. For example, the 1940s included the end of the Great Depression, World War II, and four years of postwar economic boom. Some young people experienced their maturation years (say 18–22) during the early stages of the war, while others missed most of the war and came of age in the postwar economic boom.

Alternatively, consider the term "Sixties Generation." For those who reached twenty in 1960, the "sixties" offered expanding job opportunities and an optimistic attitude toward "curing" any of society's political, economic, and cultural ills. Those who turned twenty in 1968 experienced the assassinations of the Kennedys and Martin Luther King, the frustrations with the civil rights movement, the war on poverty, and the war to "preserve democracy" for the South Vietnamese; they perceived the decade in an entirely different light.

Young people reaching twenty in the late 1990s enter a world where the end of the cold war has opened new possibilities for trade and economic growth and has greatly reduced the fear of a nuclear holocaust. Yet, other threats to their well-being include the exploding world population, crime, drugs, AIDS, pollution, and changing family values. With regard to the Social Security program, they inherit a responsibility to pay the retirement benefits of the baby boomers. At the same time they inherit a mistrust for government and its ability to address social problems.

To iterate, we are using the idea of generations in two ways: (1) within a family in which various responsibilities, expectations, claims, and duties are attached to the roles of children, parents, and grandparents; and (2) as age cohorts in which important economic and political events may trigger a sense of shared experience, worldview, and purpose. As noted, these sequences of familial generations may overlap in various ways. For example, many of the veterans returning from World War II had baby-boom children in the late 1940s who became part of the youth movement in the late 1960s. A striking feature of the youth movement in the late 1960s and early 1970s was the alienation of that generation, not only from their parents but also from any authority except that of their peers. An earlier overlapping generation matured during the Great Depression and also fought in World War II; but their families and careers were started in the mid and late 1930s, and they returned from the war with a different set of responsibilities and goals. Many of their children came of age in the late 1950s and early 1960s, with a different inheritance of values and a different assessment of individual and social possibilities. Many of the young people who turn twenty in the late 1990s are part of the generational sequence that is offset to the baby boomers. The interplay of generations with different experiences and values makes for interesting speculation. Will the trend toward more adversarial relationships in business and almost all aspects of social activity affect the relationships among generations? Will faith in the effectiveness and fairness of our political processes continue to erode?

Obviously, the nature of intergenerational "conflict" or "support" depends strongly on the perceptions and values held by each generation. If there is to be adequate support of the Social Security program, its purposes must be interpreted in terms of the values and perceptions of each generation.

THE NATURE OF THE 1983 CRISIS

Query: Was the 1983 Solution Fair and Efficient?

If the Social Security system had continued to rely on pay-as-you-go funding, it would have been vulnerable to demographic changes and economic conditions. Over the last fifty years, several important demographic changes have been occurring. First, the life spans of women and men have increased. One reason the market for retirement programs was not well developed in the 1930s was that most workers did not visualize living until sixty-five; and of those who reached age sixty-five in 1930, the remaining life expectancy was to live to age seventy-seven. By 1950 the remaining life expectancy at sixty-five had reached eighty-one for men and eighty-eight for women. Although the rate of increase in life expectancy is slowing, the trend continues upward.

Second, the phenomenon of the baby-boom years has been followed by steadily declining birth rates. The birth rate rose after World War II and reached a maximum in the mid and late 1950s. It then fell rapidly. The average woman now has fewer than two children. The proportion of our population over sixty-four has risen from 14 percent in 1950 to 21 percent in 1990. It will reach only 22 percent in 2010 but will then jump to 29 percent in 2020, 38 percent in 2030, and should be over 40 percent in 2060.

Third, the percentage of men who remain in the workforce after sixty-five is declining. The number of beneficiaries per covered worker rose rapidly over the first four decades of the program and then leveled off at a rate of 30 beneficiaries per 100 covered workers. This rate is expected to be maintained until it begins to rise again in 2015 toward a plateau by 2030 or somewhere between 40 and 50 beneficiaries per 100 covered workers (or even more under the most pessimistic assumptions).

Finally, a particular feature of the 1983 crisis was the reduction in revenues caused by the 1981–1982 recession. Unemployment during any recession automatically reduces the employee and the employer contributions to Social Security, and this recession was by far the most severe since the depression of the 1930s. At the same time, a recession reduces the employment opportunities of the elderly and thus either encourages or forces them to retire.

These difficulties combined to create a crisis for the program in the late 1970s and early 1980s. Shortfalls in revenues were quickly depleting the program's trust fund. A presidential commission headed by Alan Greenspan offered a set of recommendations to shore up the program immediately. First, a scheduled cost-of-living increase to beneficiaries was postponed. Second, the schedule of future tax increases was accelerated. Third, coverage was extended to new federal employees. While this last change brought in more revenue in the short run, it also increased future claims. A change that improves the long-run viability of the program was to raise the retirement age from sixty-five to sixty-seven starting the year 2000. There remain many inefficiencies built into the incentives of the program. The most obvious is the great disincentive against continuing work once you have reached retirement age. A restructuring of the benefit options would encourage the development of part-time work opportunities for partially retired workers Most, if not all, of the revenue loss could be recouped by taxing the additional income earned.

From the mid-1950s through 1983 the program's revenues were closely matched by expenditures. The changes instituted in 1983 will continue to lead to the accumulation of larger and larger reserves: more than $215 billion in 1990, $1,026 billion by 2000, and over $6,300 billion by 2020.

A Rational Approach to Funding over Time: Close Actuarial Balance

It was the necessity of dealing with an immediate crisis that brought about changes in funding in 1983. The administration and the Congress were forced to consider both the short-run and long-run viability of the programs. The funding program that has emerged follows a pragmatic approach. The actuarial standard used to evaluate the financial viability of the programs through time is termed *close actuarial balance*. It compares the cost (benefit rates) and the income (revenue rates) through time for various periods of the next seventy-five years. If at any time the income rate of the next seventy-five-year period becomes less than 95 percent of the cost rate, Congress is expected to cut benefits or raise revenues to restore "balance." Of course the projections of future revenues and benefit obligations depend heavily on assumptions concerning economic growth, employment rates, income levels, interest rates, fertility rates, and mortality rates.

An assessment of the long-run viability of the program and the intergenerational distribution of benefits and burdens must take into account the larger macroeconomic picture. The "claims" with which the future taxpayer must deal include Social Security payments to the elderly as well as debt instruments of the federal government. In the early 1980s the particular combination of expansionary fiscal policy and overwhelmingly restrictive monetary policy seemed designed to maximize the federal debt. Whether by design or not, the Reagan administration quickly realized that the debt was an effective constraint on any expansion of social programs that might be advocated by the Democrats in Congress. Deficits were maintained at high levels during the Reagan years, and the resultant debt will continue to act as a constraint on spending initiatives in succeeding years. The debt and the viability of the Social Security program are closely linked. During the course of the program, the benefits to the elderly have been increased regularly to levels beyond what they contributed and beyond the returns on private retirement programs. In the 2010s and 2020s, when many of the baby boomers will retire, the viability of the program will be greatly threatened. As noted, the number of retired persons will rise dramatically relative to the number of those working.

A Case Study of Immoral Public Financing:
Masking the Federal Deficit

In the 1980s and early 1990s the Reagan and Bush administrations and Congress allowed the Social Security surpluses to mask the true size of the deficits. As noted, these deficits can be attributed to an unfortunate mix of fiscal and monetary policy. The phenomenon of cost-push inflation had caused two severe recessions in the 1970s. But the monetary and fiscal policies during these recessions, although inept, were not so devastating as those that created the recession of the early 1980s. Public perceptions of the efficacy of public policies were also dimmed by the unsuccessful Vietnam War. National income per person, which had been growing from 1945 to 1973 at over 2.1 percent per year, had slowed from the mid-1970s. Declines in economic growth and fertility rates began to take their tolls on the economic health of the Social Security programs in the early 1980s. A related legacy of these events and policies is a huge federal debt. The federal debt, tax cuts, and effective resistance to tax increases make it difficult to follow rational approaches to funding the Social Security retirement and health care programs.

The role played by the Social Security and Medicare trust funds in masking federal budget deficits is shown in Table 6.1. To the extent that the surpluses play this role, the basic rationality of the Social Security and other taxes is undermined. In the first place, and most important, the rationality of building up surpluses so as to fairly and efficiently allocate taxpayer burdens and recipient benefits through time is eroded because smaller *real* surpluses are set aside. In the second place, since higher Social Security taxes essentially took the place of higher personal income taxes in providing revenue for the increased spending on defense and interest on the debt, the mix of revenue sources becomes significantly more regressive. The mix thus became less "rational" in terms of the traditional principles of tax fairness and efficiency.

Economic Growth and the Distribution of Financial Claims

At a more general level we observe that the future well-being of various age cohorts, working and retired, depends more on economic growth than on the intergenerational distribution of claims in the form of debt instruments. Only to the extent that surpluses in the Social Security trust funds lead to increased national saving (and in turn to increased capital formation, new technology, and greater productivity), will the real burden on future taxpayers be reduced. In a very real sense, all participants in a growing economy share the benefits. As economic growth occurs over time, the financial claims in the form of issues of stock and bonds that accompany real investments do not exhaust the increase in productivity. We can gain some insight into this relationship by considering the economic theory known as the *marginal productivity theory*.

TABLE 6.1
FEDERAL BUDGET AND SOCIAL SECURITY
SURPLUSES (IN BILLIONS OF DOLLARS)

Year	Total Federal Budget Deficit	OASDI Surpluses	Total
1980	−74.0	0	−74.0
1986	−221.2	+14.3	−235.5
1987	−149.8	+35.5	−185.3
1988	−155.2	+56.9	−212.1
1991	−269.5	+71.7	−341.2

Sources: Department of the Treasury and Office of Management and Budget, U.S. Department of Health and Human Services.

Two ideas inherent in the argument are useful here. First is the idea that, if capital stocks grow faster than the labor supply, productivity per unit of labor is enhanced relative to capital. More important, the productivity of labor is enhanced by new technology; not only the quantity but also the quality of real investment is increasing. Second, if we assume that market wages reflect this change in relative productivity, then the wage rate will increase faster than the rate of return. Ironically, all of this happens simply because the capital stock increases faster than the supply of labor. Put more simply, the 1945–1975 wage rates of American workers increased because they were working with more and better machines. Even if the claims represented by the Social Security trust funds grow and are designated for benefits for the elderly, these claims will not exhaust the added productivity brought about if an increase in real investment takes place in earlier periods. Those age cohorts, who in later periods will be taxpayers, will find that their real incomes will also have been enhanced by the investment taking place in earlier periods.

The question of how rapidly the economy can grow without increasing inflation is an ongoing subject of public debate. For a given growth path to be realized, savings and investment must follow certain paths. Unfortunately, the link between savings and investment is often tenuous. Increased national saving is a necessary but not a sufficient condition for increased national investment. Policies for increased productivity must encourage saving. More important, they must insure that the flow of spending in every period is sufficient to provide for a full employment of resources. At the same time, an environment must be created that encourages basic research and the realization of human potential.

Since World War II we have experienced two distinct growth paths. From 1945 until the mid 1970s the economy grew at 3.5 percent per year. Since the mid 1970s the growth rate has slowed to 2.5 percent per year. Had the former rate been maintained, the difference in annual real income per person would have been substantial, well over $3,000 per person. The slowdown in growth, particularly the recessions of the 1970s, 1980s, and 1990s, has directly affected the viability of government programs such as Social Security. Estimates of economic growth rates have become an important part of the public debate over balancing the federal budget. Much depends on macroeconomic policy, especially monetary policy. Over much of the slower growth period, the policy of the Federal Reserve has been to fight inflation by restraining the rate of growth and by keeping unemployment at or above 6 percent. If at some time the Federal Reserve discovers that a higher rate of growth is consistent with low inflation, then it will pursue a more expansionary policy. Until that time, growth is unlikely to rise above 2.5 percent.

NEW PROPOSALS: ARE THEY FAIR AND EFFICIENT?

Several recent Social Security reform proposals would make important changes in the way the system operates. Most of the reform proposals would privatize all or part of the system, seeking to take advantage of the greater efficiency promised by competitive markets. The most drastic reform would be to completely privatize the system. Simply put, this would mean that the system would be abolished. There would have to be a transition period in which the claims of those already retired or about to retire would be partially honored. The payroll tax could be phased out as well. Those who support this approach generally would allow individuals the freedom to plan or not to plan for retirement as they so choose. However, they would concede that a majority of society might insist that individuals be required to save and invest. If that is the case, they argue, we could simply require that every individual demonstrate reasonable progress toward saving for retirement. A related proposal would be to retain a safety net for the elderly poor; thus Social Security would become a "means-tested" transfer.

Other proposals would retain the present structure but would establish individual retirement accounts in which benefits would be more closely tied to an individual's contribution. A variation on this theme would be to give the individual some choice of how his or her account is invested, say, in government securities or a fund that features stocks. It is generally conceded that returns can be improved.

The assumptions implicit in these proposals can be better evaluated if we look at them separately. At least five questions can be distinguished:

1. Should the two Social Security retirement goals, a guaranteed social minimum and a base for retirement planning, be clearly distinguished and separated?

2. Would restoring and maintaining the integrity of the present system require that taxes be raised?

3. Should the Social Security trust funds be invested in ways that promise a higher return?

4. Should benefits be more closely linked to contributions?

5. Should individual participants build equity claims (i.e., equity that can be transferred)?

The analytical perspectives developed earlier can be used to dissect and analyze the inherent assumptions.

Query: Should the Two Social Security Retirement Goals Be Clearly Distinguished and Separated?

Most of the new proposals do, in fact, make the distinction between the goal of guaranteeing an acceptable social minimum standard of living for the elderly poor and the goal of providing everyone with a financial base to build their own retirement plan. Given the pervasive disposition to cut spending and taxes, public understanding and support are essential if both parts of the program are to survive. If we, as a society, are to make an informed choice, we need to have a much better understanding of the goals and what would be required for their accomplishment. Frequently, public discussion of reform proposals focuses only on the upcoming crisis created by the baby-boomer generation. The major concern becomes the burden that must be borne by future generations. The implication is that there is no way Social Security could continue to be a sound investment.

Such emphasis confuses the issue in at least two ways. First, emphasis on the investment goal ignores the equally important social-minimum goal. Second, if the demographic challenge is dealt with separately and efficiently, there is no reason why trust funds cannot be managed so that the expected retirement base remains a good investment for all participants. For both parts of the retirement program to remain viable, the public must feel an obligation to support redistribution to the elderly poor; and it must also have confidence that the retirement base insurance will remain a good buy.

It is true that the upcoming crisis will create an unfair distribution of burdens among the generations if we fail to maintain the fairness and efficiency of the system. We should not lose sight of the fact that most of the elderly are part of multigenerational families. Maintaining benefit levels for the elderly in most cases directly affects the well-being of their children and grandchildren. Conversely, if the benefits of the baby boomers are cut when they retire, their children and grandchildren will also be affected. The "savings" to many taxpayers will be illusory. The issue of separating the two goals leads directly to the issue of taxes.

Query: Would Restoring and Maintaining the Integrity of the Present System Require That Taxes Be Raised?

The answer to this question is simple and straightforward: yes, taxes should be raised. Small increases are needed now and at fairly predictable intervals so that intergenerational fairness can be restored and maintained. Close attention must be given to the expected benefits of each age cohort and the contributions they make during their working years. In theory, some other budget expenditures could be reduced and revenues shifted to the Social Security trust fund. But the chances of finding sufficient revenues in this way are remote.

Would it be fair for current taxpayers to pay even more taxes? Since current taxpayers can expect a healthier and longer retirement than preceding generations, they must expect more taxes during their working years. It was argued earlier that intergenerational fairness is roughly accomplished by adhering to close actuarial balance. In the 1983 legislation the conditions for intergenerational fairness were specified. Taxes and the trust fund are to be periodically readjusted in terms of each upcoming seventy-five-year period. It is appropriate that the present working-age generation pay taxes consistent with the claims they are generating for their own retirement years.

Unfortunately most new proposals are in the spirit of "tax revolt." Political strategists are convinced that any tax increase is politically unpopular and doomed to failure. On the other hand, if some of the common misconceptions about the Social Security program were overcome, there could be wide support for the required tax increases. Younger working-age participants are concerned that they will receive reduced benefits. Any tax increase must be backed by guarantees that future claims will be honored.

A better definition of the two purposes and how they are to be financed should be part of the public discussion. It is necessary that all participants understand the role of the trust fund and the concept of close actuarial balance.

The distinction between the two purposes could be better clarified by designating a separate tax structure and trust fund to accomplish the redistribution goal. As we have argued, if the two purposes are evaluated in terms of fairness and efficiency criteria, the appropriate tax for the social minimum is seen to be the personal income tax; whereas, the appropriate tax for the retirement base is seen to be the payroll tax. Several of the new proposals advocate that Social Security benefits be means tested. If the two goals are separated, the idea of a means test can be incorporated in the following way: every participant will build up claims by contributing through the payroll tax. For some, these contributions would provide a base to build a more comfortable retirement. Others will have enjoyed less success. The claims they will have built up will not be sufficient even to justify the acceptable social minimum. Therefore their contributions will have to be augmented by transfers from general revenues. The transfer necessitated to bring the benefit level up to the social minimum is, in one sense, means tested. One conclusion from this line of reasoning is that the personal income tax should play a much larger role in the system. If the personal income tax plays a larger role, the necessary increase in payroll taxes would be correspondingly smaller, and the retirement base part of the program would be perceived as a better buy.

As noted, the payroll tax is an appropriate revenue source for the insured-retirement-base part of the program, since the latter is essentially a private good. The benefits are individual and go directly to the recipient. Although there are externalities in the forms of benefits to the families of elderly persons and to society as a whole, the benefits are primarily private. A regressive tax is justified in the same way that any market price, although regressive, is considered fair. If, for example, a wealthy person and a poor person buy television sets for the same price, their net incomes afterwards are more unequal than before. However, this result does not seem unfair.

By contrast, if we characterize Social Security as simply a redistribution scheme, the use of a regressive tax is irrational. The personal income tax should be used instead. This brings us to the question of whether or not a separate trust fund should be established to finance the system's redistribution role in the future. Since the baby-boomer generation will include a larger number of elderly poor than preceding generations, it can be argued that they should pay more during their working years. It may be appropriate that a separate trust fund be built up for the redistribution function and paid for from current general revenues, say, the personal income tax.

Query: Should the Social Security Trust Funds Be Invested in Ways That Promise a Higher Return?

Here again the answer is straightforward: yes. Public understanding of how the trust funds are invested is important if the program is to be considered a good investment. The present system is largely misunderstood. While surpluses in Social Security financing do in fact encourage investment in the private sector as well as in the public sector, the general perception is that Social Security surpluses have no effect.

The Social Security trust funds are guaranteed as to principal and interest by law. Almost all of these assets are held in the form of special debt obligations issued by the Treasury for purchase only by the trust funds. The interest rate is required to be equal to the market yield on other government securities.

The treatment of Social Security within the budget has changed in the last two decades. In an effort to make sure that earlier program deficits not be ignored, the revenues and the expenditures were included in a "unified budget" after 1969. As noted, however, the relationship between revenues and expenditures changed after 1983. One of the recommendations of the 1982 Commission on Social Security Reform was that the OASDI and health insurance (HI) programs be removed from the unified budget; thus the surpluses would not be included when overall budget deficits were calculated. Congress, in theory at least, followed this recommendation; but the effective date was delayed until 1993. Although one provision of the Gramm-Rudman-Hollings Act of 1985 designated the OASDI programs as "off-budget" items, another provision allowed them to be included in the deficit-reduction targets.

For the present institutions to work in a rational way, it is not required that each dollar in the trust funds be invested in the stock market or to directly underwrite capital formation in specific industries. If the surpluses are used to purchase U. S. Treasury securities, as is now the case, these purchases *directly reduce federal borrowing* from lenders in the private sector. These reductions allow more private-sector savings to flow into private-sector investment. Again, although increased saving does not guarantee that productive investments will be undertaken, it will do so if other favorable factors are present. Trust fund surpluses directly increase government saving and, in turn, make other savings available to private-sector investment. Unfortunately, this effect was more than offset by the budget deficits created during the Reagan years.

Let us consider two arguments for seeking better investment opportunities for the trust funds. The first has to do with efficiency and the second has to do with fairness. Efficiency in the sense of the system's viability would be obviously enhanced by a higher return on trust fund investment. Efficiency also has to do with participants' making choices on the basis of perceived benefits and costs. The participants in the program compare the returns they expect from the payroll taxes they pay with other investment opportunities. If a substantial portion of the trust fund were prudently invested in the stock market, there is no doubt that, over time, the fund would enjoy a significantly higher return than the present policy; moreover, the investment function of the fund would be much more visible than it is under the present system. Indeed the mechanics of the present policy have encouraged the widely held perception that no real investment is taking place. It follows that a better understanding of the program's benefits and costs (the comparisons we make as voters and taxpayers) would enhance efficiency. This latter definition of efficiency, or, allocative efficiency refers to the allocation of resources in the economy as a whole. It is enhanced when allocative decisions better reflect marginal benefits and costs.

The second argument concerns fairness. We have observed that two principles of distributive justice feature prominently in the public debate: to each according to need and to each according to contribution. Assuming that the program is reorganized, citizens in their roles as voters and taxpayers will recognize that the redistribution function is being financed by income taxes; and the retirement base function is being financed by the payroll tax. It is in this latter context that it is important for each person's contribution to be reflected in the benefits they expect to receive. Emphasizing individual retirement accounting and a high profile investment policy would reinforce the conception of the system as a process in which legitimate claims are created among individuals as well as among generations. Of course, succeeding congresses and administrations must appreciate and honor these obligations.

These considerations inherently assume that a better return could be achieved and a better understanding of the two separate functions would lead to greater public support. This might not be the case. There are strong antigovernment currents within public opinion. Among the arguments in favor of privatization is that government is inept and cannot be trusted. Can government, or more specifically, Congress, be trusted to guard the integrity of the system? Given the tenor of current budget debates, such doubts seem well founded. Another set of reservations surrounds the question of whether or not government should invest in the stock market, since, it is argued, the government is generally inept and would probably squander money on risky endeavors. There is also a question of whether or not government would use its financial power to embark on an "industrial policy," say, to favor those industries that show promise of economic growth. Those who favor complete privatization argue that private individuals can do a better job of investing than government; therefore, all that is required is for the government to rescind the payroll tax.

Once the link between the system's two facets is broken, the choice between allowing government or individuals to make the investment decisions becomes a real option. Individual accounts could be established under either partial privatization or the present system. This leads directly to a related question: How closely should benefits be tied to an individual's contribution?

Query: Should Benefits Be More Closely Linked to Contribution?

The arguments related to this question have been raised in other contexts. Those who favor a closer link between contribution and benefits would include both efficiency and fairness considerations in their arguments. The efficiency argument is that resource allocation is improved when prices reflect benefits and costs. Just as consumers adjust their purchases of private goods by comparing additional costs with additional benefits, voters and taxpayers compare the benefits and costs of public programs. The fairness argument, as noted, is the familiar principle of distributive justice: to each according to his or her contribution. Throughout the history of Social Security, the benefits received by the average retiree have far exceeded contributions. In the future, however, it will be more difficult for benefits to exceed contributions, especially for those who contribute the maximum amount over a full working career. In the future, only if benefits are more closely tied to contributions will the returns to the larger contributors compare favorably with returns available elsewhere. Let us assume that the system is reorganized so that the personal income tax is used to finance the redistribution facet of the program and the payroll tax is used to finance the retirement base. The payroll tax would then become the price the individual pays for the private good, that is, the individual's retirement-insurance base. Again, what must be avoided are benefit reductions that make the program a poor investment for a significant proportion of the participants.

In the present system each working-age participant already has an individual retirement account, in that her or his expected benefits are based on contributions. What is being proposed is that benefits be based even more directly on contribution. Presumably, the individual would be more aware of the progress of his or her account and the benefits he or she could expect. These benefits would be described in terms of the annuity that the individual could expect upon retirement.

There are some arguments against closer links between individual benefits and contributions. A more egalitarian approach would be to retain the present redistribution scheme that provides generous benefits not only to the elderly poor but also to the lower-income groups in general. To the extent that benefits are tied more closely to contribution, the lower-income groups would be less well off. We would expect most conservatives to argue that justice requires that benefits be linked more closely to contributions. The choice to have distribution more closely reflect contribution than need is one that clearly calls for a balance between two moral principles.

Query: Should Individual Participants Build Equity Claims?

An extrapolation of the argument that benefits should be more closely related to contributions is the proposal that individuals build equity in their own retirement accounts. Under the present system one collects only if one lives past retirement age. For those who live long into retirement, the Social Security annuity will be paid for many years. In cases in which a person dies before retirement there are various benefits for survivors, including the privilege of spouses to the higher annuity; but there is no equity that could be transferred either before or after death.

The proposals to privatize Social Security would allow individuals more choice in how they invest. For example, they could prepare for retirement by accumulating wealth in the form of, say, stocks, bonds, and real estate. Unlike a plan that promises an annuity, an individual's wealth, or equity, can be transferred to others; it can be sold or given away. As noted, those proposals for complete privatization include a transition procedure in which the claims of current retirees and contributors are honored in full or in part.

As with any proposal to privatize a public program, it is appropriate to ask whether or not the market failures that necessitated government intervention originally have been somehow corrected. Let us begin with the assumption that society still wishes to guarantee a social minimum to all elderly persons. Can we assume that the appropriate level of benefits will be transferred to the elderly poor and financed from general revenues? Can we further assume that personal income tax rates will be increased? We should observe that under the present system even the poor are required to pay payroll taxes. In this way they build up claims to some portion of their final benefits. Under complete privatization the tax revenues and the correlative claims of low-income participants would simply disappear.

How would the new tax burdens be shifted among generations? By the time future generations of the elderly poor become eligible for a means-tested benefit, the rest of their generation will be already retired. Is that generation to be taxed or will the burden fall on younger generations? This question will become especially problematical when the baby boomers begin to retire. We can assume that the number of elderly poor will be proportional. As we have suggested in other contexts, a trust fund would be required if intergenerational fairness is to be maintained. This would allow for the baby-boomer generation to contribute during their working years. In this way they could share the burden that the elderly poor of their generation will impose in the future.

A related market failure that would reemerge under complete privatization is the free-rider problem. If low-income persons are aware that government will provide a safety net when they become elderly, they will have no incentive to save for retirement. The strength of the disincentives depends on the level of the basic social minimum and the rate the transfer is reduced as income levels increase.

Several market failures are associated with government provision of retirement insurance. In the 1930s most of the savings of the elderly were wiped out by the Great Depression. As noted, social risks, such as recession or inflation, cannot be met by private insurance companies; only government has the necessary resources.

We observe that a significant proportion of our fellow citizens are short-sighted with respect to providing for their own retirement. This raises the question of whether or not society has an obligation to play a paternalistic role. Must people be required to save for their retirement? We would all agree that government has an obligation to set speed limits and punish us when we speed. Surely a program that employs compulsion to make us save for retirement can be considered fair if it enjoys widespread approval.

The market failures associated with adverse selection would reemerge if the Social Security retirement insurance were privatized. In the absence of viable insurance pools many markets would be either incomplete or nonexistent. Where employer retirement insurance plans are available, the adverse selection phenomenon is overcome, as with health insurance. Moreover, no difficulty occurs when individuals are able to provide for retirement by accumulating assets such as stocks, bonds, and real estate. But if it were available, a retirement insurance plan would be a more viable alternative for most people. If the Social Security retirement insurance were terminated, no comparable alternative would evolve in the private sector.

This does not mean that the Social Security system could not be privatized. It simply means that the market failures that originally provoked government intervention will reemerge. It would be naive to think otherwise.

Finally, let us consider the ways that the various elements of the new proposals might be combined. There are several variations on the privatizing theme. The extreme version is to rescind the payroll tax and simply leave that income with the individual to do with as she or he pleases. This assumes that it is the individual's own responsibility to prepare for her or his retirement years. The basic needs of the elderly poor could be met by private charities or, if necessary, by government relief programs. This proposal fails to recognize or address the market failures and social goals we have considered. The implicit assumption is that society has neither the right nor the ability to address these concerns.

Another variation on the privatizing theme leaves the payroll tax in place but has a significant part, say, half, put into individual savings accounts in which each participant could invest largely as he or she chooses; and the accumulation would become his or hers at retirement. The individual still has some freedom of choice, benefits are more closely tied to payroll contributions, and the individual has a transferable equity claim. In most versions of this scheme certain limitations would be placed on the types of investments the individual could make.

The question of whether or not the equity claims are to be transferrable is perhaps the most important difference between partial privatization and the present system. The retirement-base feature of the present system promises relatively generous returns but only for those who live long enough to collect. It is essentially insurance that a retirement base will be provided if an individual retires. If not, there is no equity to be divided among heirs. If we assume a comparable return on investment under either system, the choice between privatization and the present benefits-only-for-the-retiree system is clear-cut. With the present system the returns on contributions of those who die before retirement or early in their retirement years go directly to those who live longer. With privatization the benefits for the living retirees would be comparatively lower. As these proposals are considered through public debate and the political process, this distinction should be made clear.

The comparison of proposals has highlighted another distinction. When the two social goals, a guaranteed social minimum and a retirement-base insurance, are differentiated, it becomes clear that the payroll tax is an inappropriate way to finance the redistribution necessary to guarantee the social minimum. The payroll tax can only be justified for the retirement base part of the plan when benefits are essentially private in nature. The redistribution function is clearly social in nature and should be financed through general taxes, more logically the personal income tax. Whatever the final outcome of the public debate, this distinction should be raised and considered.

A FINAL WORD

Regardless of the choices we make as to the structure of Social Security, there is a broader question of intergenerational justice. How do the claims of future retirees relate to projected burdens to future taxpayers?

Although neither proposal may satisfy some readers, we will consider two reform packages with varying degrees of privatization. Both are privatized in that some or all of the surplus would be invested in the private sector, that is a portfolio of bonds and stocks. Both would separate the social-minimum function from the retirement-base function. The major difference would be with investment decisions. Both would feature a closer relationship between expected benefits and individual contributions. The first package would allow the individual to own and direct her or his retirement portfolio.

The second package would feature individual accounts, but the investment would remain the responsibility of the system's administrators. The individual would have little or no choice as to how the funds were invested. The unique feature of the retirement base *as insurance* would remain. The individual would not acquire transferrable wealth but would acquire the right to an *annuity* during his or her retirement years.

These two proposals are organized so as to clarify the fairness and efficiency considerations of each. How far do we want to go with privatization? Is there greater efficiency with the insurance approach or with the wealth approach to providing a retirement base? What moral principles are relevant to the choice among greater or less equality in the benefits.

It is important that the proponents of various proposals be "kept honest" as to what tradeoffs are feasible. If the integrity of the present system is to be maintained, the trust fund (or the two proposed funds) must be periodically adjusted according to the principle of close actuarial balance. This requirement may not accord with politically popular efforts to cut taxes.

Unfortunately, unrealistic and misleading assumptions are the rule rather than the exception. Many proposals are presented as being consistent with substantial tax cuts and intergenerational fairness. Many of these proposals seem to be purposely misleading; but this practice is not unique to this decade. It takes its lead from the fiscal policies of the 1980s. The point to be made here is that if we, as a society, are to make informed choices on the basis of efficiency and fairness, we must be first presented with honest proposals.

Intergenerational justice depends on the entire picture of economic growth and how economic claims are distributed among individuals and among generations. The Social Security system is only part of the larger picture. Even if the Social Security system is made sound, the burdens to taxpayers in future generations depend on economic growth and a responsible tax policy.

The perspectives of generational accounting, introduced in earlier chapters, include Social Security in the broader picture of the government budgets through time. In order to fully appreciate the tax burdens facing current and future generations, it is necessary to compare projected government purchases and transfers to projected tax payments. The net of taxes paid, minus expected Social Security, Medicare, and other transfer benefits, will indicate the burden or benefit to each generation.

The Social Security Administration, we have noted, makes calculations of this nature regularly. This perspective enables policy makers to see what is required to keep the system viable and fair. However, the broader picture of generational accounting includes not only Social Security and Medicare, but Medicaid and other transfers. Equally important is the role played by the public debt. If we take the broader generational accounting perspective and exclude the Social Security surpluses from the federal deficits, we conclude that the current proposals to balance the budget will still fall short of achieving generational balance. This is because the Social Security surpluses continue to mask the deficits. The plans to balance the budget by 2002 or 2005 would still have substantial deficits if the Social Security surpluses were not counted.

The point to be made is that hard choices should be made now. While proposals to cut taxes may be politically popular, they are inconsistent with the aim of intergenerational fairness. Future benefits will almost certainly be cut, and of course there is already an approved schedule for raising the retirement age. But cutting future Social Security benefits and raising payroll taxes cannot be the full story. This is because raising payroll taxes and cutting future benefits will increase rather than decrease the net burden on future generations. If we are ever going to get our house in order, the baby boomers must pay their fair share in the years from now until they begin retiring in 2010.

There are a number of tradeoffs available, ranging from liberal to moderate to conservative, but an increase in personal income taxes would seem to be a necessary part of any honest proposal.

SUGGESTIONS FOR FURTHER READING

Henry Aaron, Barry Bosworth, and Gary Burtless, *Can America Afford to Grow Old?* (Washington, D.C.: The Brookings Institution, 1989). The answer is yes; but action to restore the integrity of the system is overdue. An excellent overview of the actuarial challenge and policy recommendations.

Peter Diamond, "Proposals to Restructure Social Security," *Journal of Economic Perspectives* (10)3 (1996) pp. 67–88. An evaluation of reform proposals.

Edward M. Gramlich "Different Approaches for Dealing with Social Security," *Journal of Economic Perspectives* 10(3) (1996) pp. 55–66. Gramlich concludes that Social

Security's money-worth-ratios for different age groups are falling. The trend must be reversed.

Robert J. Myers, *Social Security*, 4th ed. (Philadelphia: University of Pennsylvania Press, 1993). A comprehensive source on Social Security, Medicare, and allied programs.

ENDNOTES

1. Milton Friedman, *Capitalism and Freedom*, (Chicago: University of Chicago Press, 1962), p. 188.
2. John Rawls, *Theory of Justice*, p. 285.
3. *Ibid.*, p. 286.
4. *Ibid.*, p. 287.
5. *Ibid.*, p. 290.
6. *Ibid.*, p. 290.

7

Environmental Issues

The litany of ways we are damaging the environment grows longer daily. We are depleting ozone in the stratosphere, polluting the air and water, and destroying species and large areas of wilderness. We are using up nonrenewable energy sources and putting future generations at risk in a multitude of ways.

Our treatment of the environment as individuals, businesses, and nations is often immoral. And yet the thesis of this book is that we and our fellow citizens are essentially moral. We assume that, given the right opportunity, most people want to "do the right thing." The challenge of environmental ethics is to ask how we should relate to the natural environment. The challenge of formulating ethical environmental policy is to reorganize our institutions so that our economic behavior can better reflect our moral responsibilities.

As Americans, we depend primarily on our free market system to allocate resources efficiently, that is, to produce the goods we want most at the lowest cost possible. Environmental issues arise because of market failures. Some markets fail to account for our environmental concerns.

Most environmental issues can be analyzed as social benefits and costs that are *external* to the incentives that drive market transactions. We have made good use of the analytical concepts of market failure and externalities throughout our study; they also offer valuable insights into the economics of the environment.

There are three approaches to compensating for externalities. The first is to change the legal parameters of the economic transactions. In some cases, the law can be changed so that externalities are *internalized*. Property rights can be specified in ways that encourage negotiations to resolve the externalities. More specifically, liability rules can be made more explicit; that is, it can be made clear who is legally bound to make good any loss or damage caused by an economic activity.

The second approach is to use corrective taxes or subsidies. The idea is to tax those goods whose market prices do not reflect marginal social costs and to subsidize those goods whose market prices do not reflect marginal social benefits. The subsequent market adjustments will improve resource allocation.

The third approach is for a government agency to set standards and enforce them. Economists generally prefer the first two approaches since they make better use of market incentives. Although there is a preference for indirect methods to resolve environmental externalities, most government programs resort to a direct approach. Economists refer to the methods used by the Environmental Protection Agency (EPA) as *command-and-control strategies*. The primary focus of environmental economics has been to improve the efficiency of our efforts to preserve the environment.

As we shall see, the juxtaposition of efficiency and fairness takes on a different meaning in environmental ethics. There are still important concerns about the fairness of social policy, but questions of efficiency must take center stage. It becomes necessary to broaden our idea of efficiency.

The juxtaposition of efficiency and fairness so useful to us in analyzing other social issues featured a narrow definition of efficiency. The definition of neoclassical economic theory focuses on the ideal resource allocation that is accomplished in perfectly competitive markets. The term *allocative efficiency* is used to describe the market's ability to provide those goods consumers want most at the lowest cost possible. One problem with that idea of efficiency is that resources are allocated according to the effective demand of individuals as consumers. But the central theme of environmental economics is that our actions as consumers cannot fully express our environmental concerns.

The more complete definition of efficiency still contains the idea of finding the best allocation of resources, but it now refers to all of our individual and social concerns. Some of these concerns, or "preferences," can be expressed well in private markets and some cannot. The challenge of environmental economics is to find ways of restructuring institutions and incentives so that they reflect all of our concerns and preferences efficiently.

Before using the perspectives of economics and public policy to analyze environmental issues, we need to consider the related discipline, environmental ethics.

ENVIRONMENTAL ETHICS

The subject of environmental ethics can be approached on several levels. We can ask what the environmental ethic of an individual or a society is. What are their attitudes or values toward the environment? How do these attitudes and values come into play as decisions are made that affect the environment? At a deeper philosophical level we ask how, as individuals and a society, we should contemplate our relationship to the environment. What moral principles are pertinent to environmental issues and how are they to be balanced?

As with other social issues, our pluralistic approach denies that there can be a unique moral principle from which all other principles can be derived.

Even so, our environmental ethics should be consistent with the ethical principles we consider fundamental to all social issues.

Some philosophers would define environmental ethics exclusively in terms of the moral relations humans have with the natural world. It consists of the principles relevant to those relationships that define our duties to the environment. Thus the focus is on human obligations to the natural world, that is, land, vegetation, animals, and so on.

Although the human-to-nonhuman relationships are a major concern, most ethicists attempt to develop a broader perspective, one that also encompasses obligations among humans. As humans, we are concerned about how our use of the environment affects other humans. Pollution of the air or water may be considered an immoral act toward the earth's natural environment, but we must also consider the harm done to humans. Many ethicists are concerned about the effects humans have on each other through the medium of the environment.

The focus on human-to-human relationships brings up the question of whether a narrow description of well-being will be used, say something similar to the *homo economicus model* of neoclassical economics. Those ethicists who would focus on human-to-human relationships are quick to point out that they appreciate the rich complexity of what it means to be human. For example, humans experience feelings of joy and reverence when observing a pristine forest. To destroy that forest is to deprive others of enjoyment and spiritual renewal.

The beauty of the neoclassical model is that we can simply observe humans making choices in the market and assume that welfare is being maximized. The preferences of buyers and sellers are reflected in market prices; and accordingly, prices reflect the values they place on things. But once we attempt a more complex description of humans, and once we question whether market prices reflect the real value of things, we have a serious measurement problem.

The human-to-nonhuman focus adds another dimension to the measurement problem. Many of our most serious environmental questions pit the interests of humans against, say, those of trees. Are we to count those interests as equal? Do humans have an obligation to leave all trees alone to die a natural death? Assuming humans count for something, how are their interests to be weighed against those of the trees? What scale is to be used?

When faced with the complexity of ranking the interests of human and nonhuman entities, most of us would be inclined to accept an enlightened human-to-human ethic, one that allows us to include the more complex and spiritual aspects of the human character. We reason that, if these are considered, surely our definition of morality will be sufficiently broad. It is not so. The tension remains. Although it may seem that the heavy hands of humans touch every aspect of the natural order, the earth is replete with millions upon millions of ecosystems oblivious to human machinations. If we are searching for a moral theory that considers relationships among nonhuman entities, even relationships that will never be known to humans, it seems illogical to claim that our focus can be completely human-to-human.

Some History: Is Western Culture Fatally Flawed?

The tension between these two foci (human-to-nature and human-to-human) runs through many of our current environmental issues. Indeed, the perspectives we now use have interesting historical roots. We start with the doctrine that natural processes can be understood in terms of the laws of physics. With this knowledge, humans can manipulate nature for their own benefit. This view of nature was expounded by Galileo, Bacon, Descartes, Newton, and others. According to some theorists, this view of the world is also inherent in Judeo-Christian ethics. God made the world and gave man dominion over it. God made man in his own image and decreed that all other creatures were made to be exploited.

These theorists argue that such cultural foundations are responsible for our degradation of the environment. Western culture takes the Cartesian view; nature is something to be understood and mastered as one would employ machinery. If environmental damage occurs, it can easily be repaired. It is argued that Christianity reinforces the view that man and the rest of nature are different in kind. Nature's sole purpose is to furnish pleasure. By contrast, the Eastern religions tend to view man as an integral part of nature.

Most Americans are familiar with stories that feature the contrasting ideas of nature held by Native Americans and European settlers. Native Americans saw themselves as kindred spirits not only to other animals, but to all of nature. The spirits of every animal, tree, and rock were to be respected. The Western idea of owning and exploiting other parts of nature was difficult for them to contemplate.

Another flaw in the Western view of nature is said to be fostered by capitalism. Avaricious capitalists, driven by the profit motive, value natural resources simply as inputs. Meanwhile, competition allows no concern to be taken of environmental degradation.

Most of these theories are unconvincing. If Western culture shows little respect for nature, the blame cannot be placed entirely on capitalism. The breakup of communism in Eastern Europe and the Soviet Union revealed an unparalleled disrespect for the environment on the part of the centrally managed economies.

Needless to say, Christian ethicists take issue with the characterization of Christian culture as encouraging many to exploit nature. In Christian ethics, nature is seen as God's creation. Man's covenant with God is to act as steward not exploiter. Man, made in God's image, shares in the dynamics of creation but does so with an appreciation of God's purposes. Above all, Christian ethics sees God as a God of love, love not only for man but also for creation.

The argument that disrespect for nature is somehow deeply ingrained in Western culture may or may not have merit. More important for our purposes is the recognition that social institutions, particularly political and economic institutions, can lead to decisions that ignore widely-held moral values. A primary focus of environmental policy must be to reorganize those institutions so that decision-making will incorporate environmental concerns.

Query: Conservation or Preservation?

The terms *conservation* and *preservation* are used interchangeably in public debate on environmental issues. However, there is an important distinction, and it reflects the tension between the human-to-human and human-to-nature perspectives. Conservation refers to the human-to-human focus. Conservationists appreciate their individual and social responsibilities to conserve natural resources for others' future consumption. Preservation refers to human-to-nature relationships. Human beings have obligations to preserve some parts of nature as they are into perpetuity. Conservationists and preservationists may join forces on a particular issue such as saving a wilderness area from clear cutting; their motives and purposes are different. The conservationist foresees the wilderness area as being used to greater advantage by later generations. The preservationist would leave the wilderness untouched, allowing its own natural processes to determine its future.

> In environmental ethics **conservation** refers to the obligation to exercise restraint in the consumption of natural resources so that they will be available for future use. **Preservation** refers to the obligation to maintain natural phenomena in their present state.

Two important figures in the environmental movement in the United States personify these two ethical perspectives. Gilford Pinchot, the conservationist, was President Teddy Roosevelt's choice to organize and direct the U.S. Forest Service. His frequent antagonist was famous preservationist John Muir.

To Pinchot, man is morally obligated to *manage* natural resources so as to maximize the benefits received over time. First, the forests had to be protected from exploitation by business interests with short-run profit motives. Then, the latest scientific management methods would be used to improve the forests' productivity. The idea of letting nature takes its course was clearly irresponsible. Intervention could greatly increase productivity. The issue of whether or not, and to what degree, national parks should be protected against forest fires is still being debated. Say, a fire is started by a natural cause such as lightening. Some preservationists would argue that nature should be left to follow its own courses. The forest service, while never clearly adopting a completely hands-off policy, has often experimented with such a policy. At times, the results have been devastating. The argument that such devastation is nature's way is not always appreciated.

Some preservationists have difficulty deciding just what is to be preserved. Suppose, for example, an endangered species of wild goat is indigenous to a national park where forest fires are generally allowed to run their course. It is true that billions of species have evolved and later disappeared in the natural course of history. But, one of our most urgent environmental concerns is the massive destruction of species, primarily the result of man's intervention. What then should be our policy with regard to natural forest fires in national parks that are home to endangered species? Pinchot had no such dilemma; to the extent that forest fires could be, they should be controlled. Waste in this or any other form was simply not good business.

Indeed, Pinchot believed that the primary duty of the human race was to control the earth for its own benefit. Of course, a necessary corollary of conservation is some moral principle of distribution. We must ask the question: Conserved for whom and on what grounds? Pinchot's answer echoes the Utilitarian Credo: the greatest good for the greatest number. To his credit, he believed that the benefits should be widely dispersed and not be concentrated on corporations owned by the wealthy elite. Pinchot elaborated on the Utilitarian Credo to include the idea of benefits through time. Resources were to be conserved so as to attain the greatest good for the greatest number "for the longest time."[1]

The utilitarian approach remains central to the conservation movement. As we shall see, the cost-benefit tools of economics have been applied in ingenious ways to the whole spectrum of environmental issues. This will again raise the question of what role, if any, utilitarianism plays in modern economic theory. For now, let us observe that the utilitarianism of John Stuart Mill was quite broad. It could easily have encompassed Pinchot's conservationism and possibly even Muir's preservationism. But Mill would have objected to the modern uses of cost-benefit analyses. He would question whether or not individual preferences could simply be summed up by market prices. He would not allow that market prices could capture all of value.

John Muir's preservationist vision saw nature as much more than a machine to be efficiently managed. We have already examined arguments similar to Muir's objections in our earlier discussions of what we mean by the term *efficiency*. Recall that, in welfare economics, the term *allocative efficiency* has both economic and normative connotations. In perfectly competitive markets, firms are forced to produce at the lowest cost possible. At the same time, firms are responsive to the preferences of consumers; thus the array of goods produced will create maximum satisfaction. While the idea of allocative efficiency provides an attractive norm for resource allocation, there are important values that it does not capture. Muir argued that natural systems should not be evaluated in terms of efficiency. The appropriate human-to-nature relationship for wilderness areas is for man to admire and to protect, rather than to manage. Muir disagreed with the thesis that nature was made for man. Much of nature proceeds along its way perfectly well without benefiting from man's intervention. Most preservationists have a spiritual reverence for nature and natural places. Muir's losing battle to save the Hetch Hetchy Valley in Yosemite National Park has become an inspiration for generations of preservationists.

Can We Reconcile the Two Perspectives?

As pluralists, we must ask whether or not it is possible to find a balance between the two approaches to environmental ethics. We can begin by subscribing to the more enlightened version of utilitarianism; the version of John Stuart Mill, where man is seen as much more than *homo economicus*. This broader definition of human nature now accounts for the utility, enjoyment, or reverence that we experience from, say, knowing that wilderness areas are being preserved. There would be difficulty in estimating the psychic benefits we get from knowing that wilderness and species are being preserved; conservationists and utilitarians agree that policy makers should find some way to take these benefits into account. While such an approach would do much to appease the preservationists, they would argue that it still misses an essential point: nature has value in and of itself. Some environmental economists, recognizing the impossibility of quantifying such values, use the term *existence value*. The idea is that the mere existence of a species has value that can be appreciated by people, even in the absence of direct contact with it.

Let us attempt to define Muir's objection to the utilitarian approach to nature with more precision. There are two points to be made. First, Muir objected strenuously to the narrow utilitarianism in which the greatest good is defined in terms of consumption. What is narrow about this view is that the values of things are calculated in ways that approximate the market. We are left with what we think consumers-as-consumers would want. The second objection is to the human-to-human focus that is inherent in conservationism and utilitarianism. Muir and other preservationists warn us that the human-to-human focus draws our attention away from appreciating and respecting nature for its own sake.

The human-to-human focus is different in kind from the human-to-nature focus. Some would argue that the value of nature can only be expressed in deontological terms. The essential question is what duties humans have to the nonhuman parts of nature. Some would go on to ask whether or not animals have rights and whether or not trees have rights. If so, what are the correlative duties of humans?

Being good pluralists, we are not required to resolve the differences among conservationists and preservationists. We can simply observe that the tension remains. While both views base their arguments on moral principles, it is not clear that they succeed. Most conservationists seem comfortable in basing their arguments on utilitarian grounds. Some preservationists follow similar utilitarian lines of argument. However, Muir and many preservationists argue that nonhuman forms of life, and nature in general, have intrinsic value beyond what is ordinarily accounted for in human activities. They would argue that these may be expressed better in terms of rights and duties than in terms of, say, utility or efficiency.

ENVIRONMENTAL ECONOMICS

Economics Broadly Defined

There is a potential conflict between how economists and environmentalists, particularly preservationists, think about the ways we use resources. Nevertheless, if economics is broadly defined, it can be used to advantage no matter what one's philosophical or political persuasion. Some people assume that economics is simply about how businesses make profits or consumers maximize utility, and thus would pit economics against ethics whenever making profits conflicts with stewardship of the environment. This is a limited definition of the perspectives taken by most economists. As defined by Barry Field, "Economics is the study of how and why people, whether they are consumers, firms, nonprofit organizations, or government agencies, make decisions about the use of valuable resources."[2] Environmental economics asks how can we change the institutions and incentives that affect the resource-use decisions so that they better reflect environmental concerns.

We are interested in why people behave in ways that cause harm to the environment. One answer is that they are unethical, that they simply have no concern for the welfare of others or the value of nature. That may be the case for some, but it is not true for all. Most Americans care about the environment and support efforts for its protection. In recent years, there has been an awakening in moral sensitivity to environmental concerns. It is vital that this trend continues. Public awareness of the seriousness of the various threats to our environment is a necessary condition for social action.

At the same time, we need other approaches to changing the way we behave. We need to rearrange our economic and political institutions so that incentives no longer lead to environmental destruction. As noted earlier, it is not simply a matter of the profit motives of businesses. Government agencies, consumer groups, and employee groups also make choices that have detrimental effects. We observed earlier that government planners and plant managers of the former communist countries had equally harmful sets of incentives. In many situations, the peculiar benefits and costs of the environment are likely to be ignored unless they are given special consideration.

The Environment as a Public Good

According to economic theory, the market would look after the environment quite nicely if its benefits and costs were "excludable" and "exhaustible." However, many aspects of the environment are public in nature. Our concerns over conserving wilderness areas, rain forests, and endangered species are public-good concerns. The benefits accrue to us all; they are "nonexcludable and inexhaustible." The satisfaction we get from knowing that a wilderness area is being preserved can be shared by all. The satisfaction cannot be bottled and sold. If it could, the market would protect the wilderness. Clean air also has public-good characteristics. Within limits, one person can enjoy breathing fresh air without exhausting its benefits for others. Here again, the benefits are impossible to divide and sell.

Unfortunately, this means that environmental protection is subject to the free-rider problem. Since the benefits can be enjoyed whether one pays or not, there is no incentive to contribute. In an earlier chapter, we used the familiar lighthouse case to illustrate the problem. The story depicts a village of fishermen in need of a lighthouse. Since all fishermen would benefit whether or not they contribute, none of them have sufficient incentive to contribute. In some public-good situations, a voluntary program will suffice, but in others, the coercive powers of government to insure an adequate level of contributions is required. The village council can tax every fisherman and use the proceeds to build and maintain the lighthouse. Assuming that the tax is fairly administered, the results are both fair and efficient.

The analogy can easily be recast as a pollution problem. Assume the villagers all burn coal for heat and cooking. On certain days the combined effect of smoke and fog (smog) make it unpleasant and unhealthy to breathe. Suppose that everyone is asked to voluntarily switch from coal to natural gas or electricity. There will be some expense for each household. Since the program is voluntary, there is a temptation to free ride. If enough households switch, the problem will be solved, but the contribution by one does not make the difference. With moral suasion and peer pressure, a voluntary approach might well succeed. More often, a government program, complete with regulations and fines, would be required. Pollution abatement, like most environmental issues, usually requires the coercive powers of government to overcome the free-rider problem.

The story could also be told as a problem of depletable natural resources. Our fishing village is located on a lake where overfishing endangers the viability of the industry. All that is required to revive the fish population is restraint. The village council devises a quota system that will insure the long-term viability of the industry. If the village supports the quota system, it must be considered fair as well as efficient. But what criteria will the village council use? The council could opt for equal quotas for all. Or it could require each fisherman to reduce his catch by some percentage of last year's catch. Exceptions could be made for the poorer fishermen on the basis of need. Presumably, the council will consider all of the familiar distribution principles before deciding how to apportion the burden. In any case, each fisherman faces the temptation to free ride by exceeding the quota. The quota system will probably not work without some method of monitoring and fines.

These examples illustrate how the public-good character of most environmental problems leads to government action and raises questions of fairness and efficiency.

Cost-Benefit Analysis: Equating Marginal Social Benefits and Costs

Environmental economics, like all of economics, asks what is the best allocation of resources. If we define economics broadly, as we should, this "best allocation" includes keeping some resources as wilderness. But in every case, the idea of efficiency in allocation can be expressed in terms of marginal benefits and costs. The production of a private good should be taken to the point at which the marginal benefits from producing more are just equal to the marginal costs. As more of the good is consumed, the benefit received from each extra unit naturally diminishes. On the supply side, the marginal costs of producing the good increase as more is produced. At several points in our study, we have made use of the model of perfect competition as a norm for efficient resource allocation. Competitive markets insure that every private good will be produced at the point where marginal benefits equal marginal costs. This ideal model is to be contrasted to situations where market failures occur. Generally, cost-benefit analysis has to do with overcoming externalities created by different kinds of market failure.

The possible benefit-cost relationships are as follows. The essential rule is that the production of every good, private or public, should be carried to the point where marginal benefits are equal to marginal costs: MB = MC.

When there are benefits to others not involved in the transaction, those benefits will not be incorporated into the effective demand for the product. Thus, we would differentiate between the benefits that are incorporated, marginal private benefits (MPB) and those that are external, marginal social benefits (MSB). The problem arises because only marginal private benefits determine the market effective demand; the marginal social benefits will be overlooked.

Other problems can occur on the supply side, where the costs considered by the suppliers—marginal private costs, MPC—do not include costs to others, that is, the marginal social costs, MSC. The effective market supply includes only the direct costs to the suppliers. The social costs will be overlooked when a market equilibrium is reached. Thus, we can divide externality problems into two categories, those arising on the demand side and those arising on the supply side.

How do we change the incentives to buyers and sellers so that the social benefits or costs will be taken into account? Here again, there are two broad categories: incentive-based approaches and command-and-control approaches. With incentive-based approaches, the idea is to change the incentives of buyers or sellers but to otherwise leave them free to allocate resources. With command-and-control approaches, there is less room for market incentives to work. We first consider the incentive-based approaches. One method is to change the legal parameters of market transactions so that the externalities will be "internalized."

Adjusting the Legal Parameters

When externalities affect a small number of parties, there are advantages in a hands-off approach by regulatory agencies. Regulations that specify just how the externality is to be resolved will often obviate simpler, more efficient solutions. Moreover, a detailed procedure that works well in one context may not be appropriate in other situations or at other times. Finally, it is often the case that the most well-intentioned regulations have unintended consequences; it is often difficult to anticipate how regulations will affect behavior. It may be possible to achieve the desired result simply by changing the legal parameters within which negotiations take

> The **Coase Theorem** states that externalities will be resolved efficiently if transactions costs are low.

place. This idea has been explored in other contexts, but it is especially applicable to environmental issues. The most ardent advocate is Ronald Coase.
The Coase Theorem, we recall, asserts that negotiations among the affected
parties will frequently lead to efficient resolution of externalities. The negotiations are facilitated if property rights and liability rules have been specified.

Consider the following case of noise pollution. A new bowling alley opens
just across the street from a nursing home. The noise from the bowling alley
becomes an annoyance, particularly to those residents whose rooms are nearest to the street.

Obviously, the case brings up a number of questions of fairness and efficiency. The point of the story is that the probability that the most efficient
resolution of the problem will be found is greater if the parties are allowed
to negotiate. A government agency or the courts may be required to rule on
the fairness issue, but the most efficient resource allocation is more likely to
be found by the affected parties. They both have incentives to find a mutually advantageous resolution. The possibilities include the following: the bowling alley is moved to another location; the nursing home is moved to another
location; insulating materials are installed in the bowling alley; insulating materials are installed in the nursing home; the hard-of-hearing residents of the
nursing home are encouraged, say with lower rents, to move into the rooms
nearest the bowling alley; or new noiseless pins are introduced at the bowling alley.

After considerable thought, both sides agree on the most efficient strategy.
Let us say that the most efficient strategy is to bribe the hard-of-hearing residents to move to the noisier rooms. An interesting point of the theorem is that
finding the most efficient strategy does not depend on who is liable. If the
bowling alley is liable, it will reimburse the nursing home for the bribes it pays
to those who occupy the noisier rooms. If the bowling alley is not liable, the
nursing home will bear the cost itself. Coase and others argue that the assigning of property rights is the crucial step. Once that is settled, the negotiations
can proceed and the most efficient solution will be found.

The Question of Fairness

In theory, at least, the efficiency and fairness questions can be neatly separated.
The most efficient solution will be found regardless of who benefits or loses. In
chapter two, we used the story of the widow
washerwoman to highlight the fairness issue in
externalities. The story features a very meritorious, elderly widow who ekes out a meager
living from taking in laundry. She suddenly dis-
covers that the factory next door has begun to
pollute the air with soot. Since her speciality is
to dry the laundry in the fresh air, her business is now ruined.

In this case, the costs of negotiating, or,

> **Transactions costs** are usually de-
> fined as costs associated with do-
> ing business in a market; for ex-
> ample, buying, selling, or making
> contracts. In externality situations
> that feature large numbers of af-
> fected parties, the transactions
> costs could be prohibitive.

the *transactions costs*, are not a problem; the washerwoman is free to negotiate with the factory.

In the first version of the story, we suppose that the most efficient solution is for the factory to install a filter at a cost of five thousand dollars. If we assume that the factory is liable, it will pay for the filter. If the factory is not liable, the widow will have to dig into her savings. In the second version of the story, we suppose that the filter is very expensive, say one million dollars. Since the widow's business is not worth that much, the most efficient solution is for it to be discontinued. If the factory is liable, it will reimburse her for the loss of her business; if it is not, she will have no recourse. Her plight is a sad one, but at least efficiency has been served.

There are two points to the story. The first is that the efficient solution will be reached as long as transactions costs are low. The second is that fairness is a separate question. It should be decided on other grounds.

Transactions Costs Again

Although the Coase Theorem makes several interesting points, its applicability to environmental externalities is limited. The theorem's assumption of low transactions costs does not hold in most cases. Indeed, the reason the affected parties' interests are ignored in the first place is that they would find it costly to negotiate.

For example, air pollution has many perpetrators and many victims. Since each has little effect on the problem, each has little incentive to change behavior. The pollution problem in a large city is caused by the actions of individuals, firms, and government agencies. These same individuals, firms, and agencies are affected by pollution. While everyone would be willing to contribute to a solution, everyone knows that they can do little on their own. There is no effective way for them to negotiate.

A classic externality case can be used to describe how transactions costs and *organization costs* can reduce the chances of an efficient solution's being negotiated. In chapter two, we described the case of the papermill that pollutes a river with its effluent. Everyone downriver is affected: the fishermen, swimmers, homeowners, and farmers; not to mention the trout, frogs, dragonflies, and kingfishers.

Although the paper mill makes a multitude of transactions in carrying out its business, the use of the river is treated as a free

> The concept of **organization costs** is an extension of the idea of transactions costs. In addition to the usual costs of buying, selling, and negotiating contracts, the problems of organizing large numbers of affected parties are addressed. In many large-number situations, a **free-rider problem** arises, thus compounding the organizational difficulties.

good. The harm done those downriver and the environment is not accounted for and is not reflected in the price of the paper products. If some method of internalizing the pollution costs were found, the pollution would be corrected. The price of the paper products would be higher and resources would be allocated more efficiently. Since there are larger numbers affected by the externality, the costs of their negotiating with the paper mill are quite high.

Let us also assume, as in chapter two, that the most efficient solution is for the paper mill to install settling tanks. Suppose also that the question of liability is clear. If the affected parties can demonstrate that they have been harmed, the company will be required to end its pollution or pay damages. Regardless of who is liable, the efficient solution still remains the same; the settling tanks should be built. Here again, questions of efficiency and fairness are quite distinct. If the mill is liable, it will pay for constructing the settling tanks. If it is not, the affected parties will pay. However, here is the point: for the affected parties to pay would present further organizational problems. The organizational problems may now be insurmountable. In one sense, the reduction of water pollution is a public good to the affected parties. They will enjoy the river and cannot easily be excluded. If the burden of paying for the settling tanks is to be borne by the affected parties, the problem may not be resolved after all. There may be some question about whether or not voluntary contributions would suffice. As with other public-good situations, a government agency with the power to tax may be required.

To summarize, the free-rider problem adds a new dimension to the problem of transactions costs. In the paper mill case, there is some question as to whether or not the parties affected by the mill's effluent would be able to carry on transactions with the paper mill. We differentiated between the case in which the mill was liable and the case in which it was not. If the fishermen, swimmers, homeowners, and farmers must organize themselves and also make contributions for building settling tanks, the transactions costs take on a new dimension. As noted, many of the benefits of a clean river are public. Within limits, swimmers can swim and fishermen can fish without diminishing the pleasure of other users. At the same time, there may be no feasible way to exclude people from enjoying the river. It follows that there may be no effective way to get the users to contribute. The free-rider problem makes it impossible to organize and carry on transactions. The project will fail unless a government agency, with the necessary taxing powers, will fund the settling tanks.

What would the preservationist say to all of this? No doubt she or he would applaud us for demonstrating just how economic activities can damage the environment. Obviously, by analyzing the nature of the externality, we can make better policy choices. However, the preservationists would be uncomfortable with our examples and with all of the traditional cost-benefit examples. We should be forewarned that, in most of the examples we use, we will focus on the economic well-being of the affected parties. But, of course, there is much more to environmental ethics than economic well-being. Rivers are important to us not only because of their recreational and commercial values; they are important to us because we have a reverence for nature. We like to know that it is important to maintain at least some of our rivers so that they can support rich and varied ecosystems. Some preservationists will remind us that it is presumptuous to illustrate environmental problems solely in terms of human-to-human relationships. Preservationists would insist that the paper mill example be extended to include the rights of fish, turtles, and green herons, not to mention dragonflies. Obviously, their organizational problems and transactions costs are even more problematical than those of the fishermen and swimmers. With these caveats in mind, we will continue our survey of possible strategies.

Environmental Damage: Query: Who Has Standing?

While some externalities are easily resolved when liability rules have been specified, others are not. Many of the social responsibilities people feel toward the environment have no direct physical link with their day-to-day activities. They get satisfaction from knowing that various aspects of nature are being preserved. But unless a person can show that he or she suffers rather direct harm from others who are liable, he or she will not be likely to have *standing* in court.

In a case involving the Endangered Species Act, an environmentalist group (Defenders of Wildlife) sought to apply the act abroad. They claimed that several endangered species were being threatened by development projects in Egypt and Sri Lanka. Several public projects in those areas were backed by U.S. government funds. In attempting to establish standing, two members of the group said they planned to return to those areas some day and would be injured by not seeing the animals.

The Supreme Court ruled that the environmental group had no standing. The two members were not sufficiently injured to file a lawsuit. The Court found that such cases require that the injury be actual or imminent. In recent years, the Court has been narrowing its definition of standing in environment cases. At the same time, new environmental legislation has tended to specify and thus facilitate the procedures by which cases can be pursued.

Corrective Taxes or Subsidies

In economic theory, the classic treatment of externalities is to use corrective taxes or subsidies. The model of demand and supply is used to demonstrate that, when externalities are present, prices and quantities as determined by the market will be inefficient. In chapter two and earlier in this chapter, we showed how the problem can be expressed in terms of marginal benefits and costs. We recall that market demand is derived from the marginal benefits experienced by buyers, and market supply is derived from the producers' marginal costs. It follows that the market's demand-and-supply equilibrium is consistent with the rule for allocative efficiency, MB = MC. When externalities are present, however, we differentiate between marginal private benefits and marginal social benefits, the latter not being expressed in market demand. For externalities on the supply side, we differentiate between marginal private costs and marginal social costs.

In the case of marginal social benefits, the market demand is less than it should be. A good example is the social benefit of energy saved when homeowners install solar heating units or insulated windows. During the energy crises of the 1970s, public concern was raised over the depletion of the world's nonrenewable sources of energy. This concern was heightened by our awareness of dependence on OPEC. If buyers of energy-saving improvements are given subsidies, as they were in the 1970s, the market demand will increase to reflect the additional social benefits. More energy-saving improvements will be made and overall resource allocation will be improved. Essentially the same result could be accomplished by giving subsidies to the producers. The subsidy would lower the firms' net costs and, in turn, the market price. Again, more of the energy-saving home improvements would be made and overall resource allocation would be improved.

Now consider the problem of marginal social costs. Most of the pollution examples fit this description. Certain models of motorcycles make more noise than others. To some motorcyclists, the noise is half the fun, but this form of noise pollution is particularly obnoxious to many of its victims. The price of the noisier models does not reflect the social costs; however, a tax on the noisier models would raise the producers' costs and decrease market supply.

Alternatively, the tax could be imposed on the buyers of the noisier models (thus lowering the demand curve). The result would be the same whether or not the noisier motorcycle tax is collected from sellers or buyers. Overall resource allocation would be improved by reducing the use of the noisier motorcycles. Theoretically, the revenues from the tax could be used to compensate for the stress and hearing loss of those subjected to the noise.

Environmental economists use the term *green taxes* to refer to those taxes that internalize environmental costs into market prices. Theoretically, government could rearrange its taxes and subsidies in ways that promote environmentally sound resource allocation.

Corrective taxes or subsidies are more appropriate in some situations than in others. It is not always possible to design the tax or the subsidy so as to get the desired result. The advantage of using taxes or subsidies is that the market is left free to achieve efficiency under a changed set of incentives. Nevertheless, in many situations a regulatory agency is required.

Air and Water Pollution: A Brief History of Command and Control Policy

Air. The layer of gases enveloping our planet contains a combination of gases that is particularly favorable for the earth's life-forms. The surface air, the troposphere, features a combination of 78 percent nitrogen, 21 percent oxygen, and traces of several other useful gases that provide direct life support. The upper layer of the earth's atmosphere, the stratosphere, has two important roles. It contains a number of gases, particularly ozone, that act to shield the earth from the sun's ultraviolet rays. It uses other gases to produce the earth's necessary greenhouse effect.

In addition to the gases necessary for life, our air carries a large assortment of harmful gases and particles deposited there by natural events and human activities. The list of potentially dangerous pollutants and their potential harm is quite long.

Water. The earth's water resources occur in many forms and in many ecological systems. The land masses are intermeshed with systems of rivers, lakes, swamps, and streams. The oceans and seas are adjoined by saltwater bays, waterways, marshes, and wetlands.

There are many demands made on water by living things. Humans consume it and use it in food preparation, cleaning, and sewage disposal. Water is used by industry in many manufacturing processes. Farmers depend on irrigation systems to augment rainfall. A significant percentage of the world's food supply comes from salt and freshwater fishing. We use our lakes, rivers, and beaches for water sports and other recreational activities.

All of these resources and uses need different kinds of protection. Water, like air, is vulnerable to pollution from a multitude of sources such as deposits in the forms of sewage, industrial wastes, and runoff from farmlands.

The first water pollution policies occurred at the local and state levels. Later, in the mid-nineteenth century, the public became more aware of the importance of clean water to health. Local and state boards of health were instituted.

The Evolution of Federal Regulation

The federal role in environmental protection developed much later than other types of regulation. The first wave of regulation was focused on monopoly practices, unsound banking and financial practices, and consumer protection. These agencies were part of Roosevelt's New Deal, and they were seen as necessary to put the economy back in working order.

After World War II, the federal government committed itself to helping the states regulate water pollution. The Water Pollution Control Act of 1948 initiated two major efforts that remain the foundation of federal policy. Municipalities were given subsidies to build waste-treatment facilities, and regional conferences were held for the purpose of developing water-quality standards. The Water Quality Act of 1965 continued these themes, extending the waste-treatment subsidies and directing states to proceed with developing and monitoring water-quality standards.

The Air Quality Act of 1967 gave responsibility for establishing air-quality standards to the Department of Health, Education, and Welfare. However, the subsequent federal and state enforcement procedures were ineffective and this, in turn, led to the Clean Air Act of 1970. It established a much more aggressive approach that featured natural air-quality standards, and technology-based emission standards. It also established strict standards for automobile emissions.

The late 1960s and early 1970s witnessed a second wave of regulatory activities similar to that of the 1930s. The earlier focus had been on monopoly power and the stability of financial institutions; the focus of the second wave was on protecting the environment and the health and safety of consumers and workers. The new agencies, the so-called social regulatory agencies, included the Environmental Protection Agency (EPA), the Consumer Product Safety Commission, and the Occupational Safety and Health Administration.

The newer agencies, like the older agencies, were seen to be required to intervene to cure market failures. But whereas the principal justifications for the older regulatory agencies were failures due to monopoly power, the justification for the newer agencies stemmed from imperfect information and externalities. Imperfect information on the part of the workers and consumers could lead them to make choices that would endanger their health. Externalities could lead to misallocation of resources such as pollution. The social focus of the newer agencies was often quite broad. The EPA's mandates on water and air pollution, for example, cover almost every type of economic activity and thus require expert knowledge of every industry and its technology.

The EPA was born in July, 1970, when President Nixon's Reorganization Plan No. 3 was submitted to Congress. The plan consolidated the functions previously spread out among a number of departments. Accordingly, the EPA started out as a large agency with a large mandate. The agency's budget, and more important, the *compliance costs* of firms, individuals, and others subject to the regulations, are significant. But the benefits are also significant. As with other social programs, the question of "how much" should be answered by comparing marginal benefits and costs. Of course, program evaluation always involves a related question: How can we get better results and sacrifice less?

The EPA's policy agenda for water was spelled out in the 1972 Water Pollution Control Act. The act initiated a new, more direct federal role in controlling water pollution. It set a goal of zero discharges by 1985. The old approach had relied on states to monitor ambient-based standards. In practice, however, the states had often been frustrated in their attempts to demonstrate that the emissions of a particular firm had led to the degradation of water quality.

The new approach adopted more direct controls. It would set effluent standards for every source of pollution. The government would then issue discharge permits to every individual source. The EPA's task was overwhelming. Each permit would specify the nature and quantity of emissions allowed. The standards, termed technology-based effluent standards (TBES), are based on the best pollution-abatement technology available to the individual source. Theoretically, the discharge permit leaves some room for a firm or other source to choose among technologies.

This policy, the setting and monitoring of technology-based effluent standards, continues to be the EPA's principal approach to controlling water pollution. Its implementation has been difficult. The target deadlines have been pushed back on several occasions, most notably by the 1977 Clean Water Act and the 1987 Water Quality Act.

During the two Reagan administrations there was little support for environmental initiatives. Efforts were made instead to ease government restrictions on business. It was not until the 1990 Clean Air Act amendments that a number of growing concerns were addressed. The act listed 189 toxic materials to be controlled, and it addressed the problems of acid rain, ozone depletion, and urban air quality. Over the years, the EPA has become aware that some of its control methods unduly curtailed the flexibility of firms and others to respond. More recently, the EPA has reduced its role in stipulating the technology firms must use. Even so, the 1990 act specified several technological changes relative to automobile pollution.

Other Approaches to Pollution Control

With good reason, economists spend most of their time simply observing the economy. Attempts to *control* economic activities must be undertaken with caution. One difficulty is that the results are not always what were intended. A recent General Accounting Office survey of companies that discharge waste water found that more than one-third of the companies were breaking the law. For many, the risk of being caught and paying a fine was less than the cost of complying. Enforcement of environmental programs can be expensive, and it is one area of the budget that Congress frequently cuts. The use of subsidies may often be more effective than fines. However, it does not seem fair to reward companies when they stop doing something they should not have been doing in the first place.

Unexpected results of market controls are the rule rather than the exception, and so it is with environmental economics. There has been considerable criticism of the command and control methods of the EPA. It is one thing to establish goals, but another thing to develop and monitor the necessary standards. Much of the problem lies with Congress; it cannot seem to resist issuing impossible mandates to the EPA.

On the other hand, economists have not been reluctant to offer their ideas, and several innovative approaches have been adopted, with mixed results. There has been a concerted effort to develop new incentive-based approaches to replace the present technology-based emissions standards for both air and water pollution controls. Most experiments in water pollution control have been based on the principle of allowing emission permits to be traded. Since permit trading is only feasible for sources sharing a particular body of water, its use has been limited. Another approach that is being considered for water pollution control is reliance on a system of emission taxes.

Experiments in emission permit trading were authorized by the Clean Air Act of 1970 (and expanded by the 1990 Amendments). These pilot programs allowed sources to earn emission reduction credits, ERCs, by reducing emissions below a specified level. The EPA has developed four ways ERCs may be traded: offsets, bubbles, netting, and banking. *Offsets* apply to regions that are not in compliance with EPA air-quality standards. New sources, for example new factories, can begin operation only if they can purchase ERCs from existing firms. This allows for some industrial growth even in areas not meeting current standards. The trading criteria usually require that some improvement be made; that is, entering sources may be required to trade one-and-a-half ERCs for every one-unit increase in emission. *Bubbles* refers to one firm with multiple pollution sources. For example, a firm may have several plants in the region. The bubble approach places all of the firm's plants under a bubble within which emissions can be traded. If it would be less costly to reduce the emissions of one plant than another, the firm is allowed to do so.

Netting is similar to bubbles in that trading can take place within the firm. When an expansion is planned, the firm must be prepared to reduce emissions somewhere else in the plant. One advantage to netting is that the firm can avoid the costly review process required to approve new emission permits. *Banking* offers firms the option of banking ERCs for future use or sale.

These programs have facilitated a large number of transactions, especially under the netting option. The banking feature has seen little use. It may be that firms do not want it to appear that emissions can be so easily reduced.

The most ambitious trading program was introduced in the Clean Air Act of 1990. It introduced transferrable emission permits for the sulphur dioxides emitted by power plants. The aim was to reduce acid rain in the Northeast and Canada. Permits were distributed to designated plants that could then trade them. Periodic reductions are made. Those plants that encounter the greatest difficulty in meeting new quotas are allowed to purchase permits from others who have reduced emissions by more than they were required.

These attempts to introduce more flexibility into pollution controls will continue to be evaluated. There is great interest in reducing our reliance on command-and-control methods. Unfortunately, however, few good substitutes have appeared. It is interesting that, in this age of deregulation, when most of the original regulatory agencies have been severely curtailed or abolished, the regulatory responsibilities of the EPA have continued to expand.

The Tragedy of the Commons: What Should Be Held in Common?

Garret Hardin's provocative article "The Tragedy of the Commons"[3] likened the earth to a pasture open to all. The incentives faced by each herdsman inevitably lead to overgrazing and ruin for all. Among the examples of the tragedy of overuse, Hardin pointed to the national parks. In some areas, such as the Yosemite Valley, freedom of access has already led to overuse; the value that visitors seek has been seriously eroded. Efficient use of the resource requires some method of rationing.

Hardin also applied the commons analogy to pollution problems. Here, *use* refers to the waste products we deposit in the air, water, and soil. If these resources are free to be used as garbage dumps, the rational individual will use them to their limit and we will all be worse off.

To Hardin, the most pressing tragedy is "the population problem." He asserts that the freedom to breed is intolerable, especially in a welfare state: "In a welfare state, how shall we deal with the family, the religion, the race, or the class (or indeed any distinguishable and cohesive group) that adopts over breeding as a policy to secure its own aggrandizement?"[4] Hardin does not believe appeals to individual conscience will be an effective way to limit population. The only alternative is some form of coercion mutually agreed upon.

Open-Access Externalities

The term *open-access resources* is often used to describe those situations in which a resource or facility is open to uncontrolled access by individuals who benefit in some way from its use. Overuse can occur, as in the case of the commons and the case we mentioned earlier of overfishing an open-access lake. As usual, questions of efficiency and fairness arise. Suppose there is an obvious answer to the efficiency question. There is a pattern of use, grazing or fishing, that allows for the long-term viability of the resource, the commons or the lake. The solution is for the village council to issue "use permits" that will limit use to the efficient level. The fairness issue is separate; the village council must come up with a distribution formula that is fair. We are aware of a number of principles they could use: to each an equal share, to each according to need, to each according to the welfare of others, and so on.

There is another solution to the problem that does not involve government permits and monitoring. As the Coase Theorem suggests, the government could simply assign property rights to the use of the resource. As government is wont to do these days, it could simply auction off the resources. The buyer would then control access and would insure that the resource would be used efficiently.

At this point, we must return to our query: What resources should be held in common? As with most of our queries, there is room for disagreement. Our strawman individualist would want very few resources held in common. Only the profit motive can insure efficiency. Moreover, the individualist likes the freedom to own the things she or he uses—none of the sharing with others that one may be subjected to at a public beach. The individualist wants to own his own beach, or better yet, an island. Our strawperson egalitarian (egalitarians are always politically correct) enjoys sharing things on an equal basis. She or he would be offended by the idea of a private beach; beaches should be held in common. No one should be denied access, especially the poor. For resources held in common, one's wealth or position should not count.

The rest of us realize that many of the individualist and egalitarian values we share have merit. There are levels of resource use that are clearly inefficient. There are some open-access externalities that need to be resolved by private or public regulation. Most of us are agreed on the attributes of an economy in which most resources are owned as private property. We, like the egalitarians, like the idea that some resources should be held in common and enjoyed collectively. If the community playground becomes crowded, good; expand the playground. If not all kids can afford to go to the ball game, have certain days when they can get in free.

We will leave the question open. As pluralists, we remind ourselves that the solution requires that we attempt to balance the competing values and principles. With respect to environmental externalities, we must judge each case on its own merits. For some resources, we will decide that private ownership is appropriate; for others we will want open access; for others, access with a minimum charge; for others, access according to some other principle of distribution. We should not overlook the option of *no access*, or at least very limited access. For example, there are wilderness areas that many Americans prefer to leave untouched.

The Battle for Public Lands

For its first two hundred years in the land management business, the federal government's goal was to convey as much land to states, farmers, trappers, railroads, and miners as they were willing to develop. The federal government was left to manage what was left. This process was not impeded until the conservation movement at the turn of the century. It was reversed entirely in the 1970s when the general public became alarmed at the extent to which public lands were being exploited. Although much of what remained was earlier considered to have little economic value, it now holds much of what is left of our mineral resources. Moreover the continental shelf is estimated to contain 60 percent of undiscovered U.S. petroleum reserves. Federal wilderness and national forest areas contain nearly 30 percent of the nation's old-growth forests.

Of course, estimates of potential market values do not account for the roles our public lands play as parts of the environment and our natural heritage. As the naturalist Aldo Leopold argued, our federal wilderness areas and national parks represent a heritage of natural treasures. He argued that we need to preserve the land that remains as a sanctuary, so that we can better understand the natural base upon which we have built our society.

The public lands include vast areas devoted to wilderness, national parks, wildlife refuges, forests, and rangelands. The rules governing each category have occasioned fierce political conflicts over the years. These conflicts typically involve federal agencies, commercial interests, environmental groups, and Congress.

The modern conflicts can be traced to the late 1960s and early 1970s. The National Environmental Policy Act of 1969 required federal land management and other agencies to create Environmental Impact Statements when making land use decisions. Moreover, the courts and Congress expanded the influence of environmentalist groups by allowing them to sue federal agencies for not giving adequate attention to the environmental consequences of their decisions. The environmental groups began using these strategies to delay or reverse many agency policies.

In the 1980s, the Reagan administration was determined to counter the environmentalists on several fronts. Its goals were to sell a substantial percentage of the public lands to the states and to private owners and to open vast tracts to mineral exploration. Although the Western states had previously argued for more state control and privatization, they now became alarmed at the scale of resource exploitation. They turned to Congress and the courts to curtail the rate of privatization.

In the late 1980s, the "wise use" movement emerged. It is a loose alliance of interest groups that use public lands for commercial purposes. Its aim is to organize political support. It uses various philosophical and economic arguments for privatization and open access to public lands. The philosophical arguments are primarily utilitarian: as economic development is realized, more efficient use of these resources creates benefits for all of society. The familiar efficiency arguments of the privatization movement are also employed. James

G. Watt, President Reagan's notorious Secretary of the Interior, stated that he wanted to open as much land as he could. "The basic difference between this administration and liberals is that we are market-oriented, people-oriented. We are trying to bring our abundant acres into the market so that the market will decide their value."[5] Generally, wise use turns out to depend on the wisdom of the market.

In recent years, the battle lines over public lands have generally been drawn up along party lines. But environmental concerns are only a few of the many issues that politicians and voters consider. Most Americans, regardless of party affiliation, share a concern for the environment and the legacy to be left to future generations. Thus, the continuing debate over land use management will not proceed entirely along party lines.

The Global Environment

It is only in the last few decades that we have begun to see the earth as one large ecological system. This vision has been heightened by beautiful pictures of the earth shot from space and by speculation about whether there might be other planets suitable for human habitation. Over humankind's long history on earth when one place became unwelcome, they could migrate to another place. But if we humans despoil the whole planet, there will be nowhere else to go. Hardin's stark warning about the population problem depicts planet earth as the commons that we humans will inevitably ruin.

As production and trade increase, scientists recognize new threats, not just to certain areas and to certain species, but to the global environment itself. As we survey the various incentive-based and command-and-control methods available for combating international externalities, the difficulties of the tasks become apparent. If we cannot devise incentive-based programs for dealing with our own nation's environmental issues, how can we expect to deal with global issues?

Command-and-control methods seem to be a necessary feature of any successful pollution-abatement effort. But the necessity to reach international agreements on what methods to use and how the burdens will be shared makes policy formulation infinitely more problematical. The United States-Canada program to deal with acid rain demonstrated that international cooperation is possible between friendly neighbors with a clear understanding of what must be done. But even there, policy negotiations were difficult.

Of the many global environmental concerns, three seem particularly threatening: (1) ozone depletion in the stratosphere; (2) global warming, or the greenhouse effect; and (3) massive loss of species.

Ozone Depletion

The stratosphere's ozone layer protects earth from the sun's harmful ultraviolet rays. In the late 1970s, scientists discovered that the ozone layer was being rapidly depleted, first over Antarctica and then over the entire stratosphere. They found the cause of this depletion to be the increasing presence of chlorine that interrupts ozone's process of replenishment. The sources of this chlorine are a number of relatively new manufactured chemicals including the chlorofluorocarbons used extensively in refrigeration, aerosol sprays, and solvents. They are very stable chemicals that, when released, gradually make their way up to the stratosphere. The ozone threat promises to be manageable for several reasons. The scientific evidence is convincing and the sources are identifiable. In the countries involved, only a few large companies manufacture the chemicals.

In 1987, after promising starts by several countries and prior study and negotiation, twenty-four nations signed the Montreal Protocol on Substances That Deplete the Ozone Layer. Under the protocol, each country has developed it own control policies. They feature such innovations as transferable production quotas and the international trading of emission reduction credits.

The Montreal Protocol is a success story. It provides a role model for future efforts at international cooperation.

Global Warming, or the Greenhouse Effect

Several gases in the stratosphere reflect earth's radiation and produce the earth's greenhouse effect. Without this feature, life as we know it could not exist. In recent years, however, many scientists have warned that the effect is becoming too much of a good thing. Increased industrial production and the use of large amounts of energy from oil, coal, and natural gas have led to an increase in carbon dioxide and other gases. The addition of these gases to the stratosphere has increased the greenhouse effect.

Scientists predict that temperatures on the earth's surface will increase, the sea level will rise, glaciers will melt, and the polar ice caps will begin to break up. While some areas of the world will become more humid, others will become drier. Some of the countries scheduled to become drier are already straining their food supplies. For them global warming promises widespread famine.

In contrast to the concensus reached on ozone depletion, there is some disagreement as to the threat posed by the greenhouse effect. While most scientists agree that some global warming will occur, there is less agreement about the severity of the threat. Moreover, adaptation to warming would pose different problems to different countries.

The choice of strategies to reduce emissions poses further difficulties. Assigning carbon dioxide quotas for countries would involve considerable controversy. The question of how to fairly distribute the burden would be raised. What principles should be followed: equal sacrifices, equal proportional reductions, reductions where they are least costly, or some other rule? How should the risks be assessed? What sacrifices should this generation make for uncertain future benefits? Similar questions of fairness would arise if a system of taxes were instituted. Who should bear the burden? Would it be fair to burden developing countries with regressive taxes? Would it be fair to stymie the growth of the less-developed countries? So far, there has been no significant international effort to reverse global warming.

Biodiversity and Species Loss

Over the millenia, species have come and gone. But in recent years, the destruction of species has reached alarming levels. We must contemplate the consequences for the species that remain. There are at least three areas for concern: the stock of genetic material, the diversity among species, and the diversity among ecosystems. The diversity among species is crucial to the survival of each. We humans use other species of animals and plants in a multitude of ways, so their strength and survival is important. For example, many of our prescription drugs come from "cures" developed by other species. We have mutual enemies. Just as "friendly" species continuously evolve, our enemies, such as viruses and bacteria, continuously develop new modes of attack. We humans need all of the help we can get.

The extinction of species can occur because they are directly depleted or, more likely, because their habitat has been destroyed. Human commerce and industry use resources in ways that destroy habitats; thus they create environmental externalities. Logging, agriculture, and urban development are very destructive of specie habitat.

The range of possible strategies, like the range of externalities, covers many variations. Three possible approaches are zoning, privatizing, and changing the incentives of those now destroying species and their habitats. While preservation through zoning is more direct and definitive, it requires that the public or private owners forgo monetary rewards. Predictably, they would like to negotiate with someone for compensation. Privatizing, or rather, assigning property rights, would insure that the resources would be used efficiently. For example, if certain genetic resources have potential value for pharmaceutical companies, assigning property rights would encourage the owners to preserve them and to negotiate for future profits. This approach is being tried on a limited basis, but, of course, it is not applicable to many environmental externalities.

Ultimately, the incentives of those now destroying habitats must be changed. This must involve not only various types of zoning, but incentive-based programs. Few of the methods successful for other environmental problems seem to be applicable here. The basic difficulty is that the benefits are so far removed from the costs. How are the global benefits, many of which are public in character, to be measured, assigned, and paid for? A number of international meetings have addressed the problems of biodiversity and specie destruction, but little actual progress has been made.

SOME FINAL WORDS

Environmental issues, like the other issues we have addressed, are social in nature. All of society shares a concern for the environment and all agree that social action is required. Although questions of resource allocation predominate, environmental policies must address questions of fairness as well. In the public debates on these issues, it is important that the social goals be clarified. We need to be clear about the criteria to be used in formulating goals and policies.

There are many threats to the environment and they affect humans and other species in a multitude of ways. In our brief survey, only a few of the threats have been introduced: the pollution of air and water, the loss of species, the reduction in biodiversity through the destruction of habitats, the depletion of the ozone layer, and the problem of global warming. National and international efforts to formulate and execute environmental policies have met with uneven success. We can expect that public debate on environmental issues will continue, since the list grows daily and our ability to respond is tenuous.

The market-oriented economies of the West are efficient in allocating resources to private goods; but the benefits of environmental protection are public. As with other social issues, market failures occur, and their analysis offers clues as to the appropriate policy responses.

Most environmental issues involve externalities: economic activities in which social benefits or costs are ignored. The task of accounting for environmental externalities is often difficult. That scientists were able to track down the sources causing depletion of the ozone layer is remarkable. Other externalities are more difficult to trace. Moreover, assessing the severity of a threat can be problematical, as in the cases of global warming and the loss of species.

On the other hand, there are environmental externalities whose resolution depends more on politics than technology. For example, the worldwide destruction of rain forests by European, American, and Asian loggers brings short-term profits to some of the less-developed nations. The political leaders of those countries are often more concerned with those short-term profits than the long-term benefits to the nation. The more global dimensions of rain forest depletion are completely external to such transactions. Our task is to find ways, say through international forums and legislative processes, to account for these social costs. How are the incentives of the buyers and sellers to be changed? More specifically, can international commissions help to change those incentives, say by imposing penalties or offering subsidies?

In our survey of environmental economics, we encountered many of the same perspectives and methods employed with other social issues. The methods for dealing with externalities remain the same. One approach is to change the legal parameters within which trading takes place. The point is that, if the affected parties are allowed some flexibility, more efficient solutions may be found. The example of the nursing home and the bowling alley makes that point. More important, the negotiations between the United States and Canada on the acid rain problem resulted in several innovative methods being used.

For many environmental externalities, the analogy with small-number bargaining is not applicable. The paper mill example demonstrates how transactions and organization costs create particular difficulties for large-number situations. Air pollution in large cities such as Los Angeles has many sources and many affected parties. The transactions and organization costs preclude private individuals or groups from negotiating to resolve the issue. Instead, government standards must be set and various command-and-control methods must be employed. Even within command-and-control approaches, the EPA and environmental agencies at all levels seek to change incentives in positive ways. For example, the EPA's programs for reducing air pollution include standards and quotas but also allow firms to trade discharge permits and credits.

While many of the ethical questions posed are similar to those encountered with other social issues, one is unique. That question is raised by the preservationist–conservationist debate: should our ethical focus be on human-to-human relationships or should it include human-to-nature relationships? How should we, as humans, relate to nature? What are our responsibilities? The preservationists and conservationists give different answers to these fundamental questions. So, although they often agree on policy prescriptions, we can expect this fundamental difference in moral perspective to occasionally cause disagreement on policy.

With most environmental issues involving externalities, questions of fairness must be resolved. The story of the washerwoman and the smokestack made the point that the efficiency and fairness questions can be separated. But in many cases, the two questions must be settled simultaneously or no resolution will be achieved.

The *distribution principles* relating to income and tax burdens are also relevant to the burdens imposed by pollution quotas. In almost every case, legislators or government officials must devise a method for apportioning the burden. As pluralists, we would expect that the appropriateness of one principle over another would depend, in part, on the particular context. It may be useful, for example, to know which parties contributed most to the present state of environmental degradation.

The advantage of taking a pluralistic approach is that the discussion of a social issue can be framed so that participants with different values and perspectives can contribute. Environmental policy must be considered in a broad context to include the contexts of other social goals.

We do not expect complete agreement on the efficiency and fairness criteria to be used, much less agreement on the specifics of the policy prescriptions. The hope is that reasoned discussion will narrow our differences. In most deliberations, final agreement on policy is not required; but when agreement is required, being clear about the moral, political, and economic dimensions of the social issue should enhance the process.

SUGGESTIONS FOR FURTHER READING

General: Some Classics

Rachel Carson, *Silent Spring* (Boston: Houghton Mifflin, 1962).
Aldo Leopold, *A Sand County Almanac, and Sketches Here and There* (Oxford: Oxford University Press, 1949).
John Muir, "The Yosemite," reprinted in *American Environmentalism: The Formative Period 1860–1915* ed. Donald Worster (New York: Wiley, 1973).

Gifford Pinchot, *The Fight for Conservation* (Garden City, N.Y.: Anchor, 1910).
———, *Breaking New Ground* (Covelo, Ca.: Island, 1947).

Environmental Ethics

Eugene Hargrove, *Foundations of Environmental Ethics* (Englewood Cliffs, N.J.: Prentice-Hall, 1989).
Ernest Partridge, ed., *Responsibilities to Future Generations: Environmental Ethics* (Buffalo: Prometheus, 1984). A collection of essays on the intergenerational issues of the environment.
Holmes Rolston, III, *Environmental Ethics: Duties to and Values in the Natural World* (Philadelphia: Temple University Press, 1988).
Mark Sagoff, *The Economy of the Earth: Philosophy, Law and the Environment* (Cambridge: Cambridge University Press, 1988).
Donald Worster, *Nature's Economy: A History of Ecological Ideals* (Cambridge: Cambridge University Press, 1986).

Environmental Economics and Policy

William J. Baumol and William E. Oates, *The Theory of Environmental Policy* (Englewood Cliffs, N.J.: Prentice-Hall, 1975). Theoretical concepts such as externalities are applied to the economics of the environment; rather technical.
William F. Baxter, *People or Penguins: The Case for Optimal Pollution* (New York: Columbia University Press, 1974). As the title implies, Baxter comes down on the side of people and optimal pollution.
Alan S. Blinder, *Hard Heads, Soft Hearts* (Reading, Mass.: Addison-Wesley, 1987), chap. 5, Issues in environmental economics; policy proposals of economists.
Maureen L. Cropper and Wallace E. Oates, "Environmental Economics: A Survey," *Journal of Economic Literature* (30)2, (June 1992). A survey of environmental economics and recent policy.
Barry C. Field, *Environmental Economics: An Introduction* (New York: McGraw-Hill, 1994). A good introduction to the various fields of environmental economics.

ENDNOTES

1. Utilitarian philosophers and economists have been reminded often enough that two variables such as "the good" and "the number" cannot be simultaneously maximized. Therefore, when Pinchot adds a third, "for the longest time," there is no cause for consternation.
2. Barry C. Field, *Environmental Economics* (New York: McGraw-Hill, 1994), p. 3.
3. Garret Hardin, "The Tragedy of the Commons," *Science*, 162 (1968), pp. 1243–48.
4. Just to make sure that no one is left unoffended, Hardin criticizes the United Nation's Universal Declaration of Human Rights; it proclaims that the decision on how many children to have "must irrevocably rest with the family itself." Obviously, Hardin disagrees.
5. *New York Times*, July 2, 1982. Also see chapter nine of Walter A. Rosenbaum, *Environmental Politics and Policy*, 3rd. ed. (Washington, D.C.: Congressional Quarterly Press, 1995), quote on p. 311.

NAME INDEX

SUBJECT INDEX